Edward of Clarendon

The History of the Rebellion and Civil Wars in England

Edward of Clarendon

The History of the Rebellion and Civil Wars in England

ISBN/EAN: 9783742864888

Manufactured in Europe, USA, Canada, Australia, Japa

Cover: Foto ©ninafisch / pixelio.de

Manufactured and distributed by brebook publishing software (www.brebook.com)

Edward of Clarendon

The History of the Rebellion and Civil Wars in England

THE

HISTORY

OF THE

REBELLION AND CIVIL WARS

IN

ENGLAND,

Begun in the Year 1641.

With the precedent Paſſages, and Actions, that contributed thereunto, and the happy End, and Concluſion thereof by the King's bleſſed Restoration; and Return upon the 29th of *May*, in the Year 1660.

Written by the Right Honorable

Edward Earl of Clarendon,

Late Lord High-Chancellor of *England*, Privy-Counſellor in the Reigns of King Charles the Firſt and the Second.

Κτῆμα ἐς ἀεί. *Thucyd.*
Ne quid Falſi dicere audeat, ne quid Veri non audeat. Cicero.

VOL. VIII.

BASIL:
Printed and ſold by J. J. TOURNEISEN.
MDCCXCVIII.

THE
History of the Rebellion, etc.
BOOK IX.

If. I. 15.

And when you spread forth your hands, I will hide mine eyes from you; Yea, when you make many Prayers, I will not hear. Your hands are full of blood.

If. xxviii. 15.

For we have made lies our refuge, and under falshood have we hid ourselves.

WE are now entering upon a time, the representation and description whereof, must needs be the most unpleasant, and ungrateful to the Reader, in respect of the Subject matter of it; which will consist of no less weakness and folly, on the one side, than of malice and wickedness, on the other; and the most unagreeable and difficult to the Writer, in regard, that he shall, probably, please very few who acted then upon the Stage of business, but must give very severe Characters of the Persons, and severely censure the Actions of many, who wished very well,

Introduction to the Ninth Book and the year 1645.

BOOK IX. and had not the least thought of disloyalty or infidelity, as well as of those, who, with the most deliberate impiety, prosecuted their design to ruin and destroy the Crown: A time, in which the whole stock of Affection, Loyalty, and Courage, which at first alone engaged Men in the Quarrel, seemed to be quite spent, and to be succeeded by negligence, laziness, inadvertency, and dejection of Spirit, contrary to the Natural temper, vivacity, and constancy of the Nation: A time, in which they who pretended most public-heartedness, and did really wish the King all the greatness he desired to preserve for himself, did sacrifice the public Peace, and the security of their Master to their own passions and appetites, to their ambition, and animosities against each other, without the least design of Treachery, or damage towards his Majesty: A time, in which want of discretion, and mere folly, produced as much mischief, as the most barefaced Villany could have done; in which the King suffered as much, by the irresolution, and unsteadiness of his own Counsels, and by the ill humor, and faction of his Counsellors, by their not foreseeing what was evident to most other Men, and by their jealousies of what was not like to fall out; sometimes by deliberating too long without resolving, and as often resolving without any deliberation, and most of all, not executing Vigorously what was deliberated and resolved, as by the indefatigable industry, and the irresistible power and strength of his Enemies.

All these things must be very particularly enlarged upon, and exposed to the naked View, in the Relation of what fell out in this year, 1645, in which we are engaged, except we will swerve from that precise Rule of ingenuity, and integrity, we profess to observe; and thereby leave the Reader more perplexed, to see the most prodigious accidents fall out, without discerning the no less prodigious causes which produced them; which would lead him into as wrong an estimate of things, and persuade him to believe, that a universal corruption of the hearts of the whole Nation had brought forth those lamentable effects; whereas they proceeded only from the folly and the frowardness, from the weakness and the wilfulness, the pride and the passion of particular Persons, whose Memories ought to be charged with their own evil Actions, rather than that the Infamy of them should be laid on the Age wherein they lived; which did produce as many Men eminent for their loyalty and uncorrupted fidelity to the Crown, as any that had preceded it. Nor is it possible to discourse of all these particulars, with the clearness that is necessary to Subject them to Common understandings, without opening a door for such reflections upon the King himself, as shall seem to call both his Wisdom, and his Steadiness into question, as if he had wanted the one to apprehend and discover, and the other to prevent, the Mischiefs which threatened him. All which considerations might very well discourage, and even terrify me from prosecuting this part of the Work, with such a freedom and openness, as must call many things to memory which are forgotten, or were never sufficiently understood; and rather persuade me to satisfy myself, with a bare relation of what was

BOOK IX.

done, and with the known event of that miserable year (which, in truth, produced all that followed in the succeeding years) without prying too strictly into the causes of those effects, and so let them seem rather to be the production of Providence, and the instances of Divine displeasure, than shew how they proceed from the weakness and inadvertency of Men, not totally abandoned by God Almighty to the most unruly lusts of their own appetite, and inventions.

But I am too far embarked in this Sea already, and have proceeded with too much simplicity and sincerity with reference to Things, and Persons, and in the examinations of the grounds, and oversights of Counsels, to be now frighted with the prospect of those Materials, which must be comprehended within the relation of this year's transactions. I know myself to be very free from any of those Passions which naturally transport Men with prejudice towards the Persons whom they are obliged to mention, and whose Actions they are at liberty to censure. There is not a Man who acted the worst part, in this ensuing year, with whom I had ever the least difference, or Personal unkindness, or towards whom I had not much inclination of kindness, or from whom I did not receive all invitations of farther endearments. There were many who were not free from very great faults, and oversights in the Counsels of this year, with whom I had great Friendship, and which I did not discontinue upon those unhappy oversights; nor did flatter them when they were past, by excusing what they had done. I knew most of the things myself which I mention, and thereforec an Anfwer for the Truth of them; and other moft important particulars, which were tranfacted in places very diftant from me, were tranfmitted to me, by the King's immediate direction and order, even after he was in the hands and power of the Enemy, out of his own Memorials, and Journals. And as he was always fevere to himfelf, in cenfuring his own overfights, fo he could not but well forefee, that many of the misfortunes of this enfuing year, would reflect upon fome want of refolution in Himfelf, as well as upon the grofs errors, and overfights, to call them no worfe, of thofe who were trufted by him. Wherefore as I firft undertook this difficult work with His approbation, and by His encouragement, and for His vindication, fo I enter upon this part of it, principally, that the world may fee (at leaft if there be ever a fit feafon for fuch a Communication; which is not like to be in this prefent Age) how difficult it was for a Prince, fo unworthily reduced to thofe ftraits his Majefty was in, to find Minifters, and Inftruments, equal to the great Work that was to Be done; and how unlikely it was for him to have better fuccefs under their conduct whom it was then very proper for him to truft with it; and then, without my being over-folicitous to abfolve him from thofe miftakes, and weakneffes, to which he was in truth fometimes liable, he will be found not only a Prince of admirable Virtue, and Piety, but of great parts of Knowledge and Judgment; and that the moft fignal of his Misfortunes proceeded chiefly from the modefty of his Nature, which kept him from trufting himself enough, and made him believe, that others discerned better, who were much inferior to him in those faculties; and so to depart often from his own reason, to follow the opinions of more unskilful Men, whose affections he believed to be unquestionable to his Service. And so we proceed in our relation of matter of *Fact*.

What expectation soever there was, that the *Self-denying Ordinance*, after it had, upon so long deliberation, passed the House of Commons, would have been rejected and cast out by the Peers; whereby the Earl of *Essex* would still have remained General; it did not take up so long Debate there. The Marquis of *Argyle* was now come from *Scotland*, and sat with the Commissioners of that Kingdom, over whom he had a great ascendant. He was, in matters of Religion, and in relation to the Church, purely Presbyterian; but in matter of State, and with reference to the War, perfectly Independent. He abhorred all thoughts of Peace, and that the King should ever more have the Government, towards whose Person, notwithstanding the infinite obligations he had to him, he had always an inveterate malice. He had made a fast Friendship with Sir *Harry Vane*, during his late being in *Scotland*; and they both liked each other's Principles in Government. From the time of His coming to the Town, the *Scottish* Commissioners were less vehement in obstructing the Ordinance, or the new modelling the Army: so that after it came to the House of Peers, though thereby the Earl of *Essex*, the Earl of *Manchester*, the Earl of *Warwick*, and the Earl of *Denbigh* (whose power and authority, that is,

the power, credit, and authority, of the three firſt named, had abſolutely governed and ſwayed that Houſe from the beginning) were to be diſpoſſeſſed of their Commands, and no Peer of *England* capable of any employment either Martial, or Civil; yet the Ordinance found little Oppoſition, and the old Argument, "that the Houſe of Commons thought it neceſ-
" ſary, and that it would be of miſchievous Conſe-
" quence to diſſent from the Houſe of Commons," ſo far prevailed, that it paſſed the Houſe of Peers likewiſe; and there remained nothing to be done, but the Earl of *Eſſex*'s Surrender of his Commiſſion into the hands of the Parliament, from whom he had received it; which was thought neceſſary to be done with the ſame formality in which he had been inveſted with it. *Fairfax* was now named, and declared General, though the Earl of *Eſſex* made not haſte to ſurrender his Commiſſion; ſo that ſome Men imagined, that he would yet have conteſted it: but he was not for ſuch enterpriſes, and did really believe that the Parliament would again have need of him, and his delay was only to be well adviſed, in all the circumſtances of the formality. In the end it was agreed, that, at a conference of both Houſes in the Painted-Chamber, he ſhould deliver his Commiſſion; which he did. And becauſe he had no very plauſible faculty in expreſſing himſelf, he choſe to do it in Writing; which he delivered to them; wherein he declared, " with what Affection
" and Fidelity he had ſerved them, and as he had often
" ventured his Life for them, ſo he would willingly
" have loſt it in their Service; and ſince they be-
" lieved, that what they had more to do would be

BOOK IX.

The Self-denying Ordinance paſſes in the Houſe of Lords.

B 4

BOOK IX.

The Earl of Essex resigns his Commission;

And Divers other Officers.

" better performed by another Man, he submitted to
" their judgment, and restored their Commission to
" them; hoping they would find an abler Servant:"
concluding with some expressions which made it
manifest that he did not think he had been well used,
or that they would be the better for the change: and
so left them, and returned to his own House; whither
both Houses, the next day, went to attend him,
and to return their thanks for the great Service he
had done the Kingdom; which they acknowledged
with all the Encomiums, and flattering Attributes
they could devise.

By this *Self-denying Ordinance*, together with the
Earl of *Essex*, the Earl of *Manchester*, Sir *William
Waller*, the Earl of *Denbigh*, Major General *Massy*,
lost their Commands; as *Cromwell* should likewise
have done. But as soon as the Ordinance was passed,
and before the Resignation of the Earl of *Essex*, the
Party that steered, had caused him to be sent with
a Body of Horse into the West, to relieve *Taunton*,
that he might be absent at the time when the other
Officers delivered their Commissions; which was
quickly observed; and thereupon Orders were given,
to require his present Attendance in Parliament,
and that their new General should send some other
Officer to attend that Service; which was pretended
to be done; and the very day named, by which,
it was averred that he would be in the House. A rendezvous was then appointed, for their new General
to take a View of their Troops, that he might appoint
Officers to succeed those who had left their Commands by Virtue of the Ordinance; and likewise in

Their places who gave up their Commands, and refused to serve in the new Model, who were a great number of their best Commanders. From this Rendezvous, the General sent to desire the Parliament, "that they would give Lieutenant-General *Cromwell* "leave to stay with him for some few days, for his " better information, without which, he should " not be able to perform what they expected from " him." The request seeming so reasonable, and being for so short a time, little opposition was made to it : and shortly after, by another Letter, he desired with very much earnestness, " that they would allow " *Cromwell* to serve for that Campaign." Thus they compassed their whole design, in being rid of all those whose affections they knew were not agreeable to Theirs, and keeping *Cromwell* in Command; who, in the Name of *Fairfax*, Modelled the Army, and placed such Officers as were well known to Him, and to no body else; and absolutely governed the Whole Martial Affairs; as was quickly known to all Men; many particulars whereof will be mentioned at large hereafter.

Cromwell only finds means to keep his Commission, and New-models the Army under Fairfax.

Though the time spent in passing the *Self-denying Ordinance*, and afterwards in new-modelling their Army, had exceedingly retarded the preparations the Enemy was to make, before they could take the Field, whereby the King had more breathing-time than he had reason to expect; yet all the hopes he had of Recruits against that Season, depended upon the Activity of those to whose Care the providing those Recruits was committed : so that there will be little Occasion to mention any thing that was done at *Oxford*, till the Seafon of the year obliged his Majefty to leave that place, and to march with his Army into the Field. Of all the Action that was till that time, the Weft was the Scene; where the Prince, as foon as he came to *Briftol*, found much more to do (and in which he could not avoid to meddle) than had been forefeen. One very great end of the Princes Journey into the Weft, befides the other of more importance, which has been named before, was, that by His prefence, direction, and authority, the many Factions and Animofities between particular Perfons of Quality, and Intereft in thofe Parts, equal in their affections to the King's Service (yet they miferably invefted and diftracted it) might be compofed, and reconciled; and that the endeavours of all Men who wifhed well, might be united in the advancing and carrying on that public Service, in which all their joint happinefs and fecurity was concerned. This Province, befides the Prince's immediate countenance, and interpofition, required great diligence and dexterity in thofe about him, who were trufted in thofe Affairs. But his Highnefs found quickly another tafk incumbent on him than had been expected, and a Mifchief much more difficult to be maftered, and which, if unmaftered, muft inevitably produce much worfe effects, than the other could, which was, the ambition, emulation, and conteft, between feveral Officers of the Army and Parties, which were then in thofe Countries, whereby their Troops were without any Difcipline, and the Country as much expofed to Rapine and Violence, as it could be under an Enemy, and in an Article of time when a Body of the Enemy was every day expected. That this may be the better understood, it will be necessary here, in the entrance upon this discourse, to set down truly the Estate of the Western Counties, at the time when the Prince first came to *Bristol.*

The Western Counties, when the Prince of Wales came to Bristol.

The Lord *Goring* had been sent by his Majesty, before the time of the Prince's coming into the West, with such a Party of Horse, Foot, and Dragoons, and a Train of Artillery, as he desired; into *Hampshire,* upon a design of his own, of making an Incursion into *Sussex;* where he pretended " he had cor-
" respondence; and that very many well affected
" Persons promised to rise, and declare for the King,
" and that *Kent* would do the same." And so a Commission was granted to him, of Lieutenant-General of *Hampshire, Sussex, Surrey,* and *Kent,* without the least purpose or imagination that he should ever be near the Prince. Some attempts he made, in the beginning, upon *Christ-Church,* in *Hampshire,* a little unfortified Fisher-Town; yet was beaten off with loss: So that he was forced to retire to *Salisbury;* where his Horse committed the same horrid outrages, and barbarities, as they had done in *Hampshire,* without distinction of Friends or Foes; so that those Parts, which before were well devoted to the King, worried by Oppression, wished for the access of any Forces to redeem them. Whilst the Lord *Goring* lay fruitlessly in those Parts, a Party of Horse and Dragoons, under the Command of *Vandruske* a *German,* passed by him without interruption, to the relief of *Taunton,* then blocked up by Colonel

Windham, and reduced to some straits; and accordingly effected it. About the same time, Sir *Walter Hastings*, Governor of *Portland*, seconded by Sir *Lewis Dives* (who had the Command of *Dorsetshire* as Colonel-General) had surprised *Weymouth*, and possessed the Forts, and the upper Town, the Rebels having withdrawn themselves into the lower Town, divided from the other by an Arm of the Sea, and of no considerable strength: so that the speedy reducing that small place was not looked upon as a matter of difficulty. However, lest those Forces which had relieved *Taunton*, and were conceived to be much greater than in truth they were, should be able to disturb the work of *Weymouth*, and for the sooner expediting the business there, the Lord *Goring*, now pretending that his Friends in *Sussex* and *Kent* were not ready for him, was by Order from *Oxford*, upon his own desire, sent thither; whereby it was thought both the work of *Weymouth*, and *Taunton*, would be speedily effected. Thereupon the Lord *Hopton*, whose right it was to Command in those Counties as Field-Marshal of the West, being sent down by the King to compose the disorders there, upon the relief of *Taunton*, was, by special Order, recalled to *Bristol*, lest there might be dispute of Command between Him and the Lord *Goring*; the one being General of the Ordinance, the other General of the Horse; but the Lord *Hopton* was likewise Field-Marshal of the West, in which the Lord *Goring* had no Commission to Command.

Shortly after the Lord *Goring*'s arrival about *Weymouth*, with his full strength of Horse, Foot, and

Dragoons, and Artillery, confifting of above three thoufand Horfe, and fifteen hundred Foot, befides what he found in thofe parts, that place of fo vaft Importance, was, by moft Supine Negligence at beft, retaken by that contemptible Number of the Enemy, who had been beaten into the lower Town, and who were looked upon as Prifoners at Mercy. The myfteries of which fatal lofs were never inquired into; but with great plainnefs, by the Vote of the County, imputed to General *Goring*'s natural want of Vigilance; who thereupon retired with his whole ftrength into *Somerfetshire*. His Highnefs, upon his arrival at *Briftol*, found the Weft in this Condition; All *Dorfetshire* entirely poffeffed by the Rebels, fafe only what Sir *Lewis Dives* could protect by his fmall Garrifon at *Sherborne*, and the Ifland of *Portland*, which could not provide for its own Subfiftence: the Garrifon of *Taunton*, with that Párty of Horfe and Dragoons which relieved it, commanding a very large circuit, and difturbing other parts in *Somerfet-shire: Devonshire* intent upon the blocking up of *Plymouth*, at one end, and open to incurfions from *Lyme*, and prejudiced by *Taunton*, at the other end: The King's Garrifons, in all three Counties, being ftronger in Fortifications (which yet were not finifhed in any place, and but begun in fome) than in Men, or any Provifions to endure an Enemy: whilft the Lord *Goring*'s Forces equally infefted the borders of *Dorfet*, *Somerfet*, and *Devon*, by unheard of Rapine, without applying themfelves to any Enterprife upon the Rebels. *Cornwal* indeed was entire; but being wholly affigned to the blocking up of *Plymouth*, yielded no supply to any other Service, or to the providing its own Garrisons against the time that they might be visited by an Enemy.

Sir *William Waller*, and *Cromwell*, marched together about this time towards the West, and passing through *Wiltshire*, had routed, and taken the whole Regiment of Horse of Colonel *Long*, the High-Sheriff of that County, by his great defect of Courage, and Conduct; and seemed to intend an attempt upon General *Goring*; who was so much startled with the noise, at a great distance, that he drew his Forces so far West of *Taunton*, that *Vandruske* had an opportunity to retire with that Body of Horse and Dragoons with which he had relieved *Taunton*, to his fellows; whilst the King's Forces reposed themselves upon the borders of *Devonshire*, the Lord *Goring* himself, and most of his principal Officers, taking that opportunity to refresh at *Exeter*, where they stayed three or four days in most scandalous disorder, a great part of his Horse lying upon free Quarter, and plundering to the Gates of the City; which, in the beginning of the year, was an ill Presage to that People, what they were to expect. But finding that Sir *William Waller* made not that haste he apprehended, having borrowed such Horse and Foot as he could procure from *Exeter*, he returned again towards *Taunton*, and gave his Highness an account of his Condition.

The Prince, being attended at *Bristol* by the Commissioners of *Somerset*, found no one thing provided, or one promise complied with, which had been made by them at *Oxford*: Of his Guards of Horse and Foot,

which they assured him, for the proportion of that County, should be ready against his coming, not one Man or Horse provided: Of the hundred pound a Week, to be allowed by them towards his Highness's support, not one penny ready, nor like to be. So that he was forced to borrow from the Lord *Hopton*'s own private store, to buy Bread. And, which was worse than all this, we found plainly, that, what had been so particularly, and positively undertaken at *Oxford*, was upon the confidence only of three or four Men, who were governed by Sir *John Stawel*, and Mr. *Fountain*, without any concurrence from the rest of the Commissioners of that, or the other three Associated Counties; and that they who had been so confident, instead of forming and pursuing any design for raising of Men or Money, were only busy in making Objections, and preparing Complaints, and pursuing their private Quarrels, and Animosities against others. So they brought, every day, Complaints against this and that Governor of Garrisons, for the Riots and Insolences of the Lord *Goring*'s Soldiers, and, "that those parts of the Country
" which were adjacent to *Sherborne*, and *Bridge-*
" *water*, were compelled to work at those Fortifica-
" tions;" with other particulars, most of which, they well knew, in that conjuncture of time, could not be prevented; and some of which were in themselves very necessary. Yet the Prince endeavoured to give them all encouragement; told them, "that
" he was very sensible of all those disorders, of which
" they complained; and would redress them, as
" soon as they should discern it to be in his Power:

"that the Forces under the Lord *Goring* were an Army by themselves, come down into those Parts, before his Highness; and stayed then there for their Protection against the power of *Waller* (which was ready to Invade them) and the Garrison of *Taunton*, which they confessed infested their whole Country; that he was very desirous that Army might move Eastward, as soon as they should put themselves in such a posture, as might render them secure against their Enemies; wished them to propose any Expedients, how the Fortifications of the Garrisons might be finished, without some extraordinary help; or to propose the most convenient one; and he would join with them; and desired them to proceed in their Levies of Men, and Money, in the ways agreed on by themselves; and they should find all concurrence and assistance from him." But notwithstanding all he could say or do, nothing was reasonably proposed, or admitted by them, for the advancement of the Public Service.

By this time, towards the end of *March*, Sir *William Waller* having advanced with his Horse and Dragoons, by *Bath* towards *Bristol*, in hope, as hath been said before, to have surprised that City by some Treachery within, and being disappointed there, retired towards *Dorsetshire*, and the edge of *Somerset*, adjoining to that County; where *Cromwell* expected him; the Lord *Goring* having, in the mean while, fallen into some of *Cromwell's* Quarters about *Dorchester*, and taken some Prisoners, and Horses, and disordered the rest. Upon a dispute between themselves,

selves, or some other Orders, *Cromwell* retired to join
with Sir *Thomas Fairfax* toward *Reading;* Sir *William Waller* stayed in those Parts, to intend the business of the West, but made no haste to advance,
expecting some Supplies of Foot by Sea at *Weymouth.*
So that the Lord *Goring* drew back to *Bruton,* and
sent to the Prince to desire, "that two of his Council
" might meet him at *Wells* the next day, to consider,
" what course was best to be taken:" accordingly
the Lords *Capel* and *Colepepper,* the next day, met
his Lordship at *Wells.* Where, after long consideration
of the whole State of the West, and of the great importance of reducing *Taunton,* without which no
great matter could be expected from *Somersetshire,*
the Lord *Goring* proposed, and put the design in writing under his own hand, for the whole method and
manner of his proceeding, " that he would leave the
" gross of his Horse, and two hundred Foot mounted
" in such convenient place, upon the skirts of *Dorsetshire,* and *Wiltshire,* as they might be able to retire
" to their Body, if the Enemy advanced powerfully;
" and that he would himself, with all his Foot, and
" Cannon, and such Horse as were necessary, attempt the taking, or burning of *Taunton:*" and to
that purpose, desired his Highness, "to send positive
Orders to Sir *Richard Greenvil* (who, notwithstanding
his Highness's commands formerly sent to him, and
some Orders from the King himself, made not that
haste as might reasonably be expected) "to advance,
" and to direct the Commissioners of *Somerset* to give
" their Personal attendance upon that Service; and
" in the mean time to take care that sufficient Maga-

Vol. VIII.   C

"zines of Victual, and Provisions, were made for the
"Soldiers:" all which was exactly performed by his
Highness, the next day after he received the desires
of General *Goring*.

But, within three or four days, and before the
design upon *Taunton* was ready for Execution, it
appeared by constant Intelligence, that *Waller* was
advancing with a great Body of Horse, and Dragoons, and some Foot; and therefore the attempt
upon *Taunton* was for the present to be laid aside;
and the Lord *Goring* very earnestly desired the Prince
to Command Sir *Richard Greenvil*, who was now
drawn near to *Taunton*, with eight hundred Horse,
and above two thousand Foot, besides Pioneers,
with all possible speed to march to him, that so he
might be able to abide the Enemy, if they came upon
him; or, otherwise, to compel them to Fight, if
they stayed in those fast Quarters, where they then
were; which was about *Shaftsbury*, *Gillingham*, and
those places. The Prince accordingly sent his Commands positively to Sir *Richard Greenvil*, "to advance
" towards the Lord *Goring*, and to obey all such
" Orders, as he should receive from his Lordship."
But he as positively sent his Highness word, "that
" his Men would not stir a foot; and that he had pro-
" mised the Commissioners of *Devon*, and *Cornwal*,
" that he would not advance beyond *Taunton*, till
" *Taunton* were reduced; but that he made no ques-
" tion, if he were not disturbed, speedily to give a
" good account of that place." In the mean time,
the Lord *Goring*, very gallantly and successfully, by
night, fell upon Sir *William Waller's* Quarters twice,

in less than a Week; and killed and took so good a
Number, that it was generally believed, Sir *William
Waller* was lessened near a thousand Men by those
Rencounters; the Lord *Goring* still declaring, "that
"he could neither pursue his advantages upon a
"Party, nor engage the main of the Rebels, without
"the addition of *Greenvil*'s Foot;" and he, notwithstanding all Orders, as peremptorily refusing to stir,
but professing, "that, if he had an addition of six
"hundred Men, he would be in the Town within
"six days."

Whilst things stood thus, Sir *William Waller*,
much weakened with these disasters, and the time of
his Command being near expired, drew back Eastward; and was, by night-marches, retired as far as
Salisbury, before the Lord *Goring* had notice of his
Motion. Whereupon his Highness, upon consideration how impossible it was to overtake him, which
General *Goring* himself confessed by his Letters, or
to engage the Forces under the Command of *Greenvil*,
and the other Forces of those parts, in any Action,
before the business of *Taunton* should be over (which
indeed disappointed all our hopes both of Men, and
Money, in that great County) and on the other side,
considering, if that place were reduced (as Sir *Richard
Greenvil* undertook it should be in six days, and
others, who had viewed it, thought it not a work
of time) besides the terror it would strike into their
Neighbours, there would be an Army of four thousand Horse, and five thousand Foot, ready to be applied to any service they should be directed to, and
that then the Lord *Goring* might prosecute his Com-

mission in *Sussex*, and *Kent*, with such a reasonable Recruit of Foot as should be necessary, and yet his Highness enabled, in a short time, to be in the head of a very good Army, raised out of the four Associated Counties, either for the reducing the few other places which were Garrisoned by the Rebels, or to march toward his Majesty: I say, upon these considerations, the Prince (with the privity and advice of Prince *Rupert*, who was then at *Bristol*, and present at the whole consultation, and the principal adviser in it) writ, upon the eleventh of *April*, to the Lord *Goring*, being then about *Wells*, "that his
" opinion was, that the Horse and Dragoons under
" his Lordship's Command, should advance from the
" Quarters where they then were, much to the pre-
" judice of that County, into *Dorsetshire*, or *Wilt-*
" *shire*, or into both of them; and that the Foot and
" Cannon should march directly towards *Taunton*,
" according to the design formerly proposed by his
" Lordship; and referred it to himself, whether his
" Lordship in Person would stay with the Horse, or
" go with the Foot; and desired to receive his opi-
" nion, and resolution upon the whole; there being
" nothing proposed to be acted in two days." This Letter was sent by Colonel *Windham*, the Governor of *Bridgewater*, who came that day, from before *Taunton*, from Sir *Richard Greenvil*; and could best inform him of the strength of the Town, and the condition of Sir *Richard Greenvil*'s Forces.

The next day Colonel *Windham* returned, with a short sullen Letter from the Lord *Goring* to the Prince, " that he had, according to his Command,

" sent the Foot and Cannon to *Taunton*; and the
" Horse, to the other places; and that, since there
" was now nothing for him to do, he was gone to
" *Bath* to intend his Health: where he complained
" privately, that his Forces were taken from him at
" a time when he meant to pursue *Waller*, and could
" utterly Defeat him;" and much inveighed against
the Prince's Council, for sending Orders to him so
prejudicial to the King's Service: whereas it was
only an Opinion, and not Orders, grounded upon
what himself had formerly proposed, and to which
he was desired to return his present judgment, being
within half a days Journey of the Prince, upon whom
he ought to have attended in Person, or have sent
his advice to him, if what was then offered seemed
not convenient. But, after some days frolicly spent,
at *Bath*, he returned to his former temper, and waiting on the Prince at *Bristol*, was contented to be
told, " that he had been more apprehensive of Dis-
" courtesies than he had cause;" and so all misunderstandings seemed to be fairly made up.

   The Lord *Goring*'s Foot and Cannon being thus
suddenly sent to *Taunton*, under the Command of
Sir *Joseph Wagstaffe*; for the better preventing any
Mistakes, and Contests about Command, the Prince
sent the Lords *Capel* and *Colepepper* to *Taunton*, to
settle all disputes that might arise, and to dispose the
Country to assist that work in the best manner; which
proved very fortunate; for the same day they came
thither, Sir *Richard Greenvil*, having brought his
Forces within Musquet-shot, on one side of *Taunton*,
went himself to view *Wellington*-House, five Miles

distant, in which the Rebels had a Garrison, and was, out of a Window, shot in the Thigh; with which he fell, the wound being then conceived to be Mortal: so that there was no Person who would pretend to Command; those under *Greenvil*, having no experienced Officer of Reputation equal to that Charge, yet being Superior in number to the other, would not be Commanded by Sir *Joseph Wagstaffe*; so that if the Lords had not very happily been present, it is probable, both those Bodies of Foot, each being too weak for the attempt by itself, would, if not disbanded, at best have retired to their former Posts, and left those of *Taunton* at liberty to have done what they thought best. But they being there, and Sir *John Berkeley* being in that instant come thither to meet them, with an Account of the State of *Devonshire*, they persuaded him to undertake the present Charge of the whole (all the Officers of both Bodies having formerly received Orders from him) and to prosecute the former design upon the Town; all Persons submitting till the Prince's Pleasure should be farther known; those Officers under Sir *Richard Greenvil*, presently sending away an Express to *Bristol*, to desire the Lord *Hopton* to take the Command of them. But his Lordship had no mind to enter upon any particular Action with disjointed Forces, till, upon the withdrawing of the Lord *Goring*, the whole Command might be Executed according to former establishment. And so a special direction was sent to all the Officers, and Soldiers, to obey Sir *John Berkeley*, according to what had been formerly settled by the Lords. He, in few days, put the business in very good Order, and by Storm took *Wellington*-House, where *Greenvil* had been hurt. I cannot omit here, that the Lords, coming to visit *Greenvil*, in the instant that he was put into his Litter, and carrying to *Exeter*, told him, what they had thought necessary to be done in the point of Command; the which he seeming very well to approve, they desired him to call his Officers (most of the principal being there present) and to Command them to proceed in the work in hand cheerfully, under the Command of Sir *John Berkeley*; the which he promised to do, and immediately said somewhat to his Officers, at the side of his Litter, which the Lords conceived to be what he had promised: but it appeared after, that it was not so; and, very probably, was the contrary; for neither Officer, nor Soldier, did his duty after he was gone, during the time Sir *John Berkeley* Commanded in that Action.

The Prince, finding the Public Service in no degree advanced by the Commissioners of *Somerset*, and that though there was no progress made in the Association affected, and undertaken by them, yet it served to cross, and oppose all other attempts whatsoever; those who had no mind to do any thing, satisfying themselves with the visible impossibility of that design, and yet the other, who had first proposed it, thinking themselves engaged to consent to no alteration; and his Highness being informed by a Gentleman (sent by him, at his first coming to *Bristol*, to the two farthest Western-Counties, to press the execution of whatsoever was promised in order to the Association) " that those two Counties of *Devon*, "and *Cornwal*, were entirely devoted to serve the Prince, in what manner soever he should propose," he thought fit, to summon the Commissioners of all the Associated Counties, to attend upon him in some convenient place, where, upon full consideration, such conclusions might be made, as might best advance the work in hand, both for the reduction of *Taunton*, and raising a marching Army; which Counsel had been sooner given, and had in truth been fit to be put in practice upon his first coming to *Bristol*, when he discerned the flatness, peremptoriness, and unactivity of the Gentlemen of *Somerset*; from whom it was evident nothing was to be expected, till, by the unanimity and strength of the two Western Counties, that County could be driven and compelled to do what was necessary, and to recede from their own sullen and positive determinations; which had been easy to do, but that shortly after his Highness came to *Bristol*, upon what apprehensions no Man knew, there was great jealousy at *Oxford* of his going farther West; and thereupon direction given "that he should not remove from *Bristol*, but upon weighty reasons, and with which his Majesty was to be first acquainted." Whereas, by his instructions, "he was to make his residence in such a place, as by the Council should be thought most conducing to his Affairs." However, such a meeting with all the Commissioners being demonstrably necessary, and *Bristol* thought at too great a distance from the West, besides that the Plague begun to break out there very much, for the time of the year, his Highness resolved to go to *Bridge-*

The Prince summons the Commissioners of the

water for a few days, and to summon thither the Commissioners, the rather to give some countenance to the business of *Taunton*, then closely Besieged by Sir *John Berkeley*; and to that purpose, directed his Letters to the several Commissioners to attend him there, on *Wednesday* the three-and-twentieth of *April*; the King being then at *Oxford*, preparing for the Field, Prince *Rupert* at *Worcester*, levying Men, and the Rebels at *London* in some disorder and confusion about their new Model, having newly removed the Earl of *Essex*, and Earl of *Manchester*, Earl of *Denbigh*, and Sir *William Waller* from any Command, and Substituted Sir *Thomas Fairfax* General; who was, out of the other broken and almost dissolved Forces, to mould a new Army, which was then in no very hopeful forwardness.

<small>BOOK IX.
four Associated western Counties to Bridgewater.</small>

Upon the day, the Prince came to *Bridgewater*; and was attended by a great body of the Commissioners of *Somerset*, that place being near the centre of that great County; there appeared for *Dorsetshire*, as sent from the rest, Sir *John Strangewaies*, Mr. *Anchetil Grey*, and Mr. *Ryves*; for *Devonshire*, Sir *Peter Ball*, Sir *George Parry*, Mr. *Saint Hill*, and Mr. *Muddyford*; and for *Cornwal*, Sir *Henry Killegrew*, Mr. *Coriton*, Mr. *Scawen*, and Mr. *Roscorroth*. The whole Body waited on the Prince the next morning; and were then told, "that his coming thither was to
" receive Their Advice, and to give His Assistance,
" in what might concern the Peace and welfare of
" each particular County; and might best advance
" the General service of the King; that if the Association which had been proposed, seemed to them,

"by the accidents and mutations which had happened since the time of that first proposal' (as in truth very notable ones had happened) "not fit now to be further prosecuted, he was ready to consent to any alteration they should propose, and to join with them in any other expedient; and wished them therefore to confer together, what was best to be done; and when they were ready to propose any thing to him, he would be ready to receive it." After two or three days consultation amongst themselves, they were unanimously of opinion (except Sir *John Stawel*, who, against all the rest, and against all that could be said to him, continued positive for the general rising of One and All, and for that alone) "that That design was for the present to be laid aside; and that, instead thereof, those Counties, according to their several known proportions would in a very short time" (as I remember a Month was the utmost) "raise, and Arm, six thousand Foot, besides the Prince's Guards, which would be full two thousand more; not reckoning those of the Lord *Goring's* which were fifteen hundred, but including the Foot of Sir *John Berkeley*, and Sir *Richard Greenvil* then before *Taunton*;" which all Men concluded, would be reduced in less than a Month. This Proposition being approved by the Prince, all particulars were agreed upon: the several days for the Rendezvous of the new levies, and the Officers, to whom the Men were to be delivered, named; and Warrants issued out accordingly: all things requisite for the speedy reduction of *Taunton* ordered, and directed; so that,

OF THE REBELLION.

towards the taking that place, and the raising an Army speedily, all things stood so fair, that more could not be wished.

As this Journey to *Bridgewater* wrought this good effect, so it produced one notable inconvenience, and discovered another. The Prince, having before his coming from *Oxford* been very little conversant with business, had been persuaded, from his coming out, to sit frequently, if not constantly, in Council, to mark, and consider the state of Affairs, and to accustom himself to a habit of speaking, and judging upon what was said; to the which he had with great ingenuity applied himself; but coming to *Bridgewater*, and having an extraordinary kindness for Mrs. *Windham*, who had been his Nurse, he was not only diverted by her folly, and petulancy, from applying himself to the serious consideration of his business, but accustomed to hear her speak negligently and scornfully of the Council; which though at first it made no impression in Him of disrespect towards them, encouraged other People who heard it, to the like liberty; and from thence grew an irreverence towards them; which reflected upon himself, and served to bring prejudice to their Counsels throughout the whole course. She had many private designs of benefit and advantage to herself, and her Children, and the qualifying her Husband to do all Acts of power without control upon his Neighbours, and labored to procure Grants, or Promises of Reversions of Lands from the Prince; and finding that the Prince was not to transact any such thing, without the Advice of the Council, and that They were not like to comply in thofe enterprifes, fhe contrived to raife jealoufies and diflikes between them, and kindled fuch a faction in the Prince's Family, as produced many inconveniences. For from hence Sir *Charles Berkeley*, who had a promife to be made Controller of the Prince's Houfehold, and Mr. *Long*, who had the like promife to be his Secretary, when he fhould be created Prince of *Wales* (till which time thofe Officers were never made) began to think they had injury done them, that they were not prefently of the Prince's Council, to which the places they were to have, gave them Title; though they knew well, that the Lords who then attended upon the Prince, were of the King's Privy-Council, and in that capacity only, waited upon his Highnefs; and that the other were only of the Prince's own Council for his Revenue, and for the adminiftration of the Dutchy of *Cornwal*, for which his Highnefs had now his livery.

However, thefe Fancies, thus weakly grounded, and entertained, made fuch an impreffion upon thofe Perfons, that they united themfelves into a Faction, and prevailed over the weaknefs of the Earl of *Berkfhire* to join with them; and, by degrees, all of them joined with all other difcontented Perfons, to render the Council to be much neglected and undervalued. Laftly, fhe being a Woman of no good breeding, and of a Country-pride, *Nihil muliebre præter corpus gerens*, valued herfelf much upon the Power, and Familiarity, which her Neighbours might fee fhe had with the Prince of *Wales*; and therefore, upon all occafions, in company, and when the Concourfe

OF THE REBELLION.

of the People was greatest, would use great boldness towards him; and, which was worse than all this, she affected in all Companies, where she let herself out to any freedom, a very negligent and disdainful mention of the Person of the King; the knowledge of which humor of hers, was one reason that made his Majesty unwilling his Son should go farther West than *Bristol*; since he knew *Bridegewater* must be a Stage in that motion. This her ill disposition was no sooner known to the Lords, who were all absolute strangers to her before, than they took care that his Highness should make no longer residence in that Garrison.

The other inconvenience, that it discovered, was the design of the Lord *Goring* to have the Command of the West. For then it grew very apparent, that, whatever had been pretended for *Kent*, or *Sussex*, he had, from the beginning, affected that Charge; and, I fear, had some other encouragement for it, than was then avowed. And therefore, from his first coming into those Parts, he had with great industry caressed the Commissioners of *Somerset*, and *Devon*, and especially those, whom he thought not well inclined to the Lord *Hopton*; whom, by all ill Arts, he endeavoured to undervalue; inveighing against " the " too great Contribution, assigned to the Garrison of " *Bristol*; and that any should be allowed to the unne- " cessary Garrison (as he called it) at *Lamport*; which " had been lately settled by the Lord *Hopton*;" and, as appeared afterwards, was of vast importance: those discourses being most Popular to the Country, though most pernicious to the King: and promised " great

"strictness and severity of Discipline, if that Power
"under the Prince might be devolved to him." To
Bridgewater he came at the same time from *Bath*,
upon pretence of "visiting *Taunton*, and seeing
"whether the work were like to be soon done, that
"it might be worth the intending it." But, in truth,
to drive on his Project for Command with the Commissioners; who were invited by Sir *Peter Ball* to
make it one of the Propositions to the Prince, "that
"the Lord *Goring* might be constituted his Lieute-
"nant-General;" which he himself had so absolutely
digested, that, as if the matter itself had been out of
question, he proposed privately to most of the
Prince's Council, the Rules that should be observed
between them in the Government of the Army, and
the Administration of the Civil part. Some, of no
extraordinary kindness to *Goring*, wished the agreement made, and Him settled in the Command, as
the best, if not the only Expedient, for advancement
of the King's Service, and for the speedy forming an
Army worthy of the Prince's own Person in the
Head of it; apprehending, that the dividing his
Forces from the New Levies, would leave a good
body of Foot without an equal Power of Horse, and
without a Train, except a longer time were given
for the making it, than the state of Affairs promised
to permit. But when *Goring* discovered by his discourse with several of the Council (with whom he
communicated upon the Argument very freely, and
expressed in plain English, "that except he might
"be satisfied in the particulars he proposed, he should
"have no heart to proceed in the public Service)"

OF THE REBELLION.

that they would not consent to any Act that might reflect upon the Lord *Hopton;* and that some of them had such a prejudice to his Person, that they would make no conjunction with him; he resolved to compass his ends some other way; and so, pressed it no farther in any public address to the Prince at that time. It is not to be omitted, that he was then offered, and assured, " that, as soon as the business of *Taunton* " should be over, he should have such a Recruit out " of the New Levies, as would make up his own " Foot three thousand Men, besides Officers;" with " which he might well prosecute his former design;" and, in the mean time, he had the absolute Command; the Lord *Hopton* not at all interposing, or meddling with the Army.

It was now concluded by all Men who had well considered his carriage and behaviour from his first coming into the West, that, as he had formed that design in his own thoughts from the first, of being about the Prince, and resolved never to march with the Army under Prince *Rupert* (whose nature was not agreeable to him) so that he had purposely and willingly suffered *Vandruske* to Relieve *Taunton,* and even *Weymouth* to be again recovered by that handful of Men who had been beaten out of it, lest the business of the West might be done without him, by other Men; and that his presence there might not be thought necessary. For if *Taunton* had been reduced, as it must have been if that small Party had not Relieved it even in the last Article, he could have had no pretence to have stayed in those Parts, but must immediately have pursued his former design upon *Sussex*,

BOOK IX.
and those other Counties, for which he had never any reasonable foundation; or have continued his march to the King; which he had less mind to do. When he first left *Oxford*, and went into *Hampshire*, which was before the end of the Treaty at *Uxbridge*, he had, in his jovial Fits, where he was always very unreserved, declared, with great resentment, " that " his Father was ill treated by the Queen in *France*, " and that he hoped shortly to be in such a posture, " that the King should find it reasonable to use both " his Father and Himself better." And yet the King had even then, upon his Suit, made his Father Captain of his Guard of Halberdeers, and Created him Earl of *Norwich*, whereby himself had the Appellation of Lord, which he enough affected: and in his first debauches at *Exeter*, his brother *Porter*, who was Lieutenant-General of his Horse, informed some Persons of Honor in confidence, " that *Goring* resolved " to make himself Lieutenant-General to the Prince, " or else to be very discontented." This Advertisement was sent to some of the Council, upon his Highness's first coming to *Bristol;* and was the first hint that ever they received, that he had affected that Charge; and was not, with the rest of his behaviour, like to dispose them to wish that he might obtain his desire; but to do all that was in their power to prevent it.

The Commissioners of Devon complain of Sir Richard Greenvil.

The general business concerning the four Counties being agreed and settled at *Bridgewater*, the Commissioners for *Devon*, desired to be heard in what concerned that particular Country: and then informed " his Highness, " that upon Sir *Richard Greenvil's*
" first

" firſt entering upon the work of *Plymouth*, and his
" aſſurance under his hand, that he would take the
" Town before *Chriſtmas*-day, and that he would
" forthwith Raiſe, Arm, and pay twelve hundred
" Horſe, and ſix thouſand Foot, they had aſſigned
" him above one half of their whole Contribution,
" amounting to above eleven hundred pounds a
" Week; and, for the providing Arms and Ammu-
" nition, had aſſigned him the Arrears of the Con-
" tribution due from thoſe hundreds allotted to him;
" which amounted to near 6000l; he having likewiſe
" the whole Contribution of *Cornwal*, being above
" ſeven hundred pound weekly; and had received
" moſt part of the Letter and Subſcription-Money of
" that County, towards the ſame Service: that he
" had, from his firſt entering upon the charge, quietly
" enjoyed thoſe Contributions in *Devon*, which were
" duly paid; and had received the greateſt part of
" the Arrears aſſigned to him for the Proviſion of
" Arms and Ammunition: Notwithſtanding all
" which, he had never bought above twenty Barrels
" of Powder, or any Arms, but had received both
" the one and the other from Them, out of their Ma-
" gazines; and had never maintained, or raiſed,
" near half the Number of Men to which he was
" obliged, till the Week before he was required to
" march to *Taunton*; when he had called the *Poſſe-*
" *Comitatus*, and out of Them forced almoſt the
" whole Number of Foot, which marched with him
" thither, bringing them with him, as far as *Exeter*,
" unarmed; and there compelled the Commiſſioners
" to ſupply him with Arms, and Ammunition; that

Vol. VIII.   D

BOOK IX.

"having left scarce two thousand Foot, and four
"hundred Horse, before *Plymouth*, he continued
"still to receive the whole Contribution formerly
"assigned when he was to have twelve hundred
"Horse, and six thousand Foot; and would not part
"with any of it: so that he received more out of
"*Devonshire* for the blocking up of *Plymouth* (having
"all *Cornwal* to himself likewise) than was left for the
"Garrisons of *Exeter, Dartmouth, Barnstable,* and
"*Tiverton*, and for the finishing those Fortifications,
"Victualling the Garrisons, providing Arms and
"Ammunition; with which they had before not
"only supplied themselves but had sent great quan-
"tities to the King's Army, to the Lord *Goring*, and
"to the Siege of *Taunton:* That he would not suffer
"them to send any Warrants to collect the Letter
"and Subscription-Money, to settle the Excise, or
"meddle with Delinquents Estates in the hundreds
"assigned to him for Contribution; and had those
"continual contests with Sir *John Berkeley*, being
"Colonel-General of the County, and the other
"Governors of Garrisons; pretending that He had
"power to Command them; that there was such an
"Animosity grown between them, that they very
"much apprehended the danger of those divisions;
"there having been some blood shed, and Men
"killed, upon their private Contests:" and therefore
besought his Highness, "by his Authority, to settle
"the limits of their several jurisdictions, in order to
"the Martial Affairs; and likewise to order Sir
"*Richard Greenvil* to receive no more Contribution,
"than would suffice for the maintenance of those

"Men, who continued before *Plymouth*; whereby
"they could be only enabled to perform Their parts
"of the Affociation."

This was preffed with fo much earneftnefs, and reafon, that it was thought very advifable for his Highnefs himfelf to go to *Exeter*, where both the Commiffioners and Sir *Richard Greenvil* were; and there, upon the hearing of all that could be faid, to fettle the whole difpute. But, at the fame time, and whilft that matter was in confideration, Letters came from his Majefty to his Highnefs and the Lords, exprefsly inhibiting his going farther Weftward; upon what reafons I cannot imagine; and thereupon the Prince himfelf returned to *Briftol* on *Wednefday* the thirtieth of *April*, having ftaid at *Bridgewater* only feven days; and fent the Lords *Capel* and *Colepepper*; and the Chancellor of the Exchequer, to *Exeter*, with inftructions "to examine all the complaints, "and allegations of the Commiffioners, and to "fettle the bufinefs of the Contribution; and "upon view of the feveral Commiffions of Sir *John* "*Berkeley*, and Sir *Richard Greenvil*, fo to agree the "matter of jurifdiction, that the public Service might "not be obftructed."

Upon which the Prince fedds three Commiffioners of his own to Exeter and fo to return to Briftol:

As foon as the Lords appointed by his Highnefs to go to *Exeter*, came thither, they went the fame hour to Vifit Sir *Richard Greenvil*, who was ftill bedrid of his hurt. They intended it only as a Vifit, and fo would not reply, at that time, to many very fharp, and bitter complaints and invectives he made againft Sir *John Berkeley* (who was then at the Leaguer before *Taunton*) but told him, "that they would come

"to him again the next day, and confider of all bufi-
"neffes." Accordingly they came, when, with
great bitternefs, he again complained of the Governor,
and fome difrefpects from his Lieutenant-Governor:
but when he was preffed to particulars, he mentioned
principally fome high and difdainful Speeches,
the moft of which were denied by the other, and the
with-holding fome Prifoners from him, which he
had fent his Marfhal for near *Taunton*. The truth of
which, was this; whilft Sir *Richard* was before
Taunton, he had fent for one Mr. *Syms*, a Juftice of
Peace of the County, a rich and decrepit Man, who
lived within three miles of that Town. He charged
him with fome inclinations to the Rebels, and of
favoring their proceedings. The Gentleman ftood
upon his juftification, and innocency, and defired
to be upon any Trial. However, Sir *Richard* told
him, "he was a Traytor, and fhould redeem him-
"felf at a thoufand pound, or elfe he would proceed
"in another way;" and gave him three days to provide
the Money. Before the time expired, Sir *Richard*
was hurt, and carried to *Exeter*; whither he no
fooner came, but he defpatched his Marfhal to fetch
Mr. *Syms* to him; who appealed to Sir *John Berkeley*
(who had then the Command) and defired to be put
upon any Trial; and (befides that he was of a very
infirm body, and unfit for Travel) many Gentlemen
of the beft Quality gave him a very good Teftimony,
and undertook for his Appearance, when-ever he
fhould be called upon. Upon this, Sir *John Berkeley*
difcharged the Marfhal, and writ a very civil Letter
to Sir *Richard Greenvil*, of the whole matter; "and

"that he would see the Gentleman forth-coming
" upon the least warning; but that it would be an
" Act of great cruelty, to carry him a Prisoner, in
" that indisposition of health, from his House." Sir
Richard looked upon this as the robbing him of a
thousand pounds, and writ such a Letter to Sir *John
Berkeley*, so full of ill Language, and reproach, as I
have never seen the like From, and To a Gentleman;
and complained to us of the Injury. We told him,
" that neither He, nor Sir *John Berkeley*, had any
" Authority to meddle with Mr. *Syms*, or any Per-
" sons of that Quality; who could not be looked
" upon as Prisoners of War; but if in truth he should
" prove to be a Delinquent, and guilty of those
" 'crimes objected against him, his Fine and Com-
" position was due to the King, who had assigned
" the same to the Prince for the public Service; and
" that there were Commissioners, before whom he
" was regularly to be tried, and with whom he might
" only compound." He would not understand the
reason of this, but insisted upon " Sir *John Berkeley*'s
" protecting *Syms*, as a great indignity to himself."
On the other hand, Sir *John Berkeley* complained by
his Letters, "that those Soldiers brought to *Taunton*
" by *Creenvil*, every day mouldered away, and he
" had reason to believe it was by His direction; for
" that those that staid, and the Officers, were very
" backward in performing their duties; and that,
" after the taking of *Wellington*-House, he had com-
" manded that nothing should be done towards the
" defacing it, because it might possibly be fit to put
" a Garrison into it, if the Siege should be raised

"from *Taunton*; but that the Officer, who was
"under *Greenvil*, had, notwithstanding such Com-
"mand, burned it: That he proceeded in the levy-
"ing Monies, and sending out extravagant War-
"rants throughout the County; and many other
"particulars."

Sir *Richard Greenvil* denied, "that the Soldiers left
"the Leaguer, or that *Wellington*-House was burned,
"by any direction of His:" though it appeared,
that all such Soldiers as left their Colors and came to
him, were kindly used, and had Money given to
them by him; and that Lieutenant-Colonel *Robinson*,
after he had received Orders from Sir *John Berkeley*
not to slight *Wellington*-House, rode to *Exeter* to Sir
Richard Greenvil, and immediately, upon his return
from him, caused it to be burnt. *Greenvil* said, "that
"he levied no Monies, nor issued out any Warrants,
"but what he had Authority to do by his Commis-
"sion." In the end they showed him their Instructions from the Prince, "thoroughly to examine all
"differences between them; and, upon view of
"both their Commissions, to agree what limits each
"of them should observe." Thereupon, he showed
them his Commission in Paper, under his Majesty's
Sign Manual, attested by the Lord *Digby*, by which
he was authorized "to Command the Forces before
"*Plymouth*;" and in order thereunto, with such clauses of latitude and power, as he might both raise the
posse, and Command the Trained-bands, and indeed
the whole Forces of both Counties; and was to receive Orders from his Majesty, and his Lieutenant-
General; and was likewise at that time High-Sheriff

of *Devon*. Sir John Berkeley's Commission was precedent, and more formal, being under the Great Seal of *England*, "of Colonel-General of the Counties of "*Devon* and *Cornwal*, and to Command the whole "Forces of both Counties, as well Trained-bands, "as others;" so that, though their Commissions were not in intention all one, yet they included clauses, and powers, so much the same, that either of them had Authority enough to disturb the other; and he that only saw his own, might reasonably think he had power over the other: which, between Persons so disinclined one to the other as they were grown to be, might have proved very fatal, if the remedy had not been so near by his Highness's Authority.

After the perusal of their Commissions, they showed him their Instructions, concerning the regulating the Contributions, in proportionable assignments for the several Services; and desired his opinion, "what Forces were now necessary for the "blocking up of *Plymouth*, since any attempt for "the taking it was to be laid aside, at least for a "time? And that thereupon, such assignation might "be made to that purpose, as was sufficient, and the "rest otherwise disposed of." He told them, "that "the Forces then there (being about fifteen hundred "Foot and four hundred Horse, of the *Devonshire-* "side) were sufficient;" and proposed allowance little enough for the Service; and then said, "that "it troubled him to be confined to such an employ- "ment, as the blocking up a place, whilst there "was like to be so much Action in the Field; and "therefore he hoped, his Highness would give him leave to wait on him in the Army; where he thought he might do him much better Service." They told him, "they had Authority from the Prince" (for some of his Friends had mentioned the same, soon after he had received his wound) "if they found his health able to bear it, and his inclination led him that way, to let him know, that his Highness would be glad of his Service, in the moulding that Army which was then raising; which, allowing two thousand Foot to the recruiting the Lord *Goring*, would be in view six thousand Foot, and above two thousand Horse with the Guards: in which he had designed Him the Second Place of Command." But then, they said, "they knew not where to place the Command before *Plymouth*." Sir *Richard* very cheerfully received the Proposition for himself in the Army; and for *Plymouth*, he said, "no Man was fit to undertake the work There, but Sir *John Berkeley*, who had the Command of both Counties: that it was visible by the differences and breaches that had been between Them, how inconvenient it would be to have that Charge independent; whereas, if it were in one hand, the unanimous consent of both Counties, and all the Forces in them, would more easily do the business."

All things being thus agreed upon, as far as they could be without Sir *John Berkeley*'s consent, who was then before *Taunton*; the Lords resolved to return to the Prince, and in their way to dispose Sir *John Berkeley* to what had been proposed; and left the Chancellor of the Exchequer at *Exeter*, to agree with the Commiſſioners, upon the ſettlement of the Contributions, and to ſettle ſome other particulars which they had reſolved upon. The whole Contribution of the County of *Devon* amounted to two thouſand pound Weekly; whereof ſo many hundreds were aſſigned by the Commiſſioners, for the maintenance of the Forces before *Plymouth*, as amounted to the juſt proportion and eſtabliſhment propoſed by Sir. *Richard Greenvil* himſelf; and then ſo many to the Garriſons of *Exeter*, *Dartmouth*, *Barnſtable*, and *Tiverton*, as amounted to the payment of ſuch Forces, as, on all hands, were agreed to be abſolutely neceſſary for their defence, at the loweſt eſtabliſhment. All which being done, upon ſuppoſition that the whole Contribution, being two thouſand pound Weekly, would be, according to the aſſignments, exactly paid, there remained not a penny overplus, for the buying Ammunition and Arms, for the finiſhing Fortifications, for Victualling the Garriſons, or for blocking up of *Lyme*; which if it were not done, all that part of the Country would be liable to that preſſure; and ſo, unable to pay Contribution where it was aſſigned. But it was ſuppoſed, the laſt might be done by drawing out ſome Numbers from the ſeveral Garriſons, if there were no diſturbance from abroad; and the reſt muſt be ſupplied out of the Exciſe (the Major part whereof was by the King aſſigned for the Support of the Princeſs *Henrietta* left at *Exeter*) and ſome other extraordinary ways to be thought of; the Letter-Money, and Subſcription-Money, being almoſt exhauſted.

His Highneſs was no ſooner returned to *Briſtol*

BOOK IX.

Goring joins the King at Oxford.

from *Bridgewater*, which was on the last day of *April*, than General *Goring* was sent for by the King, to draw his Horse and Dragoons towards *Oxford*; that thereby his Majesty might free himself from *Cromwell*; who, with a very strong Party of Horse and Dragoons, lay in wait, to interrupt his joining with Prince *Rupert* about *Worcester*. How unwelcome soever these Orders were to the Lord *Goring*, yet there was no remedy but he must obey them: and it was now hoped, that the West should be hereafter freed from him, where he was at that time very ungracious. He marched with that Expedition towards the King, who was then at *Woodstock*, that he fell upon a Horse-Quarter of *Cromwell's*, and another Party of *Fairfax's* Horse, as they were attempting a passage over the River of *Isis*, so prosperously (the very Evening before he came to the King) that he broke and defeated them with a great slaughter, which gave him great Reputation, and made him exceedingly welcome: and it was indeed a very seasonable Action, to discountenance, and break such a Party, in the Infancy of their new model; and did break their present measures, and made *Fairfax* to appoint a new place of Rendezvous for his new Army, at a greater distance from the King's Forces.

Resolutions taken at Oxford.

Prince *Rupert*, who now met with very little opposition in Council, had, throughout the Winter, disposed the King to resolve "to march Northwards, " and to fall upon the *Scottish* Army in *Yorkshire*, " before *Fairfax* should be able to perfect his new " model to that degree, as to take the Field." This design was not unreasonable; nor the Prince to blame for desiring to take revenge on them for what passed the last year; which, now they were separated from the *English*, who had indeed defeated him, he believed was easy to be done. That purpose of marching Northward was now the more hastened, that, in the way, *Chester* might be relieved; which was closely besieged; and then they might come soon enough to *Pontefract*-Castle, before which the *Scottish* Army then was; and if they could defeat that, the King would be again, upon the matter, Master of the North: which, by the insolence of the *Scots*, and the dislike they had of the new model, was conceived to be better affected than ever. The next day after *Goring* came to the King, the Army was drawn to a Rendezvous, and consisted then of five thousand Foot, and above six thousand Horse; an Army not to be reasonably lessened in the beginning of a Campaign, when the King was to expect he should have so much to do; and if it had been kept together, it is very probable, that the Summer might have been crowned with better success.

Fairfax was then about *Newbury*, not in readiness to march; yet reported to be much more unready than he was. It was said, that his design was to carry his whole Army to the relief of *Taunton*, brought almost to extermity; which if he could bring to pass, would give him great reputation, and would make the Parliament near Sharers with the King in the interest of the West. Upon this prospect, it was thought reasonable, and accordingly proposed, "that "the King himself would march with his Army into "the West; and thereby, not only prevent the relief of *Taunton*, but compel *Fairfax* to Fight, before he should be able to join with *Cromwell*; who had not gathered his Troops together." This was the concurrent advice of the whole Council with which the King used to consult, Prince *Rupert* only excepted, and Sir *Marmaduke Langdale*, who Commanded the Northern-Horse; which were impatient to be in their own Country. Now the very contrary Affections towards each other, between Prince *Rupert* and the Lord *Goring*, began to co-operate to one and the same end. The Prince found that *Goring*, as a Man of a ready Wit, and an excellent Speaker, was like to have most Credit with the King in all debates; and was jealous, that, by his Friendship with the Lord *Digby*, he would quickly get such an interest with his Majesty, that his own Credit would be much Eclipsed. Hereupon, he did no less desire that *Goring* should return again into the West, than *Goring* did, not to remain where Prince *Rupert* Commanded. This produced a great Confidence and Friendship between them, and the Prince told him all that any of the Council had spoken freely to him, when his Highness abhorred nothing more than that *Goring* should be near the Prince of *Wales*; and *Goring* said all of the Council, which he believed would most irreconcile him to them. So they both agreed to do all they could, to lessen the Credit and Authority of the Council. The King was desired to receive the Information, and State of the West, from *Goring*; who, upon the late good Fortune he had, and by the Artifices of the Lord *Digby*, was too easily believed.

He informed the King with all imaginable confidence, " that if, by the pofitive Command of the
" Prince, contrary to his opinion and advice, his
" Forces had not been taken from him, and applied
" to the Siege of *Taunton*, he had doubtlefs totally
" ruined all *Waller's* Forces, and prevented the com-
" ing of thofe Parties who had given his Majefty fo
" much trouble at *Oxford:* that he had been always
" ufed, upon his refort to the Prince, with great dif-
" refpect, being not called into the Council, but put
" to an attendance without, amongft inferior Sui-
" ters;" and then told many particular paffages at *Bridgewater*, of which he raifed advantage to himfelf, upon the prejudice he begot to others.

Whereas the truth of the defign upon *Taunton* is before fet down, with all the circumftances; and *Waller* was marched beyond *Salifbury*, before the Lord *Goring*, knew where he was; and confeffed, there was no overtaking him; and he had always received as much refpect from the Prince, and Council, as could be given to a Subject; being conftantly called, and admitted to Council when he was prefent; and when abfent, opinions and advices fent to him from the Council, upon fuch particulars as himfelf propofed, with a full reference to his difcretion, to do, upon the place, as he judged moft meet: yet, I fay, he got fo much Credit, that the King, by his Letters of the tenth of *May* to the Prince, directed,
" that General *Goring* fhould be admitted into all
" confultations and Debates, and advifed withal, as
" if he were one of the eftablifhed Council; that
" Prince *Rupert* having granted him Power, to give

"Commissions in that Army, all Commissions to be "granted should pass by General *Goring*; and that "none should be granted by the Prince, in his own "Name, otherwise than in such Cases as were of re- "lation merely to the Association: that the Council "should contribute their opinions and advices to "General *Goring*, but that his Highness should care- "fully forbear to give unto the Lord *Goring* any po- "sitive or binding Orders;" whereas, by his Instructions, when he came from *Oxford*, he was to put both his Commissions, of Generalissimo, and of General of the Association in execution, as he found most convenient; his Majesty himself then entertaining very little hope of the Association, as it was proposed; and therefore, by his Letters to the Prince of the twentieth of *April*, which came to him at *Bridgewater*, all the assignations formerly made towards the Association, were directed to be disposed, and converted to such uses, as by the advice of his Council should be found most advantageous to the Service of those Parts; and thereupon the Levies were consented to, and directed as is before mentioned. With these triumphant Orders, the Lord *Goring* returned into the West; where we shall now leave him, and wait upon his Majesty, in his unfortunate march, until we find cause enough to lament that Counsel, which so fatally dismissed *Goring*, and his Forces, at a time, in which, if he had been born to Serve his Country, his presence might have been of great use and benefit to the King; which it was never after in any occasion.

The Lord Goring sent back into the West.

When *Goring* was thus separated from the King's Army, his Majesty marched to *Evesham*; and in his way, drew out his Garrison from *Cambden*-House; which had brought no other benefit to the Public, than the enriching the licentious Governor thereof; who exercised an illimited Tyranny over the whole Country, and took his leave of it, in wantonly burning the Noble Structure, where he had too long inhabited, and which, not many years before, had cost above thirty thousand pounds the building. Within few days after the King left *Evesham*, it was surprised by the Enemy, or rather stormed and taken for want of Men to defend the Works; and the Governor, and all the little Garrison made Prisoners. The loss of this place was an ill Omen to the succeeding Summer; and, upon the matter, cut off all the intercourse between *Worcester*, and *Oxford*; nor was it at all repaired by the taking of *Hawkesly*-House in *Worcestershire*; which the Rebels had fortified, and made strong, and which the King's Army took in two days, and therein the Governor, and one hundred and twenty Prisoners; who served to redeem those who were lost in *Evesham*. And so, by easy and slow marches the Army prosecuted their way towards *Chester*. But, in *Staffordshire*, the Lord *Byron*, who was Governor of *Chester*, met the King; and informed him, "that the Rebels, upon the noise of his "Majesty's advance, were drawn off;" and so there was no more to be done, but to prosecute the Northern design; which was now intended, and the Army upon it's march accordingly, when Intelligence was brought, "that *Fairfax* had sent a strong Party "to relieve *Taunton*, and was Himself, with his "Army, sat down before *Oxford*." This could not

BOOK IX.

Marches of the King's Army towards the North, whilst Sir Thomas Fairfax with his, sat down before Oxford.

but make some alteration, at least a pause in the Execution of the former Counsels: and yet *Oxford* was known to be in so good a Condition, that the loss of it could not in any degree be apprehended, and nothing could more reasonably have been wished, than that *Fairfax* should be thoroughly engaged before it: And it was concluded, " that the best way to " draw him from thence, would be to fall upon some " place possessed by the Parliament."

The King storms, and takes Leicester.

They had no Town so considerable near the place where the King then was, as *Leicester*; in which there was a good Garrison, under the Command of Sir *Robert Pye*; and Prince *Rupert*, who was always pleased with any brisk attempt, cheerfully entertained the first motion, and sent Sir *Marmaduke Langdale* forthwith to surround it (which was of great extent) with his Horse; and the next day, being the last of *May*, the whole Army was drawn about the Town, and the Prince, having taken a view of it, Commanded a Battery to be forthwith raised against an old high stone-Wall, on the South-side of the Town; which, by his own continued presence, was finished with admirable diligence: which done, he sent a Summons to the Governor; who returned not such an Answer as was required. Thereupon, the Battery began to play; and, in the space of four hours, made such a Breach, that it was thought Counselable, the same Night to make a general Assault with the whole Army, in several places; but principally at the Breach; which was defended with great Courage, and Resolution; insomuch, that the King's Forces were twice repulsed with great loss, and slaughter; and

and were even ready to draw off in defpair: when another Party, on the other fide of the Town, under the Command of Colonel *Page*, feconded by a Body of Horfe that came but that day from *Newark*, and, putting themfelves on Foot, advanced, with their Swords and Piftols, with the other, entered the Town: and made way for their Fellows to follow them: fo that, by the break of day, the Affault having continued all the Night, all the King's Army entered the Line. Then the Governor, and all the Officers and Soldiers, to the Number of twelve hundred, threw down their Arms, and became Prifoners of War: whilft the Conquerors purfued their advantage, with the ufual Licence of Rapine, and Plunder, and miferably facked the whole Town, without any diftinction of Perfons, or Places; Churches, and Hofpitals, as well as other Houfes, were made a Prey to the enraged, and greedy Soldier, to the exceeding regret of the King; who well knew, that, how difaffected foever that Town was generally, there were yet many who had faithful hearts to him, and who he heartily wifhed might be diftinguifhed from the reft: but thofe Seafons admitted no difference of Perfons. Though the place was well gotten, becaufe fo little time had been fpent in the getting it, yet it was not without very confiderable lofs on the King's fide; there being near two hundred Soldiers dead upon the places of Affault, with many Officers; Colonel *Saint George*, and others of Name; befides many more wounded, and maimed. The King prefently made the Lord *Loughborough*, a younger Son of the Earl of *Huntington*, and one who had served him eminently from the beginning of the War, Governor of *Leicester*; and Sir *Matthew Appleyard*, a Soldier of known Courage and Experience, his Lieutenant-Governor.

The taking of *Leicester*, the chief Town of that Province, even as soon as he came before it, and in that manner, purely by an Act of great Courage, gave the King's Army great reputation, and made a wonderful impression of terror upon the hearts of those at *Westminster*; who now revolved the conditions, which were offered at *Uxbridge*; which they had refused. They began to curse their new model; and to reproach those who had persuaded them " so " ungratefully to throw off their old General, who " was ready to foment all their discontents. It was " not above twenty days, that the King's Army had " been in the Field, and in that short time, it had " reduced two strong Garrisons of Theirs, without " giving the Soldiers any conditions, *Hawkesly* House " in *Worcestershire*, and the Town of *Leicester*: whilst " their new General *Fairfax* had only faced *Oxford* " at a distance, to try whether the Ladies would " prevail for the giving up of the Town, to pacify " their fears; and had attempted to take a poor House " that lay near, *Borstall*-House, and had been beaten " from thence with considerable loss, and had drawn " off from both, very little to his Honor." These discourses were so public in the City, and had so much Credit in both Houses of Parliament, that they exceedingly desired Peace, and exercised their thoughts only how they might revive the old Treaty, or set a new one on foot; when the evil Genius of the Kingdom in a moment shifted the whole Scene.

Leicester was a Post, where the King might, with all possible Convenience and Honor, have sat still, till his Army might have been recruited, as well as thoroughly refreshed. Colonel *Gerrard* was upon his march towards him from *Wales*, with a Body of three thousand Horse and Foot: and he had reason to expect, that the Lord *Goring* would be very shortly with him with his Horse; for he was not departed from the King above four or five days, with those Orders which are mentioned before (and with which he was so well pleased) but that the King saw cause to repent his separation, and sent other Orders to recal him as soon as was possible. But the King's fate, and the natural unsteadiness, and irresolution of those about him, hurried him into Counsels very disagreeable to the posture he was in. He knew not that *Fairfax* was gone from *Oxford*; and the Intelligence which some Men pretended to have received from thence, was, "that it was in distress." The Duke of *York* remained there; the Council, many Lords and Ladies, who sent Intelligence to their Friends, and all the Magazines were there, and if all these should fall into the Enemies hands, *Leicester* would appear a very poor recompence. These particulars being unskilfully, yet warmly pressed by those who could not be understood to mean amiss, the King resolved to march directly for *Oxford*; and in order thereunto, within five days after the taking of *Leicester*, he appointed the Rendezvous for his Army; where he might yet very reasonably have been discouraged from prosecuting that intention; for it then appeared evidently, how very much it was weakened

BOOK IX.

by, and since that Action, by the loss of those who were killed and wounded in the Storm; by the absence of those who were left behind in the Garrison; and by the running away of very many with their Plunder, who would in few days have returned.

The number of the King's Foot which remained, did not amount to above three thousand five hundred; which was not a Body sufficient to Fight a Battle for a Crown. Then, all the Northern Horse, who had promised themselves, and were promised by the King, that they should go into their own Country, were so displeased with this new Resolution, that they were with great difficulty restrained from Disbanding; and, though they were at last prevailed with to march, were not enough recovered to be depended upon in any sudden Action. Notwithstanding all this, the march was continued; the next day, at *Harborough*, the Intelligence came " that *Fairfax* was drawn off from *Oxford*, without having ever approached so near it, as to discharge one Piece of Cannon upon it; that he had been beaten off from *Borstal*-House with the loss of Officers, as well as Soldiers; and that he was marched with his whole Army to *Buckingham*." But this kindled a greater appetite to find him out, than there was before. Indeed there was less reason to march Northward, since they might well apprehend the *Scottish* Army in their Face, and *Fairfax* in their Rear. But there was the same reason still for their retiring back to *Leicester*, or to *Worcester*, where they might expect, and could not fail of an Addition of Forces to the Army; and where the Enemy, who must now

Sir Thomas Fairfax draws off from Oxford.

be obliged to find them out, muſt come with many diſadvantages. Theſe Conſiderations were all laid aſide, and every body believed, that Fairfax his Army was much diſpirited, by having failed in their two firſt Enterpriſes; and that it was now led out of the way, that it might recover Courage, before it ſhould be brought to Fight with ſo Victorious Troops, as the King's were: and therefore, that it was beſt to find them out, whilſt their fear was yet upon them: all Men concluding that to be true, which their own wiſhes ſuggeſted to them. So the Army marched to *Daventry* in *Northamptonſhire*: where, for want of knowing where the Enemy was, or what he intended to do, the King remained in a quiet poſture the ſpace of five days.

Upon the thirteenth of *June*, the King received Intelligence that *Fairfax* was advanced to *Northampton*, with a ſtrong Army; much ſuperior to the Numbers he had formerly been adverciſed of. Whereupon, his Majeſty retired the next day to *Harborough*; and meant to have gone back to *Leiceſter*, that he might draw more Foot out of *Newark*, and ſtand upon his defence, till the other Forces which he expected, could come up to him. But, that very Night, an Alarm was brought to *Harborough*, that *Fairfax* himſelf was Quartered within ſix Miles. A Council was preſently called, the former Reſolution of retiring preſently laid aſide, and a new one as quickly taken, "to Fight;" to which there was always an immoderate appetite, when the Enemy was within any diſtance. They would not ſtay to expect his coming, but would go back to meet him. And

BOOK IX.

so, in the Morning early, being *Saturday* the fourteenth of *June*, all the Army was drawn up, upon a rising ground of very great advantage about a Mile South from *Harborough* (which was left at their back) and there put in order to give or receive the Charge. The main Body of the Foot was led by the Lord *Astley* (whom the King had lately made a Baron) consisting of about two thousand and five hundred Foot; the right Wing of Horse, being about two thousand, was led by Prince *Rupert*; the left Wing, consisting of all the Northern-Horse, with those from *Newark*, which did not amount to above sixteen hundred, was Commanded by Sir *Marmaduke Langdale*; in the Reserve, were the King's Life-Guard, Commanded by the Earl of *Lindsey*, and Prince *Rupert*'s Regiment of Foot (both which did make very little above eight hundred) with the King's Horse-Guards, Commanded by the Lord *Bernard Stuart* (newly made Earl of *Lichfield*) which made that day about five hundred Horse.

The Army, thus disposed in good order, made a stand on that ground to expect the Enemy. About eight of the Clock in the Morning, it began to be doubted, whether the Intelligence they had received of the Enemy was true. Upon which the Scoutmaster was sent to make farther discovery; who, it seems, went not far enough; but returned and averred, "that he had been three or four Miles forward, " and could neither discover, nor hear any thing of " them:" presently, a report was raised in the Army, " that the Enemy was retired." Prince *Rupert* thereupon drew out a Party of Horse and Musqueteers, both to discover, and engage them, the Army remaining still in the same place, and posture they had been in. His Highness had not marched above a mile, when he received certain Intelligence of Their advance, and in a short time after, he saw the Van of their Army, but it seems not so distinctly, but that he conceived they were retiring. Whereupon, he advanced nearer with his Horse, and sent back, " that the Army should march up to him;" and the Messenger who brought the Order, said, " that the " Prince desired they should make haste." Hereupon the advantage-ground was quitted, and the excellent order they were in, and an advance made towards the Enemy, as well as might be. By that time they had marched about a mile and a half, the Horse of the Enemy was discerned to stand upon a high ground about *Naseby*; whence, seeing the manner of the King's march, in a full Campaign, they had leisure and opportunity to place themselves, with all the advantages they could desire. The Prince's natural heat, and impatience, could never endure an Enemy long in his view; nor let him believe that they had the courage to endure his Charge. Thus the Army was engaged before the Cannon was turned, or the ground made choice of upon which they were to Fight: so that Courage was only to be relied upon, where all Conduct failed so much.

It was about ten of the Clock, when the Battle began: The first Charge was given by Prince *Rupert*; who, with his own, and his Brother Prince *Maurice*'s Troop, performed it with his usual vigor; and was so well seconded, that he bore down all before him, and was Master of six pieces of the Rebels best Cannon. The Lord *Astley*, with His Foot, though against the Hill, advanced upon Their Foot; who discharged their Cannon at them, but over-shot them, and so did their Musqueteers too. For the Foot on either side hardly saw each other till they were within Carabine-shot, and so only gave one Volly; the King's Foot, according to their usual custom, falling in with their Swords, and the But-ends of their Musquets; with which they did very notable execution, and put the Enemy into great disorder and confusion. The right Wing of Horse and Foot being thus fortunately engaged and advanced, the left Wing, under Sir *Marmaduke Langdale*, in five Bodies, advanced with equal resolution; and was encountered by *Cromwell*, who Commanded the right Wing of the Enemies Horse, with seven Bodies greater, and more numerous than either of the other; and had, besides the Odds in number, the advantage of the ground; for the King's Horse were obliged to march up the Hill, before they could Charge them: yet they did their duty, as well as the place, and great inequality of Numbers would enable them to do. But being flanked on both sides by the Enemies Horse; and pressed hard, before they could get to the top of the Hill, they gave back, and fled farther and faster than became them. Four of the Enemies Bodies, close, and in good order, followed them, that they might not rally again; which they never thought of doing; and the rest Charged the King's Foot, who had till then so much the advantage over Theirs; whilst Prince *Rupert*, with the right Wing, pursued those Horse which he had broken and defeated.

OF THE REBELLION.

The King's Reserve of Horse, which was his own Guards, with Himself in the head of them, were even ready to Charge those Horse who pursued his left Wing, when, on a sudden, such a Panic fear seized upon them, that they all run near a quarter of a mile without stopping; which happened upon an extraordinary accident, that hath seldom fallen out, and might well disturb and disorder very resolute Troops, as those were, and the best Horse in the Army. The King, as was said before, was even upon the point of Charging the Enemy, in the head of his Guards, when the Earl of *Carnewarth*, who rode next to him (a Man never suspected for infidelity, nor yet one from whom the King would have received Counsel in such a case) on a sudden, laid his hand on the bridle of the King's Horse, and swearing two or three full-Mouthed *Scottish* Oaths (for of that Nation he was) said, " will you go upon your death in an in-" stant?" and before his Majesty understood what he would have, turned his Horse round; upon which a word run through the Troops, "that they should " *march* to the right hand;" which led them both from Charging the Enemy, and assisting their own Men. Upon this they all turned their Horses, and rode upon the Spur, as if they were every Man to shift for himself.

It is very true that, upon the more Soldierly word *stand*, which was sent after them, many of them returned to the King; though the former unlucky word carried more from him. By this time, Prince *Rupert* was returned with a good Body of those Horse, which had attended him in his prosperous Charge on the right Wing; but they having, as they thought, acted their part, could never be brought to rally themselves again in order, or to Charge the Enemy. That difference was observed all along, in the discipline of the King's Troops, and of those which marched under the Command of *Fairfax*, and *Cromwell* (for it was only under Them, and had never been remarkable under *Essex*, or *Waller*) that, though the King's Troops prevailed in the Charge, and routed those they Charged, they seldom rallied themselves again in order, nor could be brought to make a second Charge again the same day: which was the reason, that they had not an entire Victory at *Edgehill*: Whereas the others Troops, if they prevailed, or though they were beaten, and routed, presently rallied again, and stood in good order, till they received new Orders. All that the King and Prince could do; could not rally their broken Troops, which stood in sufficient Numbers upon the Field, though they often endeavoured it, with the manifest hazard of their own Persons. So that, in the end the King was compelled to quit the Field; and to leave *Fairfax* Master of all his Foot, Cannon, and Baggage; amongst which was his own Cabinet, where his most secret Papers were, and Letters between the Queen and Him; of which they shortly after made that barbarous use as was agreeable to their Natures, and published them in Print; that is, so much of them, as they thought would asperse either of their Majesties, and improve the prejudice they had raised against them; and concealed other parts, which would have vindicated them from many particulars with which they had asperfed them.

I shall not stay, in this place, to mention the Names of those Noble-Persons who were lost in this Battle; when the King, and the Kingdom were lost in it; though there were above one hundred and fifty Officers, and Gentlemen of prime Quality, dead upon the spot; whose Memories ought to be preserved. The Enemy left no manner of cruelty unexercised that day; and in the pursuit killed above one hundred Women, whereof some were the Wives of Officers of Quality. The King and Prince Rupert, with the broken Troops, marched by *Leicester* that Night to *Ashby de la Zouch*; and the next day to *Lichfield*; and continued two days march more, till they came to *Bewdley* in *Worcestershire*; where they rested one day; and then went to *Hereford*, with some disjointed imagination, that they might, with those Forces under *Gerrard*, who was General of South *Wales*, and was indeed upon his march, with a Body of two thousand Horse and Foot, be able to have raised a new Army. At *Hereford*, Prince *Rupert*, before any formed Counsel was agreed upon, what the King should do next, left the King, and made haste to *Bristol*, that he might put that place into a condition to resist a Powerful and Victorious Enemy; which, he had reason to believe, would in a short time appear before it. Nothing can be here more wondered at, than that the King should amuse himself about forming a new Army in Counties which had been vexed, and worn out with the oppressions of his own Troops, and the Licence of those Governors, whom he had put over them; and not have immediately repaired into the West, where

The King retires by Lichfield to Bewdley; thence to Hereford.

Thence Prince Rupert retires to Bristol.

he had an Army already formed, and a People, generally, well devoted to his Service, whither all his broken Troops, and General *Gerrard*, might have transported themselves, before *Fairfax* could have given them any interruption; who had somewhat to do, before he could bend his course that way: of which unhappy omission we shall have too much occasion to take more notice, after we have again visited the West.

The Affairs of the West in the meantime.

The Sickness which infested *Bristol*, and which was thought to be the Plague, had made it necessary for the Prince of *Wales* to remove from thence: and no place was thought so convenient for his residence as *Barnstable*, a pleasant Town in the North-part of *Devonshire* well Fortified, with a good Garrison in it, under the Command of Sir *Allen Apsley*. And as his Highness was upon his way thither, he received the Orders which the Lord *Goring*, who was now returned, had procured from the King; which he carefully transmitted to his Highness, as soon as he arrived. At the same time, the Lord *Colepepper* received another Letter from the Lord *Digby*, dated four days after the former Orders, by which he signified "the King's express pleasure, that the Lord
" *Goring* should Command those Forces in Chief;
" that Sir *Richard Greenvil* should be Major-General
" of the whole Army; that Sir *John Berkeley*, as
" Colonel-General of *Devon* and *Cornwal*, should
" intend the work before *Plymouth*; and that Prince
" *Rupert* would send his Ratification of all these; that
" the Lord *Hopton* should attend his Charge at the
" Army, as General of the Artillery." To which

purpose, his Majesty with his own hand writ to the Lord *Hopton*; "and that the Prince should not be in "the Army, but keep his residence in a safe Garri- "son; and There, by the advice of his Council, "manage and improve the business of the West, and "provide reserves, and reinforcements for the "Army:" with an Intimation, "Mr. *Smith's* House, "near *Bristol*, would be a convenient place for his "residence."

The Prince and Council were much amazed at these Orders and Resolutions, so different from those which had been made; and therefore they thought it fit to conceal them, till they might represent faithfully to his Majesty the state and condition of those parts, and their advice thereupon: well knowing, that if it were believed in the Country, that the Prince's Authority was in the least manner superseded, or diminished, besides other inconveniences, the hopeful Levies, upon the agreement at *Bridgewater*, would be in a moment determined; the Gentlemen who were to raise Regiments, professing, "that they "would receive no Commissions but from his High- "ness." But whatever care They used to conceal the matters of those Letters, and to hasten away a despatch to the King concerning them, the Lord *Goring* took as much care to publish them; and from that time expressed all possible contempt at least of the Council attending the Prince. However, within three days, there was another change; for the Lord *Digby* (sending at the same time express Orders from the King to the Lord *Goring* to that purpose) by his Letters to the Lords of the Council, of the nineteenth of

May, within five days after the former, signified " his Majesty's pleasure, that the Lord *Goring* should " march forthwith towards *Northamptonshire* with " all the Forces could be spared; and that the Prince " himself should stay at *Dunstar*-Castle, and encourage " the new Levies:" it being (I presume) not known at Court, that the Plague, which had driven him from *Bristol*, was as hot in *Dunstar*-Town, just under the Walls of the Castle. At the same time, a Letter to the Lord *Hopton* from the King, ordered him " to " Command the Forces under the Prince." The Prince was then, as was said before in his way to *Barnstable*; having left five hundred of his Guards to keep the Fort in *Bristol*, the Garrison being then very thin there, by reason of so many drawn from thence for the Service before *Taunton*.

General *Goring*, upon his return from the King, found *Taunton* relieved by a strong Party of two thousand Horse, and three thousand Foot, which unhappily arrived in the very Article of reducing the Town, and after their Line was entered, and a third part of the Town was burned. But this Supply raised the Siege, the Besiegers drawing off without any loss; and the Party that relieved them, having done their work, and left some of their Foot in the Town, made what haste they could, to make their Retreat Eastward; when *Goring* fell so opportunely upon their Quarters, that he did them great mischief; and believed that, in that disorder, he had so shut them up between narrow passes, that they could neither retire to *Taunton*, nor march Eastward: and doubtless he had them then at a great advantage, by the opinion of all

Men that knew the Country. But, the extreme ill disposing his Parties, and for want of particular Orders (of which many Men spoke with great licence) his two Parties sent out, several ways, to fall upon the Enemy at *Petherton*-Bridge, the one Commanded by Colonel *Thornill*, the other by Sir *William Courtney* (both diligent, and sober Officers) they fell foul on each other, to the loss of many of their Men; both the chief Officers being dangerously hurt, and one of them taken, before they knew their Error; through which the Enemy with no more loss got into, and about *Taunton*; notwithstanding which untoward accident, General *Goring* was, or seemed, very confident that he should speedily so distress them, that the place would be the sooner reduced, by the relief that had been put into it, and that in few days they would be at his Mercy.

This was before the latter end of *May*; when, upon the confidence of speedily despatching that work, all possible and effectual care was taken to supply him with Provisions, and to send all the new Levied Men, and 'his Highness's own Guards thither. Insomuch, as he had within few days a Body of full five thousand Foot, and four thousand Horse; which he Quartered at the most convenient places; rather for ease, than duty; having published Orders, under pretence of preserving the Country from plunder, and with a promise of most exemplary Discipline, " that six pence a day should be collected for the " payment of each Trooper;" to which he got the Commissioners consent; by virtue whereof, he raised great Sums of Money, without the least abatement of the former diforders: yet he proceeded with fuch Popular circumftances, fending moft fpecious Warrants out, and Declarations for Reformation; fometimes defiring, "that folemn Prayers might be faid " in all Churches for him; and to defire God to blefs " fome attempt he had then in hand;" always ufing extreme Courtfhip to the Commiffioners (whom he barefaced informed, "that he was to have, or rather, that he " had the abfolute Command of the Weft under the " Prince, without reference to his Council)" that with his Promifes, Proclamations, and Courtfhip, together with laughing at thofe Perfons they were angry at, he had wrought himfelf into very Popular confideration till they found, that he promifed and publifhed Orders, to no other purpofe than to deceive them; and that, whilft he feemed with them to laugh at other Men, he made them Properties only to his own ends.

In this conjuncture, the King's Letter came to the Lord *Goring*, to march towards *Northamptonfhire*; to which he returned an Anfwer by an Exprefs, before he defired the Prince's directions; though he was diligent enough to procure his Highnefs's opinion for the refpite of his march. The truth is, the affurance that he gave of his reducing thofe Forces within very few days; the leaving all the Weft to the Mercy of the Rebels, if he went before they were reduced; the danger of their marching in his Rear, and carrying as great an addition of ftrength to the Enemy, as General *Goring* could carry to the King, except he carried with him the Forces of the feveral Garrifons, which were then joined to him, made it very Counfelable to fufpend a prefent Obedience to thofe Orders, till his
Majefty

Majesty might receive the full and true State of his Affairs in those parts; to which purpose, an express was sent likewise by his Highness to the King. In the mean time, General *Goring* was so far from making any advance upon *Taunton*, that he grew much more negligent in it, than he had been; suffered Provisions, in great quantities, to be carried into the Town, through the midst of his Men; neglected, and discouraged his own Foot so much, that they ran away, faster than they could be sent up to him; and gave himself wholly to Licence: insomuch that some times he was not seen abroad, in three or four days together. At this time came the news of the fatal blow at *Naseby*, which freed him from any fear of being drawn out of the West; yet he used no expedition to attempt any thing upon the Enemy, who were exceedingly disheartened; but suffered the Guards to be more negligently kept; insomuch that his Quarters were often beaten up, even in the day-time; whilst some Principal Officers of his Army, as Lieutenant-General *Porter*, and others, with His leave, had several Parleys with the Officers of the Rebels, to the very great scandal of the rest; who knew not what interpretation to make of it, at a time that he used to mention the Person of the King with great contempt, and avowed in all places a virulent dislike of the Prince's Council. Thus, after about six Weeks lying about *Taunton*, the Forces whereof he promised to confound (I mean those that marched to the relief of it) within few days, he was forced himself to retire, and suffer them to join with Sir *Thomas Fairfax*;

BOOK IX.

The Prince of Wales *...* to Barnstable.

who in the beginning of *July* marched towards those parts.

After the Prince came to *Barnstable*, though he very seldom received any account from the Lord *Goring* of what happened, he was informed by several Persons of Credit, "that he was much discontented; and expressed a great sense of disrespect, and unkindnesses that he had received." Therefore it was wished by them, "that some means might be found out, to settle a good understanding with him, whereby he might be encouraged to an Alacrity in so important a Season:" and he having appointed to be at *Tiverton* on such a day, the Prince sent thither Sir *John Berkeley*, Sir *Hugh Pollard*, and Colonel *Ashburnham*, to confer with him, and to know what he desired; the Prince having never denied to assist him, in any one particular he had ever proposed, or to grant him any thing he had expressed a desire of. Upon their meeting there, he carried himself very high; "talked only of general neglects put upon him by the Prince's Council; that he had been promised by the King to have the Command of the West, but that they had hindered it; which affront he required to have repaired, before he would do any Service upon the Enemy;" with many bitter Invectives against particular Persons; "whereof, he said, Prince *Rupert* had told him that some thought him not a Man fit to be trusted." They had indeed spoken freely to his Highness to that purpose, upon his very frankly discoursing of him. In the end, these three Persons pressing him as Friends to deal particularly with them, what would

OF THE REBELLION. 67

satisfy him; he told them, "if he might be presently "made Lieutenant-General to the Prince, and admitted of his Council, and be promised to be "Sworn of the Privy-Council, as soon as might be, "and to be Gentleman of the Prince's Bed-Chamber, "he would then proceed roundly and cheerfully in, "the business; otherwise, the Prince's Council "should do the work themselves for Him." All this being so extravagant, it cannot be thought any Answer could be given to it, especially it being said to them as Friends, and not expressly sent to the Prince.

When the Prince first apprehended the advance of Sir *Thomas Fairfax* to the West, he very earnestly recommended to the Lord *Goring* the state of the Garrisons about *Bridgewater*, especially the Garrison of *Lamport*, which was of so great importance, that, being well supplied, it had secured *Bridgewater*, and all that part of the Country. This Garrison had been settled by the Lord *Hopton*, upon his first coming down to *Taunton*, after *Vandruske* had raised the Blockade that Colonel *Windham* had laid to it; and Sir *Francis Mackworth* (who, having been formerly Major-General to the Marquis of *New-Castle*, was now, that Army being dissolved, returning to his Command in the Low-Countries by his Majesty's leave) was engaged by him to take the Command of it till, upon the Prince's coming into those Parts, a worthier Command could be provided for him; and before the Lord *Goring's* coming to *Taunton*, he had Fortified it to a good degree. This Garrison, from the first Establishment, had been much maligned by Colonel *Windham*, who defired not to have another Governor fo near him, who was to receive fome of the fruit that he had before looked on as his own, though never affigned to him: and then, upon fome differences between Sir *John Stawel*, and Sir *Francis Mackworth*, it was more inveighed againft: infomuch as at the firft coming down of the Prince to *Briftol*, moft of the time was fpent in complaints from Sir *John Stawel* of this Garrifon, and of the forcing the Country to work, and contribute to thofe Fortifications. After the Lord *Goring*'s coming to *Taunton*, he had, as a compliment to *Bridgewater*, and to all the Gentlemen, who were grown angry with my Lord *Hopton*, upon their own fancies, befides the former unkindneffes he had to Sir *Francis Mackworth* upon fome difputes they had Had in the North (where they were both General-Officers) very much neglected, and oppreffed that Garrifon; not only by countenancing all complaints againft it, but by taking away all the Contribution affigned for the fupport of it, for the fupplying his own Army; and exprefsly inhibiting him by force to Levy thofe Rates, which the Prince himfelf had affigned to him. Infomuch as when the Club-men of the County affembled together in great Numbers, and, having taken fome Officers and Soldiers of that Garrifon Prifoners, for requiring their juft Contributions in Money, or Provifions, came up to the Walls of *Lamport*, and difcharged their Mufquets upon the Works, and Sir *Francis Mackworth* thereupon with his Horfe Charged them, and killing one or two of them, forced the reft to run away, the Lord *Goring* sent him a very strict reprehension for so doing, and positively Commanded him "to do so no more; nor "in any Case to disturb or injure those People." This brought that Garrison so low, that when it might have preserved that Army, it had not two days Provisions in it; Sir *Francis Mackworth*, having been called to wait on the Prince's Person, as well by his own choice (when he saw the carriage towards him, believing that some prejudice to his Person brought a disadvantage to the place) as by Prince *Rupert*'s advice; who promised, when he left the Prince at *Barnstable*, and visited *Goring*, and *Bridgewater*, " to settle that Garrison of *Lamport*, and make Colo- " nel *Windham* Governor of it."

Here I cannot but say somewhat of the Club-men; who began then to rise in great Numbers, in several parts of the Country, about the time that the Prince went from *Bath* to *Bridgewater*, in his Journey to *Barnstable*; and that night his Highness lay at *Wells*, which was the second of *June*, a Petition was delivered to him, which had been agreed upon that day at *Marshal's Elme*, where there had then assembled five or six thousand Men, most in Arms; and the Petitioners were appointed to attend the next day at *Bridgewater* for an Answer. It was evident, though the avowed ground for the rising, was the intolerable Oppression, Rapine, and Violence, exercised by the Lord *Goring*'s Horse, that, in truth, they received encouragement from many Gentlemen of the Country; some of them thinking, it would be a good Expedient to necessitate a Reformation of the Army; others believing it would be a profitable rising for

the King, and would grow into the matter of the first Affociation, One and All. Therefore fome principal Agents of Sir *John Stawel's* were very active in thofe Meetings; and he himfelf was very folicitous, that a very gracious Anfwer might be returned to their Petition; which was followed by fome Farmerly Men, and others of the Clergy, both which had good Reputation of affection, and integrity to the King's Service. The Prince expreffed a great fenfe of the Oppreffions they fuffered, by the diforder of the Army, which he promifed to do his beft to reform; to which end, he writ earneft Letters to the Lord *Goring*. But his Highnefs told them, "that this un-
"warrantable courfe of affembling together, and
"being their own Judges, would prove very per-
"nicious: for though many of them might mean
"well, yet fome active Minifters would mingle
"with them, on the behalf of the Rebels, and having
"once brought them to a kind of Neutrality, and
"Unconcernednefs for the King, would, in a mo-
"ment, be able, againft all their good wifhes, to
"apply them againft him; and therefore ftraitly inhi-
"bited them to meet any more in that manner, except
"they firft lifted themfelves in Regiments, and
"chofe Gentlemen of the Country to Command
"them;" to whom his Highnefs offered to grant Commiffions to that purpofe.

This Anfwer feemed to fatisfy thofe who attended on the behalf of the Petitioners, until they were perfuaded by fome Gentlemen not to fubmit to it; and fo they continued their meetings; many inferior Officers of the Army quitting their Charges, and living amongſt them, and improving their diſcontents. When the Prince went to *Barnſtable*, he gave General *Goring* Advertiſements " of the great danger " that might ariſe out of the licence that People took " to themſelves;" and therefore adviſed him, " as on " the one hand, to ſuppreſs and reform the crying " diſorders of the Army by good Diſcipline, and " ſeverity upon enormous Tranſgeſſors; ſo on the " other, ſeaſonably to diſcountenance, and puniſh " thoſe Aſſemblies of Club-men; which would other- " wiſe, in time, prove as dangerous to him, as any " other ſtrength of the Rebels." But, whether it were to ſhow his greatneſs, and ſo, Popularly to comply with what the Prince had diſcountenanced, or whether in truth he belived he ſhould be able to make uſe of them, and perſuade them to become a part of his Army, he did uſe all poſſible compliance with them, and would not ſuffer any force to be uſed againſt them. So that they grew to be ſo powerful, that they kept Proviſions from the Army, and the Garriſons; and when he moved from *Taunton*, upon the coming down of Sir *Thomas Fairfax*, they killed many of his Soldiers; and did him more miſchief, than all the power of the Rebels.

When the Prince came to *Barnſtable*, he received the fatal news of the Battle of *Naſeby*, by the noiſe and triumphs which the Rebels made in thoſe parts for their Victory, without any particular information, or account from *Oxford*, or any Credible Perſons; which left ſome hope that it might not be true, at leaſt not to that degree that diſaffected People reported it to be. However, at the worſt, it concerned

him the more to be solicitous to put the West into such a posture, that it might be able to repair any loss the King had received; which he might have done, if the Jealousies and Animosities between particular Persons could have been reconciled, and a Union been made amongst all Men who pretended to wish, and really did wish, prosperity to the King's Affairs; which were disturbed, and even rendered desperate, by the intolerable Pride of incorrigible Faction. Notwithstanding the Orders, which had been made by the Commissioners of *Devonshire*, for distributing the Contributions of that County, which have been mentioned before, and in which such a proportion was assigned for the maintenance of the Forces before *Plymouth*, as in Sir *Richard Greenvil's* own judgment was sufficient for them; he had still continued to Levy the whole Contribution, which he had done formerly, for six thousand Foot, and twelve hundred Horse; and said, "he could not
" submit to the other division and retrenchment; for
" that there was nothing assigned, or left for the
" payment of his Men before *Taunton*." He was told by the Commissioners, " that they were now a part
" of the Army, and lived as their fellows did; that
" they had received no Money from him since their
" going thither, but had Had free Quarter as the rest
" of the Army; and that it would prove of ill Con-
" sequence, and beget a Mutiny, if they should
" receive a Weekly pay, when none of the rest did,
" nor any Army the King had in *England*: that he
" could not but confess, by the State of the whole,
" that the dispensation was very reasonable; and

"that it could not be expected that the County
"would be contented to pay their Contribution for
"the payment of other Forces, not of their own
"County, when their own Garrisons, that were
"kept for their defence, should be compelled for
"want of pay, to disorders, or to disband. But that,
"if he thought any thing in those Establishments
"unnecessary, or that he thought Provision could
"be otherwise made for them, they would be con-
"tented that the Overplus should be disposed as he
"desired." He Answered none of their reasons; but
positively said, "He would spare none of the Con-
"tributions formerly assigned to him;" though the
Commissioners had the same Authority now to take
it away, as they had then to dispose it to him; and
though it appeared to be assigned for the maintenance of so great a Force, as was before spoken of,
and upon his undertaking, under his hand, "to take
"the Town before *Chriſtmas-day.*

When this Account was presented to the Prince, *Tranſactions at Barnſtable: eſpecially complaints againſt Sir R. Greenvil.* he found it necessary, and resolved, to confirm what was proposed by the Commissioners, without which those Garrisons could not be supported; yet deferred the settling thereof, till he came to *Barnſtable*, being resolved speedily to go thither; and, before his coming thither, had sent to the Commissioners both of *Devon* and *Cornwal* to attend him; which they did within a day or two after he came thither, together with Sir *John Berkeley*, and Sir *Richard Greenvil.* The Commissioners for *Devon* very earnestly pressed the settling the Contributions in the manner before proposed, and the regulating the Exorbitant Power of

BOOK IX.

Sir *Richard Greenvil*, who raised what Money he pleased, and committed what Persons he pleased; and the Commissioners from *Cornwal* presented a very sharp complaint against him, in the Name of the whole County, for several Exorbitances, and strange Acts of Tyranny exercised upon them: " That he " had committed very many honest substantial " Men, and all the Constables of the East part of " the County, to *Lydford* Prison in *Devonshire*, for " no offence, but to compel them to Ransom them- " selves for Money; and that his Troops had com- " mitted such outrages in the Country, that they had " been compelled, in open Sessions, to declare against " him; and to Authorize the Country, in case that " he should send his Troops in such manner, to rise, " and beat them out;" which Declaration was produced, signed by all the Commissioners, who were most eminently and zealously affected to his Majesty; and was indeed no other than a denouncing War against *Greenvil*; and was excused by them " as an " act of necessity to compose the People, who would " otherwise in the instant have risen, and cut the " Throats of all his Men." So that, whoever would have made a judgment, upon what he heard from the Commissioners of *Devon* and *Cornwal* at that time, must have concluded, that Sir *Richard Greenvil* was the most justly odious to both Counties, that can be imagined. And no doubt he had behaved himself with great Pride, and Tyranny over them; though the Discipline he exercised over his Men at *Plymouth*, in keeping them from committing any disorder, or offering the least prejudice to any Man (which, considering the great assignment of Money he had, and the small Numbers of Men, was no hard matter to do) had raised him much Credit among the Country-People, who had lived long under the Licence of Prince *Maurice's* Army; and the fame of it had extended his Reputation to a greater distance.

There hath been too much said already, to discover the nature and the temper of this Gentleman, if the current of this discourse did not make it absolutely necessary to mention many particulars, with which the Prince was troubled almost in all places, and which exceedingly disordered the whole business of *Devon* and *Cornwal*; and, indeed, thereby the whole West. There was one particular that made a great noise in the Country: shortly after he was deputed to that Charge before *Plymouth*, upon the hurt of Mr. *Digby*, one *Brabant*, an Attorney-at Law (who had heretofore solicited the great Suit against Sir *Richard* in the Star-Chamber, on the behalf of his Wife and the Earl of *Suffolk*, living in those parts, and having always very honestly behaved himself towards the King's Service) knowing, it seems, the nature of the Gentleman, resolved not to venture himself within the Precincts where he Commanded; and therefore intended to go to some more secure Quarter; but was taken in his Journey, having a Mountero on his head. Sir *Richard Greenvil* had laid wait to apprehend him; and he likewise had concealed his Name; but, being now brought before Sir *Richard*, was immediately, by his own direction, without any Council of War, because he said he was disguised, hanged as a Spy: Which seemed so strange and incredible, that one of the Council asked him, "whether it was true? And he answered very "unconcernedly, yes, he had hanged him, for he was "a Traytor, and against the King; and that he had "taken a Brother of his, whom he might have "hanged too, but he had suffered him to be ex- "changed." He said, "he knew the Country talked, "that he hanged him for revenge, because he had "solicited a cause against him; but that was not the "cause; though having played the Knave with him," he said smiling, "he was well content to find a just "occasion to punish him."

The Prince was very unwilling to enter so far, and so particularly upon the passionate complaint of either County, as thereby to be compelled to censure, or to discountenance Sir *Richard Greenvil*; who, he thought, might be applied very usefully to the Public Service. Therefore his Highness resolved, according to the former design, to commit the business of *Plymouth* to Sir *John Berkeley*; who might, without any reproach to the other, discharge such from Imprisonment as had lain long enough there, and who made no other pretence to the Contribution, than according to the Assignments made by the Commissioners; and to dispose Sir *Richard Greenvil* to the Field, according to his own Proposition; for which there was now the more seasonable opportunity, the Lord *Goring* having then written to the Prince, "to "desire him, that, in regard very many of Sir *Ri-* "*chard Greenvil*'s Soldiers before *Taunton* were run "away, insomuch that of the two thousand two "hundred brought thither by him, there were not

OF THE REBELLION.

" fix hundred left, and that there could be no fuch
" expedient to bring them back, or to encourage the
" new Levies, as by his prefence in that Army, that
" he would fend Sir *Richard Greenvil* thither; where
" he fhould Command as Field-Marfhal:" To
which purpofe he had likewife written to Sir *Richard
Greenvil*, perfuading him, " that he fhould fix a
" Quarter towards *Lyme*, and have the whole mana-
" ging of that Province:" and fo a very good correfpondence was begun between them. Thereupon,
his Commiffion of Field-Marfhal of the Affociated
Army was delivered to him, with direction, " in the
" mean time to abide with the Lord *Goring*;" who
deputed him to Command in the fame place. It is
true that he then defired, " to continue the Com-
" mand before *Plymouth* in *Commendam*, and to exe-
" cute the fame by his Major-General; but, he was
" told, that it was otherwife fettled by his own Pro-
" pofition, and Advice, and therefore that it could
" not be altered:" And indeed would have prevented the fatisfaction, which was to be given to the two
Counties. Then he infifted very much upon fome
Affignment of Contribution for the Army; for, he
faid, "he neither would, nor could Command Men
" who were not paid." But after fome fharp invectives againft the excefs and lazinefs of Governors,
and the needlefs Contribution affigned to Garrifons,
finding that the fubfiftence for the Army muft be
provided out of *Somerfet* and *Dorfet*, he took his leave
of the Prince; and with his Commiffion of Field-
Marfhal, went to the Lord *Goring* before *Taunton*;
Sir *John Berkeley* being at the fame time defpatched
to *Plymouth*.

Sir T. Fairfax with his Army enters Somersetshire.

About the beginning of *July* Sir *Thomas Fairfax* entered into *Somersetshire*; so that General *Goring* found it convenient to draw off from *Taunton*, and seemed to advance towards him, as if he intended to Fight; fixing his Quarters between the Rivers about *Lamport*, very advantageously for defence, having a Body of Horse and Foot very little inferior to the Enemy, although by great negligence he had suffered his Foot to moulder away before *Taunton*, for want of Provisions, and Countenance; when the Horse enjoyed Plenty, even to Excess and Riot. He had been there very few days, when the Enemy, at Noon-day, fell into his Quarters, upon a Party of Horse of above a thousand, Commanded by Lieutenant-General *Porter*; who were so surprised, that though they were in a bottom, and could not but discern the Enemy coming down the Hills, half a Mile at the least, yet the Enemy was upon them, before the Men could get upon their Horses; they being then feeding in a Meadow; so that this Body was entirely routed, and very many taken; and, the next day, notwithstanding all the Advantages of Passes, and Places of Advantage, another Party of the Enemies Horse and Dragoons fell upon the whole Army; routed it; took two pieces of Cannon; and pursued *Goring*'s Men through *Lamport* (a place, which if it had not been with great industry discountenanced, and oppressed, as is said before, might well have secured his, and resisted their Army) and drove them to the Walls of *Bridgewater*; whither the Lord *Goring* in great disorder retired; and spending that Night there, and leaving with them the Cannon,

Beats Goring near Lamport.

Ammunition, and Carriages, and such Soldiers as were desired, in equal disorder, the next day, he retired into *Devonshire;* the Club-men and Country-People infesting his march, and knocking all Stragglers, or wearied Soldiers, on the head. Upon that rout, which was no less than a defeat of the whole Army, the Lord *Goring* retired to *Barnstable:* from whence (the Prince being gone some days before to *Launceston* in *Cornwal*) he writ to the Lord *Digby*, " that there was so great a terror, and distraction " among his Men, that he was confident, at that pre- " sent, they could not be brought to Fight against " half their number." In the Letter he writ, "that " he had then" (being within three days after their rout, when very many Stragglers were not come up) " between three and four thousand Foot" (Prince *Rupert's* Regiment being left in *Bridgewater,* consisting of above five hundred Men, and two hundred in *Burrow,* and five-and-twenty hundred Horse, besides Sir *Lewis Dives's* Regiment, and all the Western-Horse) so that, by his Account, considering that there were not less than one thousand Men killed, and taken Prisoners, in those two unlucky days, and that very many were run to *Bristol,* and others not come to him, it appears, that, when he rose from *Taunton,* he had a strength little inferior to the Enemy.

Sir *Thomas Fairfax* then no more pursued them, after this running away, but left them time enough to refresh, and recover themselves; whilst he himself intended the recovery of *Bridgewater;* which was exceedingly wondered at; though it was quickly discerned, he had good reason to stop there. In the mean time General *Goring* spent his time at *Barnstable*, and those parts adjacent; his Army Quartering at *Torrington*, and over the whole North of *Devon*, and his Horse committing such intolerable insolences and disorders, as alienated the hearts of those who were best affected to the King's Service. Instead of endeavouring to recruit his Army, or to put himself in a readiness and posture to receive the Enemy, he suffered all, who had a mind, to depart; insomuch, as he writ to the Lord *Colepepper*, on the 27th of *July*, "that he had not above thirteen hundred Foot left." When he was at *Barnstable*, he gave himself his usual Licence of drinking; and then, inveighing against the Prince's Council, said, "he would justify that "They had been the cause of the loss of the West;" inveighing likewise in an unpardonable dialect against the Person of the King, and discoursing much of the revenge he would take upon those who had affronted him: and in this manner he entertained himself to the end of *July*, writing Letters of discontent to the Prince, and the Lords; one day complaining for want of Money and desiring the Prince to supply that want, when he well knew he wanted Supply for his own Table; and never received a penny of the public Collections, or Contributions: Another day, desiring, "that all Straggling Soldiers might be sent out of "*Cornwal*, and drawn from the Garrisons, that he "might advance upon the Enemy;" and the next day proposing, "that all the Foot might be put into "Garrisons, for that they could not be fit for the "Field;" so that before an Answer could be sent to

his

his laſt Letter, another commonly arrived of a different temper.

Sir *Richard Greenvil* grew again no leſs troubleſome and inconvenient, than the Lord *Goring*. He had left the Prince at *Barnſtable*, well pleaſed with his Commiſſion of Field-Marſhal, and more that he ſhould Command alone the blocking up of *Lyme*; which, he reſolved, ſhould bring him plenty of Money; and in order to that, it was agreed, that, on ſuch a day appointed, " ſo many Men from the Garriſons of " *Dartmouth*, *Exeter*, and *Barnſtable*, ſhould be drawn " to *Tiverton*; where they ſhould receive Orders " from Sir *Richard Greenvil*, and join with ſuch as " he ſhould bring from the Lord *Goring*, for making " a Quarter towards *Lyme*; and Orders iſſued from " his Highneſs accordingly." Thoſe from *Exeter*, according to order, appeared, at the time; and thoſe from *Barnſtable* and *Dartmouth*, marched a day's Journey and more, towards *Tiverton*; but then, hearing that the Lord *Goring* was riſen from *Taunton*, made a halt; and ſent back to the Prince for Orders; who conceived that, upon the riſing of the Lord *Goring*, the deſign of fixing a Quarter upon *Lyme*, would be diſappointed, and that it would be neceſſary to ſtrengthen *Barnſtable*; where his own Perſon was; and recalled thoſe Men back thither; having deſpatched Letters to Sir *Richard Greenvil*, to acquaint him with the accidents that had diverted thoſe from *Dartmouth* and *Barnſtable*; but letting him know, "that, " if the deſign held, thoſe of *Barnſtable* ſhould meet, " where and when he would appoint."

Sir *Richard Greenvil* took an occaſion, from the

Soldiers failing to meet, at the day appointed, at *Tiverton* (though if they had met, there could have been no progress in the former design) to exclaim against the Prince's Council; and, the next day, in a Cover directed to Mr. *Fanshaw*, who was Secretary of the Council, without any Letter, returned the Commission of Field-Marshal, formerly given him by the Prince; and within two or three days after, on the fifth of *July*, he sent a very insolent Letter to the Lords of the Council, complaining of " many unde-
" served abuses offered to him;" implying, " that
" the same were fastened on him by Them, on the
" behalf of Sir *John Berkeley*; told them, that when
" they moved him to give over the Command of
" the Forces before *Plymouth* to Sir *John Berkeley*,
" they had promised him the Principal Command of
" the Army under the Prince:" whereas the truth is before set down, that the Proposition was made by Himself, both of quitting that Charge, and of Sir *John Berkeley*'s taking it, as the only fit Person. He said, " he had hitherto served the King upon his own
" Charge, and upon his own Estate, without any
" allowance; and that, when he went from *Barn-*
" *stable,* he was promised a Protection for his House
" and Estate; but when, after he was gone, his Ser-
" vant brought a Protection ready drawn, all the
" Clauses that comprehended any thing of favor,
" were left out; and such a Protection sent to him
" as he cared not for." He concluded, " that he
" would serve as a Volunteer, till he might have op-
" portunity to acquaint his Majesty with his Suffer-
" ings." Here it will be necessary, upon the mention

of this Protection (which he took so ill to be denied) and the mention of Serving the King, without allowance, upon his own Estate, which he very often, and very insolently objected both in his Letters, and in his discourse to the Prince himself, to say somewhat of his Estate, and what small allowance, as he pretended, he had from the King for his Service.

When he came first into that Country, he had no Command at all; armed only with a Commission to raise a Regiment of Horse, and a Regiment of Foot; of which, he never raised Horse or Man, till long after, that he came to the Command about *Plymouth*. Estate he had none, either there, or; that I have heard, any were else. It is true, his Wife had an Estate, of about five hundred Pounds a year, about *Tavistock* and other parts of *Devon*; but it is as true, that it was Conveyed before Marriage, as hath been said, in such a manner, to Friends in trust, that upon long Suits in Chancery, and in other Courts, in the time of Peace, there were several Judgments and Decrees in Chancery against him. So that he had never, since the difference with his Wife, which was many years before, received the least benefit, or advantage from it. The first thing the King granted to him, was the Sequestration of all his Wife's Estate to his own use (she living then in the Rebels Quarters) upon which Title he settled himself in her House near *Tavistock*; and, by virtue of that Grant, took all the Stock upon the Ground; and compelled the Tenants to pay to him all the Arrears of Rent, or as much as he said was in Arrear; which amounted to a very considerable value. When Colonel *Digby* received his unfortunate hurt, which rendered him for that time incapable to exercise his Command, Sir *John Berkeley* very earneftly, and He only, moved Prince *Maurice*, to confer that Charge upon Sir *Richard Greenvil*, and, though it was within a County of which he himfelf had the principal Charge as Colonel-General, procured a full Commiffion for the other to Command thofe Forces in Chief; and delivered, or fent the fame to him; having, from the time of his firft coming down, ufed him with much kindnefs. He had not then Commanded long, when the Earl of *Effex* came into thofe Parts; whereupon he was compelled to rife; and after joined with the King.

When the Earl of *Effex*'s Forces were diffolved, he was again defigned for that Service; and before the King left the Country, he granted him the Sequeftration of all the Eftate of the Earl of *Bedford* in *Devonfhire*, all the Eftate of Sir *Francis Drake* (by which he had *Buckland Monachorum*, which was his Quarter whilft he blocked up *Plymouth*; and *Worington* by *Launcefton*) in *Devon*, and the Lord *Roberts* his Eftate in *Cornwal*; all which, and his Wife's Eftate, he enjoyed by the Sequeftration granted from his Majefty, and of which he made a greater Revenue than ever the owners did in time of Peace. For, befides that he fuffered no part of thefe Eftates to pay Contribution (whereby the Tenants very willingly paid their full Rents) he kept very much ground, about all the Houfes, in his own hands; which he ftocked with fuch Cattle as he took from Delinquents; for though he fuffered not his Soldiers to plunder, yet he was, in truth, himfelf the greateft plunderer of this War; for whenever any Person had disobeyed, or neglected any of his Warrants, or when any Man failed to appear at the *Posse* (which he summoned very frequently after he was Sheriff of *Devon*, and for no other end but the penalty of Defaulters) he sent presently a Party of Horse to apprehend their Persons, and to drive their Grounds. If the Persons were taken, they were very well content to remit their Stock to redeem their Persons. For the better disposing them thereto, he would now and then hang a Constable, or some other poor fellow, for those faults of which a hundred were as guilty: and if, out of the terror of this kind of Justice, Men hid themselves from being apprehended, they durst not send to require their Stock; which was from thence quietly enjoyed: so that he had a greater Stock of Cattle, of all sorts, upon his Grounds, than any person whatsoever in the West of *England*. Besides this, the ordering of Delinquents Estates in those Parts being before that time not well looked to, by virtue of these Sequestrations, he seized upon all the Stock upon the Grounds, upon all the Furniture in the several Houses, and compelled the Tenants to pay to him all the Rents due from the beginning of the Rebellion. By these, and such like means, he had not only a vast Stock, but received great Sums of Money, and had as great store of good Household-Stuff, as would Furnish well those Houses he looked upon as his own. This was his own Estate, upon which, he said, he had maintained himself, without any allowance from the King; which, I am confident, besides what he got by his Contributions, which would always pay double the Men he had, and were strictly levied, and by his other Arts, and Extortions of several kinds, was more, and more worth in Money to him, than his Majesty bestowed upon all his General-Commanders of Armies, and upon all his Officers of State, since the beginning of the Rebellion to that time. This computation would seem too enviously made, if I should proceed here to take any view of the Services he ever did; and therefore (though they that are very good Witnesses, say, that notwithstanding all the bold promises of taking *Plymouth* within few days, " his farther Guards were never nearer the " Town, than the Lord *Hopton*'s head-Quarter was " the first day that he came thither)" I shall leave that to other Men to make the particular Estimate.

Now when Sir *Richard Greenvil* desired at *Barnstable* a Protection for his Houses and Estates, it was conceived, that he apprehended there might, under pretence of Claim, some attempt be made upon his Stock by the Owners; or that he feared, that there might be too strict an inquiry, by him that succeeded, for such things as being designed for the Public Service, had been applied to his particular private Use; as having, with great importunity (as a thing upon which the Service depended) gotten from the Commissioners of *Devon* above a thousand Deal-boards, to make huts for the Soldiers, he employed them all in the building a great riding-House at *Buckland*, for his own Pleasure. However, so severe and terrible a Person might easily be thought liable to many trespasses, when he should be removed from the place where he Governed so absolutely. The Protection was no sooner asked by him, than promised by the Prince; but, after his departure, his Servant bringing such a Protection drawn, as exempted all those Estates which the King had Granted to him in Sequestration, from the payment of any Contributions (the which had been already so scandalous, that most of the principal Persons of *Cornwal* had by that example, and with indignation at it, forborn to pay their Rates; and he was told the ill consequence of it; and, "that "no Person there in Council, whereof some had "Had very much greater Commands in Armies than "He, and though others thought their Services "deserved any reasonable Privilege, had been ever "freed from Contribution)" thereupon those clauses were struck out, and the Protection in a fuller manner still than ordinary, signed by the Prince; and Sir *John Berkeley*, then present, declared (of which his Servant was advertised, though it was not fit, for the Example, to put it in writing) "that he would "not require any Contribution for that Estate which "was his Wife's, and enjoyed by him only by virtue "of the Sequestration;" and the denying of this Protection was his great grievance. And yet he did not only never pay a penny Contribution before, or after, for all these Estates, but refused to pay the Fee-farm Rent, due to the King out of the Earl of *Bedford*'s Estate, being two hundred Marks *per annum*, though the Auditor was sent to him to demand it; but this was merely an Act of his own Sovereignty.

After this angry Letter to the Lords, and the throwing up his Commission without a Letter, and so having no Commission at all to meddle in Martial

Affairs, he fixed a Quarter, with his own Horse and Foot, at St. *Mary Ottree*, within nine or ten Miles of *Exeter*; where he governed as imperiously as ever; raised what Money he would, and imprisoned what Persons he pleased. In the end, Sir *John Berkeley*, having appointed the Constables of those Hundreds which were assigned for *Plymouth*, to bring in their Accounts of what Money they had paid to Sir *Richard Greenvil* (which, he protested, he did only that thereby he might state the Arrears, without the least thought of reproach to the other) he caused a Warrant to be read in all Churches in the County (that is, ordered it to be read in all, and in some it was read) "that all Persons should bring him an Account " of what Monies, or Goods had been plundered " from them by Sir *John Berkeley*, or any under " him;" with several Clauses very derogatory to his Reputation. This, as it could not otherwise, begot great resentments; insomuch as the Commissioners of *Devon* sent an Express to the Prince, who was then in *Cornwal*, beseeching him " to call Sir " *Richard Greenvil* from thence, and to take some " Order for the suppressing the Furious inclinations " of both sides, or else they apprehended, the Ene- " my would quickly take an advantage of those " Dissensions, and Invade the Country before they " otherwise intended;" and, in their Letter, sent one of the Warrants that Sir *Richard* had caused to be read in the Churches; which indeed was the strangest I ever saw.

Hereupon, the Prince sent for Sir *Richard Greenvil* to attend him; who accordingly came to him at

Liskard; where his Highness told him "the sense he
"had of his disrespect towards him, in the sending
"back his Commission in that manner; and of his
"carriage after;" and asked him, "what Authority
"he now had either to Command Men, or to pub-
"lish such Warrants?" He answered, "that he
"was High-Sheriff of *Devon*, and by virtue of that
"Office he might suppress any Force, or inquire
"into any grievance his County suffered; and, as
"far as in Him lay, give them remedy." He was told,
"as Sheriff he had no power to raise or head Men,
"otherwise than by the *Posse-Comitatus*; which he
"could not neither upon his own head raise, with-
"out Warrant from the Justices of Peace: that, in
"times of War, he was to receive Orders, upon
"occasions, from the Commander in Chief of the
"King's Forces; who had Authority to Command
"him by his Commission." He was asked, "what
"he himself would have done, if when he comman-
"ded before *Plymouth*, the High-Sheriff of *Cornwal*
"should have caused such a Warrant concerning
"Him to be read in Churches?" He answered little
to the Questions, but sullenly extolled his Services,
and enlarged his Sufferings. Afterwards, being reprehended with more Sharpness than ever before, and
being told, "that, whatever discourses he made of
"spending his Estate, it was well understood, that
"he had no Estate by any other Title than the mere
"bounty of the King; that he had been courted by
"the Prince more than he had reason to expect;
"and that he had not made those returns on His
"part which became him; In short, if he had Incli-

"nation to serve his Highness, he should do it in that manner he should be directed; if Not, he should not, under the Title of being Sheriff, satisfy his own Pride, and Passion" (Upon which reprehension being become much gentler, than upon all the gracious Addresses which had been made to him) he Answered, "he would serve the Prince in such manner, as he should Command;" and thereupon he was discharged, and returned to his House to *Worrington*, one of those places he had by Sequestration (It belonged to Sir *Francis Drake*) where he lived privately, for the space of a Fortnight, or thereabouts, without interposing in the Public business. Let us now see how this Tragedy was acted in other places.

We left the King at *Hereford*, not resolved what course to steer; Prince *Rupert* gone to *Bristol*, from whence he had made a short visit to the Prince at *Barnstable*, to give him an account of the ill posture he had left the King in, and from thence went to *Goring* to consult with Him: and it was exceedingly wondered at, that when he saw in what condition he was (for he was then before *Taunton*) and the Number of his Horse and Foot (which every body then thought had been his business to be informed of) he did not then hasten advice to the King, for his speedy repair thither; but his chief care was to secure *Bristol*; which, sure, at that time he made not the least question of doing; and believed the Winter would come seasonably for future Counsels.

The King goes to Abergavenny

The King quickly left *Hereford*, and went to meet the Commissioners for South *Wales* at *Abergavenny*, the Chief-Town in *Monmouthshire*. As they were for the most part Persons of the best Quality, and the largest Fortunes of those Counties, so they had manifested great Loyalty and Affection, from the beginning of the War, by sending many good Regiments to the Army, and with their Sons, and Brothers, and nearest Kindred; many of whom had lost their lives Bravely in the Field: They now made as large and ample Professions as ever, and seemed to believe, that they should be able, in a very short time, to raise a good Army of Foot, with which the King might again look upon the Enemy; and accordingly agreed what Numbers should be levied upon each of the Counties. From thence his Majesty went to *Ragland*-Castle, the Noble House of the Marquis of *Worcester*; which was well Fortified, and Garrisoned by him; who remained then in it. There he resolved to stay, till he should see the effect of the Commissioners mighty promises. But he found in a short time, that, either by the continued successes of the Parliament-Armies in all places, the particular information whereof was every day brought to them, by Intelligence from their Friends, or the Triumphs of their Enemies in *Monmouth* and *Glocester*, or by the renewed troubles, which the presence of their Governor, General *Gerrard*, gave them (who had been, and continued to be, a passionate and unskilful manager of the affections of the People; as having governed them with extraordinary rigor, and with as little courtesy and civility towards the Gentry, as towards the Common-People) there was little probability of raising an Army in those

BOOK IX.

parts: where all Men grew lefs affected, or more frighted, which produced one and the fame effect. The King ftayed at *Rugland*, till the News came " that *Fairfax*," after he had taken *Leicefter* (which could not hold out longer than to make honorable conditions) " was marched into the Weft, and had " defeated *Goring*'s Troops at *Lamport*; and at the " fame time, that the *Scottifh* Army was upon its " march towards *Worcefter*, having taken a little " Garrifon that lay between *Hereford* and *Worcefter* " by Storm; and put all within it to the Sword." And Prince *Rupert* fent for all thofe Foot which were levied towards a new Army, and part of thofe which belonged to General *Gerrard*, to fupply the Garrifon of *Briftol*: fo that his Majefty feemed now to have nothing in his Choice, but to tranfport himfelf over the *Severn* to *Briftol*, and thence to have repaired to his Army in the Weft; which would have been much better done Before, yet had been well done Then; and the King refolved to do fo; and that the Horfe under *Gerrard*, and *Langdale*, fhould find a Tranfportation over the *Severn* (which might have been done) and then find the way to him, wherever he fhould be.

Thence to Chepftow:

This was fo fully refolved, that his Majefty went to the Water-fide near *Chepftow*; were Veffels were ready to Tranfport him, and where Prince *Rupert* from *Briftol* met him, very well pleafed with the Refolution he had taken, though he had not been Privy to the Counfel. Here again the unhappy difcord in the Court, raifed new obftructions; they who did not love Prince *Rupert*, nor were loved by him, could not endure to think that the King should be so wholly within his power; and he himself was far from being importunate that his Majesty should prosecute his purpose, which he had not advised, though he liked it well enough; and so would not be answerable for any success. His Majesty himself being too irresolute, the Counsel was again changed, and the King marched to *Cardiff*; where he had been very little time, when he was informed, that *Bridgewater* was lost: and then they, who had dissuaded the King's Embarcation for *Bristol*, were much exalted, and thought themselves good Counsellors; though, in truth, the former resolution had been even Then much better pursued; for nothing could have hindered his Majesty from going to *Exeter*, and joining all his Forces; which would have put him in a posture much better than he was ever afterwards. Indeed the taking *Bridgewater*, which the King had been persuaded to believe a place impregnable, could not but make great impressions upon him, to think that he was betrayed, and consequently not to know whom to trust. It was in truth matter of amazement to all Men, nor was it any excuse, that it was not of strength enough against so strong an Army; for it was so strongly Situated, and it might well have had all those additions which were necessary, by Fortifications, that it was inexcusable in a Governor (who had enjoyed that Charge above three years, with all allowances he had himself desired, and had often assured the King, " that it was not to be Taken") that it did not resist any the greatest strength that could come before it for one Week; and within less than that time, it was Surrendered, and put into *Fairfax*'s hand.

That this prodigious success on the Enemies side, should break the Spirits of most Men, and even cast them into despair, is not at all to be wondered at; but that it should raise the hopes of any that it would produce a Peace, is very strange; yet this imagination did so much harm, that Men generally neglected to make that preparation against a powerful and insulting Enemy, that was in their power to have made, out of confidence that the offer of a Treaty would now prevail, and produce a Peace; and every Man abounded so much in his own sense on this point, that they were not capable of any reason that contradicted it. The Commissioners of all Counties, which were the best Gentlemen, and of best Affections, upon whom the King depended to apply the Common-People to his Service, were so fully of this opinion, that they made Cabals with the principal Officers of the Army, to concur with them in this judgment, and to contrive some way how it might be brought to pass; and too many of them were weary of doing their duty, or so much ashamed of not having done it, that they professed themselves to desire it, at least as much as the rest. This temper spread itself so universally, that it reached to Prince *Rupert* himself; who writ his Advice to that purpose to the Duke of *Richmond*, to be presented to the King; who took that occasion, to write the ensuing Letter to the Prince, with his own hand; which was so lively an expression of his own Soul, that no Pen else could have written it and deserves to be transmitted to Posterity, as a part of the Portraiture of that excellent Person, which hath been disguised by false, or erroneous Copies from the true Original; and follows in these words.

From Cardiff, in the beginning of the Month of Aug. 1645.

Nephew,

"This is occasioned by a Letter of yours, that the Duke of *Richmond* showed me yesternight. And first, I assure you, I have been, and ever will be, very careful to advertise you of my resolutions, as soon as they are taken; and if I enjoined silence to that which was no secret, it was not my fault; for I thought it one, and I am sure it ought to have been so now. As for the opinion of my business, and your Counsel thereupon, if I had any other Quarrel but the defence of my Religion, Crown, and Friends, you had full reason for your advice. For I confess, that speaking either as to mere Soldier, or Statesman, I must say, there is no probability but of my ruin; but as to Christian, I must tell you, that God will not suffer Rebels to prosper, or His Cause to be overthrown: and whatsoever Personal punishment it shall please him to inflict upon me, must not make me repine, much less to give over this Quarrel; which, by the Grace of God, I am resolved against, whatsoever it cost me; for I know my obligations to be both in Conscience, and Honor, neither to abandon God's Cause, injure my Successors, nor forsake my Friends. Indeed I cannot flatter myself with expectation of good success, more than this,

The King's Letter to Prince Rupert against Treating of Peace at that time.

"to end my days with Honor, and a good Conscience; which obliges me to continue my endeavour, as not despairing that God may in due time avenge his own Cause. Though I must avow to all my Friends, that he that will stay with me at this time, must expect, and resolve, either to die for a good Cause, or, which is worse, to live as miserable in the maintaining it, as the violence of insulting Rebels can make him. Having thus truly and impartially stated my Case unto you, and plainly told you my positive resolutions, which, by the Grace of God, I will not alter, they being neither lightly nor suddenly grounded, I earnestly desire you not in any ways to hearken after Treaties; assuring you, as low as I am, I will not go less than what was offered in my Name at *Uxbridge*; confessing that it were as great a Miracle that they should agree to so much reason, as that I should be, within a Month, in the same Condition that I was immediately before the Battle of *Naseby*. Therefore, for God's sake, let us not flatter ourselves with these Conceits; and, believe me, the very imagination that you are desirous of a Treaty, will lose me so much the sooner. Wherefore, as you love me, whatsoever you have already done, apply your discourse according to my resolutions, and judgment. As for the *Irish*, I assure you they shall not cheat me; but it is possible they may cozen themselves: for be assured, what I have refused to the *English*, I will not grant to the *Irish* Rebels, never trusting to that kind of People (of what Nature soever) more than I see by their Actions

" Actions; and I am sending to *Ormond* such a des-
" patch, as I am sure will please You, and all honest
" Men; a Copy whereof, by the next opportunity,
" you shall have. Lastly, be confident I would not
" have put you, nor myself, to the trouble of this
" Letter, had I not a great estimation of you, and a
" full confidence of your Friendship to"
                                           Your, &c.

When the King came to *Cardiff*, he was entertained with the News, "that the *Scottish* Army was set
" down before *Hereford*, and that, if it were not
" relieved within a Month, it must fall into their
" hands." To provide for this, there could be no better way found out, than to direct the Sheriffs of those *Welsh* Counties to Summon their *posse-Comitatus*, whereby the King was persuaded to hope, that there would be Men enough to wait upon him in that expedition; who with the Horse he had, would have been equal to any attempt they could make upon the *Scots*. But it was quickly discovered, that this Expedient had raised an unruly Spirit, that could not easily be suppressed again; for the discontented Gentlemen of those Counties, now they had gotten the People legally together, put them in mind of "the
" Injuries they had received from General *Gerrard*,
" and the intolerable exactions they lay under, which
" would undoubtedly be increased, if he continued
" in that Government." So that, instead of providing Men to march with the King, they provided a long list of grievances; from all which they desired to be relieved before they would apply themselves towards the relief of *Hereford*. All this was so sturdily urged,

that a Body of no lefs than four thoufand Men, of thofe who were thus called together, continued together many days, and would not be feparated, till the King was even compelled to give them fatisfaction in the particular they moft infifted upon; which was the removal of General *Gerrard* from having any Command over them; and that Charge was prefently conferred upon the Lord *Aftley*, the Major-General of the Army; who was moft acceptable to them; and they afterwards conformed themfelves as much to his directions, as from the diftraction of the time, and the continual ill Succeffes, could be expected by him.

But it was the hard fate of the King, that he could not provide what was fit for his own Service, except he provided likewife for the fatisfaction of other Men's Humors and Appetites. *Gerrard* had now, upon the matter, the Command of all the Forces the King had to truft to in thofe Parts; and he was of too impetuous a Nature, to fubmit to any thing for Confcience, or Difcretion, or Duty; fo that the King was compelled to fatisfy his Ambition for this prefent degradation, by making him a Baron; and which was an odd and a very fantaftical circumftance that attended it, for no other reafon, than becaufe there was once an Eminent Perfon, called *Charles Brandon*, who was afterwards made a Duke, he would be Created Baron of *Brandon*, that there might be another *Charles Brandon*, who had no lefs afpiring thoughts than the former; when he had no pretence to the Lands of *Brandon*; which belonged to, and were, at that time, in the poffeffion of a Gallant and

Worthy Gentleman Sir *Thomas Glemham*; who at the same time (very unluckily upon that account) came to the King at *Cardiff*, with about two hundred Foot, which he had brought with him out of the Garrison of *Carlisle*; which place he had defended for the space of eleven Months against *David Lesley*, and till all the Horses of the Garrison were eaten, and then had rendered, upon as honorable Conditions, as had been given upon any Surrender; *David Lesley* himself conveyed him to *Hereford*; where he joined with the other part of that Army, and from thence Sir *Thomas Glemham* (who was by his Conditions to march to the King wherever he was) came to his Majesty at *Cardiff*, at the time when the Title of his own Land, which came to him by Inheritance, was conferred upon a Gentleman of another Family: who, how well extracted soever, was of less Fortune, and, as many thought, of no greater Quality, or Merit. This unseasonable Preferment more irritated the Country, from which the King then expected Assistance, that when they believed they had accused him of Crimes which deserved the highest Censure, they saw him pretend to, and rewarded in, a higher degree than he could ever probably have arrived to, but for that Accusation. Here the King, after all his endeavours were rendered fruitless, entertained a new imagination, that he might get into *Scotland* to the Marquis of *Mountrose*, who had done wonders there; and thereupon left *Cardiff*; and, over the Mountains of *Brecknock*, and *Radnor*, passed the *Scottish* Quarters, and came to *Ludlow*, before that Army had any notice of his march.

BOOK IX.

When the King came first to *Ragland*, he had sent an Express to the Prince, by which he wished "that " the Lord *Colepepper*, and the Chancellor of the " Exchequer, might, as soon as was possible, attend ", his Majesty." The danger of the way was such, and the passage so difficult, that the Messenger came not quickly to his Highness. The Chancellor being then unfit to Travel by reason of the Gout, the Lord *Colepepper* made all possible haste out of *Cornwal*, where the Prince then was, and found his Majesty at *Cardiff*, when he was departing from thence; and waited on him to *Brecknock*; from whence he was again despatched with this Letter, to the Prince; which, being the first direction the King gave of that Nature, is necessary to be here inserted in so many words.

Brecknock 5th *August* 1645.

Charles,

The King's Letter to the Prince of Wales from Brecknock.

" It is very fit for me now to prepare for the worst, " in order to which I spoke with *Colepepper* this " Morning concerning you; judging it fit to give " it you under my hand, that you may give the " readier Obedience to it. Wherefore know that my " Pleasure is, whensoever you find yourself in ap- " parent danger of falling into the Rebels hands, that " you convey yourself into *France*, and there to be " under your Mother's care; who is to have the " absolute full Power of your Education in all things, " except Religion; and in That, not to meddle at " all, but leave it entirely to the care of your Tutor, " the Bishop of *Salisbury* or to whom he shall appoint

" to supply his place, in time of his necessitated ab-
" sence. And for the performance of this, I Com-
" mand you to require the Assistance and Obe-
" dience of all your Council; and, by their Advice,
" the service of every one whom You and They
" shall think fit to be employed in this business;
" which I expect should be performed, if need re-
" quire, with all Obedience, and without grumbling:
" This being all at this time, from

Your loving Father, Charles R.

After the Lord *Goring* had lain some time in the ill humor we left him at *Barnstable*, he entered into correspondence with Sir *Richard Greenvil*; who, he knew well, was as uninclined to the Council about the Prince as Himself; and finding that the Enemy troubled him not, but had given him rest, whilst the Army was employed upon other important Service, They two met privately; and, upon the Encourage-ment and Money he received from *Greenvil*, he writ to the Chancellor a very cheerful, and a very long Letter, bearing date first of *August*, in which he in-serted several Propositions; which, he said, had been framed "upon conference with Sir *Richard Greenvil*;
" which he desired might be presented to the Prince;
" and if they should be consented to, and confirmed
" by his Highness, he said, he would engage his
" life, that he would in a very short time have an
" Army of ten or twelve thousand Men, that should
" march wheresoever they should be commanded;
" and should be in as good order, as any Army in
" the World:" and concluded his Letter with these

BOOK IX.

"words; "I see some light now of having a brave Army very speedily on Foot, and I am sending a Copy of this inclosed Letter to the King, with this profession, that I will be content to lose my Life, and my Honor, if we do not perform our parts, if these demands be granted.

Which the Prince granted.

This Letter being presented to his Highness, then at *Launceston*, found so gracious a reception, that the next day, being the second of *August*, the Prince returned him an Answer of full consent; and the same day Signed all the particulars proposed by him; expressing a further resolution "to add whatever else should be proposed to him, and within his Power to grant;" so that there was once more a hope of looking the Enemy in the face, and having a fair day for the West. The next day, or thereabouts, Sir *Richard Greenvil* himself attended the Prince, in a seeming good humor; all the Propositions were immediately confirmed; some of which were, "that Sir *Richard Greenvil* should receive such a proportion of the Contributions of *Cornwal*, and five thousand pounds of the Arrears, for the payment of the Officers of the Army; and thereupon Sir *Richard* would gather up all the Stragglers, who were returned into *Cornwal* from their Colors; who, he said, would amount to three thousand Foot, and he would raise three thousand Foot more in *Devonshire*." So he betook himself again to Action, sending out his Warrants, and Levying Men and Money; having lent two hundred pounds to the Lord *Goring* at their first meeting, and calling the *posse* of *Devon* to meet at several places, where himself was still present, by which, he pretended, he should speedily recruit the Army. But before the end of *August*, that Friendship grew colder; Sir *Richard* observing a better correspondence between the Lord *Goring*, and Sir *John Berkeley*, than he hoped would have been, and hearing that the Lord *Goring* used to mention him very slightly (which was true) he writ a very sharp Letter to him, in which he said, "he would have no more to do with him." However he continued as Active as before, being now in *Devon*, and then in *Cornwal*, where he Commanded absolutely without any Commission, and very seasonably Suppressed an Insurrection about St. *Ives*, which might else have grown to a head; and hanged two or three fellows, who, I believe, were guilty enough, by his own order without any Council of War; and raised what Money he pleased upon others; then returned to his House at *Worrington*. All the Vivacity that had so lately appeared in the Lord *Goring*, upon the news of the loss of *Sherborne*, declined; and then there was nothing, but complaint of want of Money, and a Proposition to put the Army into Garrisons; although the Enemy gave them the same leisure, to pursue the former design, *Fairfax* being then engaged with his Army before *Bristol*.

As soon as the Prince, who was then at *Launceston*, had read the Letter, which the Lord *Colepepper* brought to him from the King, he returned it to the Lord *Colepepper* to keep, and to Communicate it to the Lords *Capel*, *Hopton*, and the Chancellor of the Exchequer; for it was a misfortune, that there was not so good Correspondence with the Earl of *Berk-*

shire (through some jealousies that were infused into him) as might have been wished; and from the Prince's first coming into *Cornwal*, some of his Servants of the best Quality, who had from the beginning been discontented, and upon strange pretences thought themselves undervalued that they were not of the Council, and, since the King's misfortune at *Naseby*, expressed their indispositions with more Licence, and whispered abroad " that there was a pur-
" pose of carrying the Prince into *France*, not that
" they believed it," but thereby thought to render the Council odious and suspected, had wrought so far upon the Earl of *Berkshire*, that He seemed to believe it too, whereby they got so much interest in him, that he always Communicated whatsoever passed in Council to them; so that a Letter of so great importance was not thought fit to be communicated to him, nor to the Earl of *Brentford*, who (though he was very kind, and just to the other four) was not without his jealousies, and was an ill treasurer of Secrets. They were very much troubled at the sight of the Letter, not at the Command of leaving the Kingdom, for, though they had never Communicated their thoughts to each other upon that Subject before, they found themselves unanimous in the Resolution, "that rather than he should be taken by the
" Rebels, they would carry him into any part of the
" Christian World." For the better doing whereof, from that minute, they took care that there was always a Ship ready in the Harbour of *Falmouth*. But it troubled them, "that the King's Command was so
" positive for *France*, against which they could

"make to themselves many Objections." Besides that, one of the Prince's Chamber, who was newly returned from *Paris*, brought a Letter from the Earl of *Norwich*, then the King's Ambassador there, to one of the Council; in which taking notice of a report there of the Prince of *Wales*'s coming thither, he passionately declared against it, "as a certain Ruin "to the Prince;" of which the Messenger, by His direction, gave many instances of moment. And they were the more troubled, because the Lord *Colepepper*, who brought that Letter from the King, averred, "that he had Had no conference with the King "upon the Argument, but had wholly declined it, "as a matter too great for him:" so that they had nothing before them but that Letter. After two or three sad Debates between themselves, they agreed upon "a Letter to be prepared in Cipher, presenting "their reasons, and what they had been informed "concerning *France;* and therefore offered it to his "Majesty, whether he would not leave the choice "of the place to them, or nominate some other, "against which so many exceptions might not be "made; and proposed *Ireland* (if the Peace were "made there) or *Scotland*, if the Marquis of *Mount-* "*rose* was as Victorious as he was reported to be; "withal assuring his Majesty, that in case of danger, "they would run any hazard, or into any Country, "before the Prince should fall into the hands of the "Rebels" This Letter after it was Communicated, with the Prince, as the Debates had been, was forthwith sent by an Express.

Towards the end of *August*, the Lord *Goring*, after

he had, in all his secret discourses, and in the hours of his jollity, spoken very bitterly of the Council about the Prince, as the Authors of all the Miscarriages, sent the Lord *Wentworth* to *Launceston* to his Highness, with certain demands, as he called them on his behalf; but with direction, "that before he "presented them to the Prince, he should Commu- "nicate them to the Lord *Colepepper*, or to the Chan- "cellor, and be advised by them, in what manner "to present them."

His Demands were, and so he styled them (1) To have a Commission to be Lieutenant-General of all the West, and to Command immediately under the Prince, Garrisons as well as the Army, and to be sworn of the Council as soon as might be. (2) That all Commissions to Officers of the Army, when his Highness is present, be given by the Prince; but that his Highness should Sign none but such as he should prepare for him. (3) That in the Prince's absence he should Sign, and grant all Commissions; and that, if any Governments of Towns should fall vacant, he might have the absolute recommendation of those that are to succeed, or, at least, a Negative Voice. (4) That all designs of Consequence should be debated, in the Prince's presence, by the Prince's Council, and such Officers of the Army as he should chuse to assist at it. (5) That the Number of the Prince's Guards should be limited; and many other particulars, which seemed so unreasonable, and unfit to be publicly urged, that the Lord *Colepepper* persuaded the Lord *Wentworth*, to suspend the presenting them; "the rather (as he said) because the Chan-

" cellor was then abfent" (being fent by his Highnefs to *Pendennis*-Caftle, under pretence of giving fome direction in the matter of the Cuftoms, but, in truth, to take care that the Frigate provided for the Prince's Tranfportation might be in readinefs, and Victuals be privately made ready, to be prefently put on Board, when the occafion fhould require) " and like-
" wife becaufe his Highnefs intended to be fhortly
" at *Exeter*, where the Lord *Goring*, being prefent,
" might better confider, and debate his own bufi-
" nefs;" to the which the Lord *Wentworth* confented.

For the Commiffioners of *Devon* had befought his Highnefs to interpofe his Authority, in the regulating and difpofing the Army to march towards the relief of *Briftol*; declaring, " as the pofture of it then was,
" that both that County, and Garrifons, muft in a
" fhort time be as much undone, and loft by Them,
" as by the Invafion of the Enemy; that all the Foot
" fubfifted by, and lived upon, the Magazines of
" the Garrifons; and the Horfe poffeffed the other
" part of the Country to themfelves; and would
" neither fuffer provifions to be brought to the Mar-
" cets, for the replenifhing their Stores; nor War-
" rants to be executed for any payments; pretending
" they were to defend their own Qarters; whilft
" themfelves levied what Monies they pleafed, and
" committed all forts of infolencies and outrages."
By this means both before in *Somerfetfhire*, and afterwards in *Devonfhire*, when the King's Army was forced to retire, the Enemy found great plenty of Provifions in thofe Quarters, where His Forces had been in danger of ftarving: as, all about *Taunton*,

there were very great quantities of Corn, when the King's Forces had caused all their Bread to be brought out of the Stores of *Bridgewater*, and *Exeter*; which proceeded partly from the negligence, and laziness of the Officers and Soldiers, who would not be at the trouble of threshing out the Mows, and Ricks, which were there; but principally by the Protection given by the Horse; who would not suffer any thing to be carried out of their Quarters; and such as sent their Provisions to Market, were sure to have their Money taken from them in their return. Insomuch as it was affirmed by the Commissioners of *Exeter*, "that before the Enemy had any Quarter "within ten miles, there was not so much provision "brought into that City in a Fortnight, as they "spent in a day:" which was only by reason of the disorder of our own Horse, General *Goring* being all this time in *Exeter*, breaking Jests, and Laughing at all People, who brought complaints to him; as one day, when the Fishermen complained to him, "that as they came to the Market, they were rob- "bed by his Troopers, who took all their Fish from "them," he said, "that they might by this see "what great Injury was done to his Men, by those "who accused them of great Swearing; for if they "did Swear, you know (said he) they could catch "no Fish."

Upon these reasons, and the very earnest desire of the Lord *Goring*, and the Commissioners, the Prince, on *Friday* the 29th of *August*, went from *Launceston* to *Exeter* in one day; leaving Sir *Richard Greenvil* (who then seemed to be in good humor) to bring up the Soldiers in *Cornwal*, and to haften his Levies in the North and Weft-parts of *Devon*. The Army having now lain ftill from the beginning of *July* to the end of *Auguft*, without the leaft Action, or Alarm from the Enemy, and fo being fufficiently refrefhed, and, as their Officers faid, awakened to a fenfe and a fhame of their former amazements, it was unanimoufly agreed at a Council of War, his Highnefs being prefent, " that the Foot fhould prefently ad" vance to *Tiverton*; and the Horfe to the Eaft of " *Exeter*; and that, as foon as Sir *Richard Greenvil* " could come up with his Men, they fhould all ad" vance to the relief of *Briftol*;" which was underftood to be in a very good condition; the laft Meffenger that came thence, affuring the Prince, as from Prince *Rupert*, that he was fufficiently provided with all Neceffaries for fix Months.

There had been, from the time of the firft going of the Prince into *Cornwal*, feveral rumors difperfed, as hath been faid, by thofe who were difcontented or angry with the Council, " that there was an in" tent to carry the Prince into *France*; which begot infinite prejudice to all that was advifed. Of this difcourfe General *Goring* had made great ufe, to the difadvantage of all thofe whom he defired to difcredit, which was indeed one of the Motives of his Highnefs' Journey to *Exeter*, that he might difcountenance that Report; which had wrought fo far amongft the Gentlemen of the feveral Weftern Counties, who were retired thither for Safety, that there was a Refolution among them " to Petition the " Prince to interpofe between the King and the Par-

A defign to Petition the Prince to fend Conditions of Peace, prevented.

"liament; and to send a Message to the latter with
"Overtures of Peace:" and to that purpose, meetings had been amongst those Gentlemen, to agree upon what Articles the Prince should propose a Peace; every Man declaring his opinion, what condescension should be in the matter of the Church, of the Militia, and of *Ireland*, upon consideration of what had passed at *Uxbridge*. When my Lords of the Council heard of these consultations, they apprehended great inconveniences might arise from thence to the King's Service, and to the Prince; who, by being pressed by their desires, and importunities, would lose the honor and thanks of the good Success that might attend it: Besides that, if he should send any Message upon their Motion, they would quickly make Themselves Judges of the matter of it, and Counsellors of what was to be done upon it: therefore they were of opinion, "that all endeavours were
"to be used to divert, and prevent any Petition of
"such a nature from being presented to his High-
"ness;" which, with great difficulty, was at last effected.

A Conference between the Lord Goring and one of the Prince's Council.

Shortly after the Prince's coming to *Exeter*, the Lord *Goring* being not then well, but engaged in a course of Physic, desired that he might have a free Conference with one of the Council in private; in which, he professed he would discover his heart, and whatever had stuck with him. Whereupon, according to appointment, the Person he had desired, went to him one Morning to his Lodging; when he caused all Persons to withdraw; and bid his Servant not to suffer any Man to disturb them. When they

were by themselves, he began with the discourse
of " unkindnesses he had apprehended from the
" Council, and from that Person in particular; but
" confessed he had been deceived, and abused by
" wrong information: that he was now very sensible
" of the damage that had befallen the Public by those
" Private Jealousies and Mistakes; and desired, that
" if any thing had indiscreetly or passionately fallen
" from him, it might be forgotten; and that they
" might all proceed vigorously in what concerned
" the King's Service; in which he could not receive
" a better encouragement, than by an assurance of
" that Person's Friendship. From this, he discoursed
" at large his apprehensions of his Brother *Porter*, of
" his Cowardice, and of his Treachery, with very
" great freedom in many particular instances;" and
concluded, " that he resolved to quit himself of him;"
and after two hours spent in those discourses, and in
somewhat that concerned his Father, in which he
said, " he was to receive this Person's advice by his
" Father's direction (it being about the Government
of *Pendennis*) as if he had said all he meant to say,
he asked the other negligently, " what he thought
" of the Demands he had sent by the Lord *Went-*
" *worth?*" Protesting, " he had no private thoughts,
" but only an Eye to the Public Service; towards
" the doing whereof, as the exigents of Affairs then
" stood, he did not think himself sufficiently qua-
" lified." The other told him, " that whatever He
" thought of them would not signify much, being
" but a single voice in Council; by the concurrent
" Advice whereof, he presumed, the Prince would

BOOK IX.

"govern himself. However, if he would have him tell him his opinion as a Friend, he would show himself so ill a Courtier, as to tell it him frankly; which, except he reformed him in his judgment, he should declare where it should be proposed, and, he believed, it would be the opinion of most of the Lords, if it were not His." Thereupon he told him very freely and plainly, "that he thought his Demands not fit for the Prince to grant, nor seasonable for Him to ask; his Authority being the same, as to the Public, all his Orders being Obeyed, and the Prince giving Him the same Assistance, as if he were his Lieutenant-General: that the Prince had not hitherto interposed his Authority in the governing that Army; and therefore, that he conceived it unseasonable, at that time, for his Highness to interest himself in the Command thereof; which he should do by making him Lieutenant-General: that the King having directed the Prince to make the Lord *Hopton* his Lieutenant-General, it would not become Them to advise the Prince to alter that designation, without receiving his Majesty's Command:" therefore he advised him, "since the alteration was no way necessary, and would inevitably beget much trouble, that he would defer the pressing it, till the King's Affairs should be in a better Posture." Satisfied he was not, yet he forbore to importune the Prince to that purpose at this time.

Prince Rupert delivers up Bristol.

About the middle of *September*, the Prince being still at *Exeter*, the News came of the fatal loss of *Bristol*; which, as all ill accidents at that time did, cast

cast all Men on their Faces, and damped all the former Vigor and Activity for a march. However, the former Resolution continued of drawing to *Tiverton*, and at least of defending those Passes, and keeping the Enemy from Invading *Devon:* for the better doing whereof, and enabling them to Fight, if *Fairfax* should advance, the Prince returned to *Launceston*; whither he Summoned all the Trainedbands of *Cornwal*, and an appearance of the whole Country; which appeared very cheerfully, and seemed well inclined to march to *Tiverton*. In the mean time the same negligence and disorder continued in the Army, and the Lord *Goring*, with the same Licence and Unconcernedness, remained at *Exeter*, to the great Scandal of the Country, and disheartening of the Army. About the latter end of *September*, his Lordship writ a Letter to the Lord *Colepepper*; in which he remembered him of the Propositions formerly sent by the Lord *Wentworth* to *Launceston*; and recounted at large, but very unjustly, the discourse which had passed between the other Counsellor and Him, at *Exeter*, upon that Subject; in which he charged the other with Answers very far from those he had received from him; and desired his Lordship, " that, by His means, he might know " positively what he was to trust to;" concluding, " that without such a Commission as he desired, he " could not be answerable for the Mutinies and Dis- " orders of the Army." Whereupon his Highness, upon full consideration of the mischiefs that would attend his Service, if he should consent to the Matter of those Demands, or comply with the Manner of the demanding, sent him word, "that he would "not for the present, grant any such Commission;" and wished him "to pursue the former Counsels and "Resolutions, in advancing towards the Enemy; "all things being in a good forwardness in *Cornwal* "to second him." And so there was no further pressing that Overture; however, he presumed to style himself, in all his Warrants, and Treaties with the Commissioners, and in some Orders which he Printed, "General of the West."

The sudden and unexpected loss of *Bristol*, was a new Earthquake in all the little Quarters the King had left, and no less broke all the Measures which had been taken, and the designs which had been contrived, than the loss of the Battle of *Naseby* had done. The King had made haste from *Ludlow*, that the *Scottish* Army might no more be able to interrupt him; and with very little rest passed through *Shropshire*, and *Derbyshire*, till he came to *Wellbeck*, a House of the Marquis of *New-Castle* in *Nottinghamshire*, then a Garrison for his Majesty; where he refreshed Himself, and his Troops, two days; and, as far as any resolution was fixed in those days, the purpose was, "to march directly into *Scotland*, to join with the "Marquis of *Mountrose*;" who had, upon the matter, reduced that whole Kingdom. During his Majesty's short stay at *Wellbeck*, the Governor of *Newark*, with the Commissioners for *Nottingham* and *Lincoln* repaired to him, as likewise all those Gentlemen of *Yorkshire* who had been in *Pontefract*-Castle (which, after a long and worthy defence, was lately, for mere want of all kind of Provisions, Surrendered upon good conditions; whereby, "all the Soldiers

"had liberty to repair to their own Houses, and might
"live quietly there)" whereupon the Gentlemen
assured the King, "they were as ready as ever to
"serve him when they should be required." Whether
the wonted irresolution of those about the King, or
the imagination, upon this report of the Gentlemen,
that a body of Foot might be speedily gathered together in those parts (which was enough encouraged
by the cheerfulness of all the Gentlemen of the several
Counties) prevailed, or not, so it was, that the
King was persuaded, "that it was not best to con-
"tinue his march, with that speed he intended, to-
"wards *Mountrose*; but that it would be better to send
"an Express to him, to agree upon a fit place for their
"meeting; and in the mean time, his Majesty might
"be able to refresh his wearied Troops, and to raise a
"Body of Foot in those parts." To which purpose
Doncaster was proposed as a fit place to begin in: and
to *Doncaster*, thereupon, the King went; and the Gentlemen so well performed their undertaking, that, within three days there was an appearance of full three
thousand Foot; who undertook, within four-and-twenty hours, to appear well armed, and ready to
march with his Majesty what way soever he would go.

Here again the King's froward Fortune, deprived
him of this opportunity to put himself into a posture
of war. That very Night, they received Intelligence,
"that *David Lesley* was come to *Rotherham* with all
"the *Scottish* Horse;" which was within ten miles
of *Doncaster*. The news whereof so confounded
them (as beaten and baffled Troops do not naturally, in a short time, recover courage enough to

BOOK IX.

The King goes to Doncaster.

endure the fight of an Enemy) that they concluded "he came in pursuit of the King, and therefore that "it was now too late to proceed upon their Northern "Expedition, and that the King must speedily remove "to a greater distance for his own security." Whereupon, he made haste (without expecting that recruit of Foot) from *Doncaster*, back again to *Newark*; Resolving then to go directly to *Oxford*; whereas, in truth, *David Lesley* knew nothing of the King's being in those parts; but, upon sudden Orders from *Scotland*, was required to march, with all possible expedition, with the Horse, to relieve his own Country from being totally overturned and subdued by the Marquis of *Mountrose*; who had then actually taken *Edinborough*. The Orders had no sooner come to the *Scottish* Army before *Hereford*, but he begun his march, without the least apprehension of any Enemy in his way, till he should come into *Scotland*; and so, as he had made a very long march that day he came tired and wearied with his Troops that Night into *Rotherham*. And he confessed afterwards, "if the King had then fallen upon him, as "he might easily have done, he had found him in a "very ill posture to have made resistance, and had "absolutely preserved *Mountrose*." But by his so sudden retreat, *David Lesley* was at liberty to pursue his march for *Scotland*, and came upon *Mountrose*, before he expected such an Enemy; and so prevented his future triumph, that he was compelled with great loss to retire again into the Highlands; and *Lesley* returned time enough to relieve and support the *Scottish* Army, after they were compelled to rise from *Hereford*.

The King now, with great expedition, prosecuted his Journey to *Oxford*, though not without making some Starts out of the way; by which he had opportunity to beat up some Quarters of new-levied Horse for the Service of the Parliament; and before the end of *August*, he arrived at *Oxford*; where he did not stay more than two days, but departed from thence again to *Worcester*, with a resolution to attempt the relief of *Hereford*; which had defended it self bravely, and very much weakened the *Scottish* Army by frequent Sallies. They had only a Body of eight hundred tired Horse remaining, which *David Lesley* left behind him when he marched with the rest into *Scotland*; and therefore the raising that Siege was thought the less difficult; and with this resolution his Majesty left *Oxford* the third day after he came thither. Upon his arrival at *Ragland*, he was certainly informed, " that *Fairfax* had Besieged " *Bristol*," for which no body underwent any trouble, for all Men looked upon that place as well Fortified, Manned, and Victualled; and the King even then received a very cheerful Letter from Prince *Rupert*; in which, " he undertook to defend it full four Months." So that the Siege being begun so late in the year, as the beginning of *September*, there was reasonable hope that the Army might be ruined, before the Town taken. Therefore the King prosecuted his former resolution, at least to endeavour the relief of *Hereford*. And as he was upon his March thither, he received Intelligence, " that the *Scottish* Army, upon " the notice of his Purpose, was that Morning risen " in great disorder and confusion, and resolved to

BOOK IX

The Scots rise from before Hereford and march into the North.

"make their retreat on the *Welsh* side of the River, "and so to pass through *Glocester*." This news was so welcome, and his Majesty was received with so full joy into the City of *Hereford*, that he slipped the opportunity he then had of discommoding at least, if not ruining the *Scottish* Army; which now passed through a strange Country, where they had never been, and where the whole Nation was extremely odious to the People. Nor would the Governor of *Glocester* suffer them to pass through his Garrison, till they sent him word plainly "that if they might not "pass through that Town," they "knew they should "be very welcome to pass through *Worcester*;" by which Argument he was convinced; so that he permitted them to go through that Town, from whence they prosecuted their march into the North. If, in all this time, they had been pursued by the King's Horse, considering the small Body they had of their own, there is little doubt to be made very many, if not the greater part of that Army, had been destroyed.

But the King's heart was now so wholly set upon the Relief of *Bristol*, that nothing else was thought upon, which might in any degree delay it. And so the King, from *Hereford*, advertised Prince *Rupert*, "that he had raised the Siege of *Hereford*, and that "the *Scots* were marched Northward; that he intend- "ed speedily to relieve him; and in order to it, that "he had then commanded General *Goring*, to draw "what force he could out of the West; and to march "to the *Somersetshire* side of *Bristol*; and that his Ma- "jesty would himself have a Body of three thousand "Foot, drawn out of the several Garrisons of those

OF THE REBELLION.

"parts, which fhould pafs over the *Severn* about
"*Berkeley*-Caftle or *Glocefterfhire*-fide; and that his
"Horfe, which were then above three thoufand,
"fhould at the fame time Ford the *Severn* not far from
"*Glocefter* (as they might have done)" and fo join
"with his Foot; and by this means all things being
"concerted, they might hopefully fall on *Fairfax*
"his Quarters on both fides." And the better to
bring all this to pafs, the King himfelf went the
fecond time to *Ragland*, the Houfe of the Marquis
of *Worcefter*; fending the Horfe to thofe feveral
places, as might beft facilitate the execution of the
defign that was formed for the relief of *Briftol*.

But when the King came to *Ragland*, he received
the terrible information of the Surrender of *Briftol*,
which he fo little apprehended, that if the evidence
thereof had not been unqueftionable, it could not
have been believed. With what indignation, and
dejection of mind, the King received this Advertife-
ment. needs no other defcription and enlargement,
than the fetting down, in the very words of it, the
Letter which, the King writ thereupon to Prince
Rupert; which, confidering the unfpeakable indulgence his Majefty had ever fhowed towards that
Prince, is fufficient evidence, how highly he was
offended and incenfed by that Act; which yet he took
fome time fadly to think of, and confider, before
he would allow himfelf to abate fo much of his
natural candor towards him. As foon as he received
that furprifing Intelligence, he prefently removed
from *Ragland*, and returned to *Hereford*, the Poft
he chofe wherein to confider the defperatenefs of the

condition he was in, and to enter upon new confultations. To that purpofe, he fent Orders "for all "the Officers, and their Troops, which had been "fent into *Shropſhire*, *Worceſterſhire*, and South- "*Wales*, to provide for the relief of *Briſtol*, to attend "him there." And as foon as he came to *Hereford*, he defpatched an Exprefs with this Letter to Prince *Rupert*.

Hereford 14th *Sept.* 1645.

The King's Letter to Prince Rupert upon his Surrender of Briſtol.

Nephew,

"Though the lofs of *Briſtol* be a great blow to me, "yet your Surrendering it as you did, is of fo much "afflidion to me, that it makes me not only forget "the confideration of that place, but is likewife the "greateſt Trial of my conſtancy that hath yet be- "fallen me; for what is to be done, after one that is "fo near me as You are, both in Blood and Friend- "ſhip, fubmits himſelf to fo mean an Aćtion? (I "give it the eaſieſt terms) fuch—I have fo much to "fay, that I will fay no more of it: only, left raſh- "nefs of judgment be laid to my charge, I muſt re- "member you of your Letter of the 12th of *Auguſt*, "whereby you affured me, that if no Mutiny hap- "pened, you would keep *Briſtol* for four Months. "Did you keep it four Days? Was there any thing "like a Mutiny? More Queſtions might be aſked, "but Now, I confefs, to little purpofe: My con- "cluſion is to defire you to feek your Subfiſtence, "until it ſhall pleafe God to determine of my Condi- "tion, fomewhere beyond Sea; to which end I fend "you herewith a Pafs; and I pray God to make you

" sensible of your present Condition, and give you
" means to redeem what you have lost; for I shall
" have no greater joy in a Victory, than in a just
" occasion without blushing to assure you of my
" being"

Your loving Uncle, and most faithful Friend, *C. R.*

With this Letter, the King sent a Revocation of all Commissions formerly granted to Prince *Rupert*, and signified his Pleasure to the Lords of the Council at *Oxford*, whither Prince *Rupert* was retired with his Troops from *Bristol*, " that they should require " Prince *Rupert* to deliver into their hands his Com- " mission." And whether the King had really some apprehension that he might make some difficulty in giving it up, and make some disorder in *Oxford*, or whether it was the effect of other Men's Counsels, his Majesty, at the same time, sent a Warrant like- wise for the present Imprisonment of Colonel *Leg* (who was Governor of *Oxford*) as a Person much in the Prince's favor, and therefore like to be subservient to any of his Commands. But this circumstance of rigor, made the other judgment upon the Prince thought to be over-sudden, " that He should be made the " first Example of the King's Severity, when so many " high Enormities, and Miscarriages of others, had " passed without being called in question." And as no body suspected the Prince's want of Duty in sub- mitting to the King's Pleasure, so Colonel *Leg* was generally believed to be a Man of that entire Loyalty to the King, that he was above all temptations: this circumstance of committing the Governor, made the other to be likewife fufpected to be more the effect of the power of fome Potent Adverfaries, than of the King's own Severity.

When the Prince of *Wales* came to *Launcefton* from *Exeter* (which was about the middle of *September*) after the lofs of *Briftol*, and the motion of the Enemy inclined Weftward, it was then thought fit to draw all the Trained-bands of *Cornwal* to *Launcefton*, and as many of them as could be perfuaded, to march Eaftward; it being agreed at *Exeter*, " that, if the " Enemy gave time, the force of both Counties (fafe " what was neceffary to be continued at *Plymouth*) " fhould be drawn to *Tiverton*, and, upon that Pafs, " to Fight with the Rebels; for the better compaffing " whereof; it was Ordered, that Sir *Richard Greenvil* " fhould Command all the *Cornifh* Trained-bands, " whereunto fhould be added his own three Regi- " ments, which he had formerly carried to *Taunton*;" who took themfelves to be fo difobliged, both Officers and Soldiers (as in truth they were) by the Lord *Goring*, that they were abfolutely difbanded, and could by no other means be gotten together, but upon affurance that they fhould be Commanded by Sir *Richard Greenvil*. Things being thus fettled, *Green- vil* feemed well fatisfied, having all the refpect, and encouragement from the Prince that was defired, or could be given; and without any other indifpofition, than that, once in two or three days, he would write a Letter either to the Prince himfelf, the Lords, or Mr. *Fanfhaw*, Extolling himfelf, and Reproaching the Lord *Goring*'s plundering Horfe, and fometimes Sir *John Berkeley*; in all which he ufed a very extra- ordinary Licence.

During the Prince's being at *Exeter*, Sir *John Berkeley* had defired, " that, in refpect his continual " prefence would be neceffary at *Exeter*, fince the " Enemy apparently looked that way, his Highnefs " would difpofe the Command of the Forces before " *Plymouth*, to fuch a Perfon as He thought fit; who " might diligently attend that Service." There was a general inclination to have fent back Sir *Richard Greenvil* to that Charge, which it was vifible he looked for; but there were three great points to be confidered; The firft, the pretence that General *Digby* had to that Command; to whom it Originally belonged; and both He, and the Earl of *Briftol*, expected it upon this alteration; he being at that time fo well recovered in his health, that he was well able to execute the Command: The next, that if it fhould be offered to *Greenvil*, he would infift upon fuch affignations of Contributions, as would make the fubfiftence of the Army, and of the Garrifons impoffible; the laft and the greateft, was, that the whole defign being now to draw fuch a Body together, as might give the Rebels Battle, this could not be without the *Cornifh* Trained-bands, and thofe other Soldiers, who had run from their Colors; neither of which, would march without Sir *Richard Greenvil*; and it was apparent, if he went to *Plymouth*, thofe old Soldiers would go to him. Befides, his experience and activity was then thought moft neceffary to the marching Army; where there was a great dearth of good Officers. Hereupon, it was refolved that General *Digby* fhould again refume the Charge about *Plymouth*, but upon any extraordinary occafion, and advance of the Enemy, he was to receive Orders from Sir *Richard Greenvil*; and accordingly, upon Sir *Richard Greenvil*'s advancing into *Devon*, and fixing a Quarter at *Okington*, *Digby* was ordered so to do; which he observed accordingly.

In the beginning of *October*, the Lord *Goring* persuaded the Commissioners of *Devon*, upon his promise to punish and suppress all disorders in the Soldiery, and that the Markets should be free, " to double the " Contribution of the County for six Weeks, and " to assign half thereof to his Army;" by virtue whereof he raised vast Sums of Money; but abated nothing of the former disorders, and pressures: and the Money so raised, instead of being regularly distributed amongst the Soldiers, was disposed to such Persons as he thought fit by his Warrants to direct. But no sooner was Sir *Thomas Fairfax* advanced as far as *Cullampton*, than the Lord *Goring* gave over the thought of defending *Devon*, and, by his Letter of the eleventh of *October* to the Lord *Colepepper*, said, " that he had sent all the Horse, but one thousand, " Westward, under the Command of the Major-Ge- " neral, to join with the *Cornish*; who were to ad- " vance; and that Himself, with one thousand Horse, " and all his Foot, resolved to stay in *Exeter* to defend " that Town, if the Enemy came before it; or to be " ready to attend their Rear, if they marched for- " ward;" and therefore desired, " that his Highness " would appoint whom he thought fit, to give Or- " ders to the Lord *Wentworth*, his Major-General, " who was prepared not to dispute Orders sent by " any Substituted by the Prince." Hereupon, the

Prince had appointed Sir *Richard Greenvil* " to ad-
" vance with the *Cornifh* to *Okington,*" and directed
the Major-General " to receive Orders from him:"
But, by that time they two had difpofed themfelves
in Order, as they did very handfomely and cheerfully,
General *Goring* changed his mind, and within four
days after his former Letter, he retired with his thoufand Horfe out of *Exeter* to *Newton-Bushell*; and then
fent to the Prince, by a Letter to the Lord *Colepepper,*
to know " whether Sir *Richard Greenvil* fhould receive
" Orders from him; and offered to undertake any
" defign with Sir *Richard Greenvil,* or by Himfelf, as
" the Prince fhould direct; or that if his Prefence
" and Command fhould be thought, on the account
" of any indifpofition in the *Cornifh* towards him,
" probable to produce any inconvenience to the Ser-
" vice, he would willingly, for that Expedition,
" refign his Command to any Perfon the Prince
" would defign for it:" intimating withal, " that if
" the Lord *Hopton* had it, the Lord *Wentworth* would
" willingly receive Orders from him." His Highnefs,
the next day, writ to him, " that he committed the
" management of the whole to his Lordfhip; and had
" Commanded Sir *Richard Greenvil* to receive Orders
" from him, who had then a good Body of *Cornifh*
" with him, and power to draw off the Men from
" *Plymouth,* if there fhould be occafion."

The King's having been in that perpetual motion,
as hath been mentioned before, kept the Exprefs that
had been fent to him from the Counfellors, upon
the firft fignification of his Pleafure concerning the
Prince's Tranfportation into *France,* from delivering

that Letter for some time. So that it was the middle of *October*, before they received his Majesty's further direction. Then this Letter to the Lord *Colepepper* was brought back by the same Express.

The King's Letter concerning the Prince of Wales.

Colepepper,

"I have seen and considered your despatches; and for this time you must be content with Results without the Reasons, leaving you to find them; Lord *Goring* must break through to *Oxford* with his Horse, and from thence, if he can, find me out, wheresoever he shall understand I shall be; the Region about *Newark* being, as I conceive, the most likely place. But that which is of more necessity, indeed absolute, is, that, with the best conveniency, the most secrecy, and greatest expedition, Prince *Charles* be Transported into *France*; where his Mother is to have the sole care of him, in all things but one, which is his Religion; and that must still be under the care of the Bishop of *Salisbury*, and this I undertake his Mother shall submit unto: concerning which, by my next despatch, I will advertise Her; this is all;" So I rest

Your most assured Friend, *Charles R.*

Though this Letter was writ after the loss of *Bristol*, yet when it arrived, the hopes of the West were not thought desperate; and it was absolutely concluded between the Lords, " that, as the Person of the Prince was never to be in hazard of being surprised, so he was not to be Transported out of the King's Dominions, but upon apparent, visible "neceffity, in point of fafety:" And the very fufpicion of his going had been, both by the Lord *Goring* and others, envioufly whifpered, to the great difheartening of the People; fo that (befides that an unfeafonable attempt of going, might have been difappointed) they faw that the lofs of the whole Weft, both Garrifons, and Army, would immediately have attended that Action, and therefore they thought, they fhould be abfolved, in point of duty, by the King, if they only preferved themfelves in a power of obeying him, without executing his Command at that time; efpecially fince General *Goring* thought it not reafonable to obferve the Orders, which were fent to him at the fame time, for marching towards the King, nor fo much as advifed with his Highnefs, or Communicated that he had received any fuch Orders; and yet his Highnefs let him know; "that he was well content, that he fhould break "through with his Horfe to the King; which he "might have done."

The Enemy, having gained *Tiverton*, made no great hafte to the Weft of *Exeter*, but fpent their time in Fortifying fome Houfes near the Town, on the Eaft-fide, without receiving the leaft difturbance from the Army; the Lord *Goring* entertaining himfelf in his ufual jollity between *Exeter*, *Totnefs*, and *Dartmouth*; it being publicly fpoken in *Exeter*, "that the "Lord *Goring* intended to leave the Army, and "fpeedily to go beyond Seas, and that Lieutenant- "General *Porter* refolved to go to the Parliament;" long before the Prince underftood General *Goring*'s refolution to go into *France*, by any intimation from himself. The twentieth of *November*, his Lordship writ a Letter from *Exeter* to the Prince by the Lord *Wentworth*, " that, now that the Enemy and his " Lordship were settled in their Winter-Quarters " (whereas the Enemy was then as stirring as ever) " he did beg leave of his Highness to spend some " time for the recovery of his health, in *France;* " intimating, " that he hoped to do his Highness some " notable Service by that Journey;" and desired, " that his Army might remain entirely under the " Command of the Lord *Wentworth*" (whereas, not above a Fortnight before, he had writ, " that the " Lord *Wentworth* was very willing to receive Or- " ders from the Lord *Hopton*) until his return; which, " he said, should be in two Months;" and so having despatched the Lord *Wentworth* with this Letter to the Prince to *Truro*, his Lordship, never attending his Highness' leave or approbation, went the same, or the next day, to *Dartmouth;* where he stayed no longer than till he could procure a passage into *France;* whither, with the first wind, he was Transported; Lieutenant-General *Porter*, at the same time, declining the Exercise of his Command, and having received several Messages, Letters, and a Pass from the Enemy for his going to *London*. After the knowledge whereof, General *Goring* signed a Warrant for the Levying two hundred pounds upon the Country for the bearing his Charges. The Lord *Wentworth*, at the time of his being then at *Truro*, told some of his confidents, " that the Lord *Goring* intended to return " no more to the Army, or into *England;* but relied " upon Him to preserve the Horse from being " engaged,

The Lord Goring retires into France.

OF THE REBELLION.

" engaged, till he could procure a Licence from the
" Parliament to Tranfport them, for the Service of
" a Foreign Prince, which would be a fortune to
" the Officers. And the Major-General faid after-
" wards at *Launceſton*, that he could not underſtand
" the Lord *Goring*'s defigns; for that, at his going
" from the Army, he gave the Officers great charge
" to preferve their Regiments, for he had hope to
" get leave to Tranfport them;" and within few
days after he arrived at *Paris*, he fent Captain *Por-
ridge* into *England*, to fetch all his Saddle-Horfes,
and Horfes of Service, upon pretence that he was to
prefent them in *France*; though at the fame time he
affured his Friends, " that he was returning fpeedily
" with Men and Money;" which was not the more
believed by his fending for his Horfes.

Though there had been no great Modeſty uſed in
the difcourfes of the People towards General *Goring*,
from the time of his firſt faſtening in the Weſt, eſpecially of the *Corniſh*, whom he had moſt unfkilfully
irreconciled to him, by his continual neglects and
contempts of them (as he would ufually before *Taunton*, when he viewed his Foot, clap an *Iriſh*-man,
or one of thofe Soldiers who came out of *Ireland*, who
doubtleſs were good Men; on the Shoulders, and
tell him, in the hearing of the reſt, " that he was
" worth ten *Corniſh* Cowards," the greateſt part of
his prefent ſtrength. and all his future hopes depending upon the *Corniſh*, many whereof had reaſon to
believe themfelves not inferior to any who had
ferved the King) yet from the time that he left the
Army, and went for *France*, they gave themfelves

VOL. VIII.   K

a greater Licence; and declared, "that he had, from
"the beginning, Combined with the Rebels; and
"having wasted and ruined all the Supplies which
"had been sent him, had now left a diffolute and
"odious Army to the Mercy of the Enemy, and to a
"County more juftly incenfed, and confequently
"more mercilefs than they. They compared the lofs
"of *Weymouth*, in the view of his Army, after he
"had been in the Town, and when the whole direc-
"tion was in him, with the Counter-fcuffle at *Pether-
"ton*-Bridge, when two of his own Parties, pur-
"fuing the Orders they had received, Fought with
"each other, whilft the Enemy retired to their own
"ftrengths: they remembered the voluntary, want-
"on, incenfing the Country; the difcountenancing
"the Garrifon of *Lamport*, and diffolving it; the
"eating the Provifions of the reft; the cherifhing
"the Club-men; and the lying with his whole Army
"before *Taunton* full fix Weeks (after he had decla-
"red the Enemy to be in his Mercy, within fix days)
"and in that time (pretending that he would in few
"days ftarve them) he fuffered great quantities of
"Provifions to be carried into them, through his
"own Quarters, and feveral Interviews, and private
"Meetings to be by his Brother *Porter* (whofe
"Integrity he had before fufpected) and the chief-
"Officers of the Rebels: the neglecting his Body of
"Foot, during the time that he lay before *Taunton*,
"by which he fuffered above two thoufand to run
"away. They talked of the beating up his Head-
"Quarter the day before the Rout at *Lamport* at
"Noon-day, for which no Man was ever called to

" a Council of War; and that total Rout at *Lamport*,
" as two of the moſt ſupine, and unſoldierly Defeats,
" that were ever known; before which, or in thoſe
" ſtraits, or upon any other occaſions of Advice,
" that he never called a Council of War to conſider
" what was to be done; and in that laſt buſineſs of
" *Lamport*, himſelf was ſo far from being preſent,
" that coming in great diſorder to *Bridgewater*, he
" ſaid, he had loſt his Foot, and Cannon; which
" indeed were brought off entirely by the care, and
" diligence of the Lord *Wentworth*, and Sir *Joſeph*
" *Wagſtaff*. They talked of his unheard of neglecting
" the Army, after that Retreat at *Bridgewater*, inſo-
" much as of between three and four thouſand Foot,
" which himſelf confeſſed he had after that buſineſs
" (and if his loſs had been no greater than he owned,
" muſt have been a far greater Number) within ſix-
" teen days, he had not thirteen hundred, nor even
" after recovered a Man, but what was gotten up
" by the Activity and Authority of the Prince. Laſtly,
" they remembered his lying in *Devonſhire* from the
" beginning of *July*, which was about the time of
" his Retreat from *Lamport*, to the end of *November*,
" when he went to *France* (which was five Months)
" with a Body of above four thouſand Horſe and
" Foot; deſtroying, and irreconciling the Country
" to the King, and the Cauſe, without making the
" leaſt attempt, or in any degree looking after the
" Enemy; whilſt the Rebels, by formal Sieges,
" took in the Garriſons of *Bridgewater*, *Sherborne*,
" and *Briſtol*, and many other important holds."

Upon the whole matter, comparing his Words,

K 2

and his Actions, laying his doing and his not doing together, they concluded, "that if he had been "confederate with the Enemy, and been corrupted "to betray the West, he could not have taken a "more effectual way to do it; since he had not "interest enough by any Overt-Act to have put it "into their power;" and therefore they who had a greater opinion of his Wit, Courage, and Conduct, than of his Conscience, and Integrity, presumed the failing was in the latter; towards which opinion they were the more inclined, by many discourses negligently let fall by the Enemy in their Quarters, "that they were Sure enough of *Goring*; and by Sir *Thomas Fairfax*'s applying himself to the taking those strong places after the Rout at *Lamport*, without ever considering or looking after the Lord *Goring*'s Army; which he could not but know consisted of a Body of Horse, equal in Number to his own; and had reason to apprehend those two Populous Counties of *Devon* and *Cornwal*, could quickly recruit the Foot; "which negligence (said they) "*Fairfax* could never be guilty of, if he had not "been well assured, that those Forces should work "them no inconvenience;" besides that, being unpursued, *Goring* might easily have made an escape, and joined with the King, and so have diverted all the Enemies designs upon the West.

Others, who were not enough in love with the Lord *Goring*, to desire to be joined with him in any Trust, yet in their opinions clearly absolved him from any Combination with the Enemy, or design of Treachery, and imputed the slow managing the business, at his first coming into the West, and overslipping some opportunities of advantage, to his desire of being settled in that Command, and so not making haste, lest, the work being done, he might be necessitated to leave those Parts, and be called to the King; for without doubt, though there was a reconciliation made between Him and Prince Rupert, to that degree, that all the Countenance General *Goring* received from Court in prejudice of the Prince's Authority, and of his Council, was procured for him purely by that Prince; who in one of his Letters to him, at such time as he was before *Taunton*, used these words; "what you desire in your Letter, "on the 22ᵈ of *May*, shall be observed; and assure "yourself that Prince *Rupert* shall maintain General "*Goring*'s Honor and Power, and shall lose his Life, "rather than General *Goring* shall suffer for Prince "*Rupert*;" which Letter (as he did any others, which he received from his Majesty, or the Secretaries, in Cipher) he Communicated to the Company in all his Acts of good fellowship; yet, I say, it was very evident, he was resolved never to be in the same Army with Prince *Rupert* under his Command; and all his loose and scandalous Speeches, they imputed to an innate licence he had always given himself; and his gross and unfortunate Oversights, to the laziness and unactivity of his Nature; which could better pursue, and make Advantages upon good Successes, than struggle and contend with difficulties and straits. And they who had been nearest the Observation, found a great difference between the presentness of his Mind and Vivacity in a sudden Attempt, though never so full of Danger, and an Enterprise that required more deliberation, and must be attended with patience, and a steady circumspection; as if his Mind could not be long bent. And therefore he had been observed to give over a Game, sooner than Gamesters that have been thought to have less Fire. Many other passages must be attributed to his perfect hatred of all the Persons of the Council, after he found they would not comply with his desires, and to his particular Ambition; and both those Passions of Ambition, and Revenge, might transport his Nature beyond any limits. But what he meant by his discourse at parting to the Officers, for the keeping the Horse for the Service of some Foreign Prince, was never understood, except he did really believe, that he should shortly return with a Body of Foot; and so that they should not be forward to engage with the Enemy, or else to keep such a dependance upon him from the Officers, that they should always hope for employment under him.

Whilst Sir *Richard Greenvil* stayed at *Okington*, he had several strange designs; which he always communicated to the Prince, or Lords, in Writing; one of which was, "to cut a deep Trench from "*Barnstable* to the South-Sea, for the space of near "forty Miles; by which, he said, he would de-"fend all *Cornwal*, and so much of *Devon*, against "the World," and many such impossible Undertakings; at which they who understood matters of that Nature, thought him besides himself. Notwithstanding the Trained-bands of *Cornwal* returned to their Homes (having ſtayed out their Month; which was their firſt Contract) Sir *Richard Greenvil* ſtayed ſtill at *Okington*, with his three Regiments of old Soldiers, having barricadoed the Town; the Paſs being of very great importance to hinder the Enemy from any Communication with *Plymouth*. And indeed the Reputation of his being there with a greater Strength than in truth he had at any time, was a great means of keeping the Rebels on the Eaſt-ſide of *Exeter*; as appears by their ſudden Advance, as ſoon as he removed from that Poſt; which he did about the end of *November*, without giving the leaſt advice to the Prince of ſuch his purpoſe, and contrary to the expreſs deſire of the Lords *Capel*, and *Colepepper*, who were then at *Exeter*, and hearing of his Reſolution, had written to him very earneſtly "not to remove." He ſuddenly retired with his three Regiments from *Okington* into *Cornwal*, and Muſtered his Men upon the River *Tamar*, that divides *Cornwal* from *Devon*, with expreſs Command "to Guard "the Paſſes, and not to ſuffer any of the Lord *Goring*'s "Men, upon what pretence or warrant ſoever, to "come into *Cornwal*." For the better doing whereof, he cauſed the Country to come in to work at their Bridges, and Paſſes, as he had done before, moſt unreaſonably, for the Fortifying of *Launceſton*; and cauſed Proclamations, and Orders of his own, to be read throughout *Cornwal*, in the Churches, "that "if any of the Lord *Goring*'s Forces" (whom in thoſe Writings he charged with all the odious Reproaches for Plundering) "ſhould offer to come into *Cornwal*, "they ſhould Ring the Bells, and thereupon the "whole County should Rise, and beat them out;" by these unheard of, and unwarrantable means, preparing the Country to such a hatred of the Lord *Goring*, and his Forces, that they rather desired the Company of the Rebels; so alienating all Men's Spirits from resisting of the Enemy; and all this without so much as Communication with the Prince, till it was executed.

About the last week of *November*, he came himself to *Truro* to the Prince, on the same day that his Highness had received Letters from the Lords at *Exeter*, of the extreme ill Consequence of Sir *Richard Greenvil's* drawing off from *Okington*; upon encouragement whereof, a strong Party of the Enemy was come to *Kirton*. Whereupon his Highness sent for Sir *Richard Greenvil*, and, in Council, acquainted him with those Letters, and other Intelligence that he had received of the Enemy, and desired him to consider what was now to be done. The next day, without attending his Highness any more, but returning to his House at *Worrington*, he writ a long Letter to Mr. *Fanshaw* of his Advice, which he desired might be Communicated to the Lords; which was, "that his Highness should send to the Parlia-
" ment for a Treaty, and should offer, if he might
" enjoy the Revenue of the Dutchy of *Cornwal*, and
" that they would not advance to disturb him in that
" County, that he would not attempt any thing
" upon them, but that they should enjoy the free-
" dom of all their Ports in *Cornwal* for Trade,
" without any disturbance by his Majesty's Ships:"
and so, in plain *English*, to sit still a Neuter between

the King and the Parliament, at a time when there was a Body of Horse Superior to the Enemy in those Parts; and when an equal proportion of Foot might have been gotten together; and when his Majesty had not the face of an Army in any other part of *England*. The Prince was very much troubled at this Letter, and the more, because he found Sir *Richard Greenvil* had contracted a great friendship with such of his Highness's Servants, as he had reason to believe less zealous and intent upon the Honor, and Prosperity of the King; and because he had discovered he labored very much to infuse a jealousy into the Governor of *Pendennis*-Castle, " that the " Prince intended to remove him from that Command, and to confer it upon the Lord *Hopton*;' to which purpose he had written to the Governor from *Okington* (when the Lord *Hopton*, and the Chancellor, were sent down thither to assist him in the Fortifying and Supplying that Castle; which if they had not done, it would not have held out, as it did afterwards) " that the Lord *Hopton* had a Commission to " take that Charge from him; but that he should not " suffer such an affront to be put upon him; for He, " and all his Friends, would stick to him in it:" Whereas there was never the least thought or intention to make any alteration in that Government.

Shortly after that Letter of the 27th, Sir *Richard Greenvil* writ again to Mr. *Fanshaw*, to know how his Propositions were approved; to which, by direction, he returned, " that the Council had not been " yet together since the receipt of them; the Lords " *Capel*, and *Colepepper*, being not then returned

" from *Exeter*; and that therefore his Propositions " had not been yet Debated." He proceeded in the mean time in his Fortifications there, and, about the middle of *December*, the Prince continuing at *Truro*, he sent several Letters to the Gentlemen of the County "to meet him at *Launceston:*" One of which Letters I saw, to Colonel *Richard Arundel*, in which, " He desired him to bring as many Gen-
" lemen, and others of Ability, as he could, as well
" the disaffected, as well-affected; for that he in-
" tended to Communicate to them some Propofi-
" tions, which he had formerly preferred to the
" Prince, and though they were not hearkened to
" There, he believed would be very acceptable to
" his Country-men of *Cornwal:*" but the Prince's sudden going to *Tavistock* disappointed that meeting.

Shortly after the Lord *Goring's* going into *France*, the Prince, being informed from *Exeter*, " that the
" Enemy, at the same time having finished their
" works, which kept the City from any Relief on
" the East-side, were now drawing their Forces to
" the West-side, whereby that City would be spee-
" dily Distressed;" thought it necessary to send the Lords *Brentford*, *Capel*, *Hopton*, and *Colepepper*, to confer with the Lord *Wentworth*; who lay then at *Ash-Burton*, six miles from *Totnefs*, and with Sir *Richard Greenvil*, who was ready to draw some Foot into *Devon*, to the end that such an understanding might be settled between them two, that the Service might proceed: their Lordships being directed, by Instructions under his Highnefs' hand, upon confi- deration of the state of the Forces, and conference

with the the Lord *Wentworth*, and Sir *Richard Greenvil*, to advife what fpeedy courfe fhould be taken for the Relief of *Exeter* (the Prince having at the fame time difburfed a thoufand pound ready Money to two Merchants of *Exeter*, for Provifion of *Corn* for that City) prefuming that both the one and the other would have been very ready to have received, and followed the advice which their Lordfhips fhould give.

The place of meeting was appointed to be *Taviftock*; where every body was, fafe the Lord *Wentworth*; but He failing, the Lords, having directed Sir *Richard Greenvil* how to difpofe of himfelf, went themfelves to *Afh-Burton*, near twenty Miles farther, to the Lord *Wentworth's* Quarter; where they fpent a day or two, but found not that refpect from him they had reafon to have expected. His Lordfhip was very jealous of diminution in his Command, which General *Goring* had devolved to him, and expreffing himfelf often-times to them very unneceffarily, " that he would receive Orders from none " but the Prince Himfelf;" whereupon, and upon the importunate calling for Relief from *Exeter*, their Lordfhips " thought it abfolutely neceffary, that the " Prince Himfelf fhould advance in Perfon, as well " to bring up as great a Body of the *Cornifh*, as was " poffible (which without his Prefence was not to " be hoped for) as to difpofe of the Command of the " whole Forces in fuch manner, as might probably " be for the beft advantage; the beft that was to be " hoped for being to bring the Enemy to Fight a " Battle; and that they might be enabled to that

"purpose, by joining with the Foot that were in
"*Exeter*; which was a confiderable Body." For
the conducting fo great a defign, upon which no lefs
than three Crowns depended, the Lord *Wentworth*
could not be thought of Intereft, Experience, or
Reputation enough; and yet there was fo great regard, that he fhould not fuffer in his Honor, or the
imaginary Truft devolved to him by General *Goring*,
or rather indeed that no notable hazard might be
run, by any unneceffary mutation in Commands;
at a time when the Soldier was to be led to Fight,
that it was refolved, " that he fhould be rather Ad-
" vifed, than Commanded; and that if he comport-
" ed himfelf with that Temper and Modefty, as
" was expected, all Refolutions fhould be formed
" in Council, and all Orders thereupon fhould iffue
" in His Name."

The next day after *Chriftmas*-day, the weather
being very fharp, the Prince went from *Truro*, to
Bodmin; and the next day to *Taviftock*; where the
Lords of the Council attended; the Lord *Wentworth*
continuing at *Afh-Burton*, and his Horfe fpread over
that part of the Country which was at any diftance
from the Enemy. Sir *Richard Greenvil*, who attended
likewife at *Taviftock*, had fent three Regiments of
Foot to *Okington*, under the Command of Major-
General *Molefworth*; which were fecured by the
Brigade of Horfe under Major-General *Web*, who
was Quartered near thofe parts, and the *Cornifh*
Trained-bands were to come up within a week; the
Blockade before *Plymouth* was maintained by General *Digby*, with about twelve or thirteen hundred

Foot, and six hundred Horse; but the whole Contribution assigned for the support of those Forces, was taken by the Lord *Wentworth's* Horse; so that the Prince was compelled to supply those Men, out of the Magazines of Victual which he had provided in *Cornwal* for the Army when it should march; and to leave his own Guard of Horse upon the skirts of *Cornwal*; there being no Quarter to be had for them nearer his own Person.

About this time, Sir *Thomas Fairfax* Quartered at a House about two miles East of *Exeter*, Sir *Hardress Waller* with a Brigade of his Army at *Kirton*, and another part of the Army had possessed *Powdram*-House, and the Church, *Hulford*-House, and some other Holds on the West-side; so that no Provisions went in, and it hath been said before, how long the Army under *Goring* had subsisted upon the Provisions within, and kept all supply from entering: the advice taken at *Tavistock*, upon the Prince's coming thither, was, "that as soon as the *Cornish*
" Foot should be come up, his Highness should
" march with those, his own Guards, and as many
" Foot as might conveniently be taken from before
" *Plymouth*, by leaving Horse in their place, to
" *Totnes*; where a Magazine should be made of
" Provisions for the whole Army, both by Money
" (for which the County would yield great store
" of Provisions) and by Victuals brought out of
" *Cornwal* by Sea;" for which likewise directions were given: "From that place it was concluded,
" that the Prince might join with the Forces in
" *Exeter*, except the Rebels should draw their whole

"Body between them; and then that Garrison
"would be able both to relieve itself, and to infest
"the Enemy in the Rear; and the Prince might
"retire, or Fight, as he found it most convenient
"and advantageous to him." Resolutions being
thus fixed, and the *Cornish* being not expected in
full Numbers till the Week following, the Prince
chose to go to *Totness*; where all things necessary
might be agreed with the Lord *Wentworth*, who
might conveniently attend there, his Quarters being
within six miles; and where directions might be
given for making the Magazine, towards which
Money had been returned out of *Cornwal*.

The next day after the Prince came thither, the
Lord *Wentworth* attended him, and was informed in
Council, what had been thought reasonable at *Tavistock*; the which he approved of; the Prince then
called to see a List of the Quarters, that thereupon
it might be agreed how the whole Army should be
Quartered when they came together; to which end,
the next day, the Lord *Wentworth* brought the
Quarter-Master-General *Pinkney*, who indeed governed him. At the first Council, the Lord *Wentworth* told the Prince, "that he was to declare one
"thing to him, at the entrance into business, and
"for the prevention of any mistakes, that he could
"receive no Orders from any Person but his Highness; the Lord *Goring* having reposed that trust in
"him, and given him a Commission and Instruc-
"tions to that purpose;" which he often repeated
afterwards in Council; and, in the Debate of Quartering, talked very imperiously, and very disrespect-

OF THE REBELLION. 143

fully, and one day, after he had been drinking, very offenfively to fome of the Council, in the prefence of the Prince. The time was not conceived feafonable for the Prince to declare how the Army fhould be commanded, till he had brought it together, and till he had his own Guards about him; and fo the Prince, though he was nothing fatisfied in the Lord *Wentworth's* carriage, only told him " that he would take the Command of the Army " upon Himfelf, and iffue out Orders as he fhould " think fit;" and having vifited the Port and Garrifon of *Dartmouth*, and taken fufficient courfe for the providing the Magazines, and fettled the differences about Quartering, he returned to *Taviftock*; refolving, with all poffible expedition, to march with the whole Body of Foot to *Totnefs*, according to former appointment.

The day before the Prince begun his Journey to *Taviftock*, he received a Letter from the King his Father, dated upon the feventh of *November*, in thefe words:

Oxford, 7th *of November* 1645.

Charles,

A Letter from the King to the Prince.

" I leave others to tell you the News of thefe parts, " which are not fo ill, as, I believe, the Rebels " would make you believe: that which I think fit " to tell you is, I command you, as foon as you " think yourfelf in a probable danger of falling into " the Rebels hands, to Tranfport yourfelf into " *Denmark*; and, upon my bleffing, not to ftay too " long upon uncertain hopes within this Ifland, in

"case of danger as above said. For, if I mistake
"not the present condition of the West, you ought
"not to defer your Journey one hour; in This I
"am not absolutely positive; but I am directly posi-
"tive, that your going beyond Sea is absolutely
"necessary for me, as I do, to command you; and
"I do not restrain you only to *Denmark*, but permit
"you to chuse any other Country, rather than to
"stay here; as for *Scotland* and *Ireland* I forbid you
"either, until you shall have perfect assurance, that
"Peace be concluded in the one, or that the Earl
"of *Mountrose*, in the other, be in a very good con-
"dition; which, upon my word, he is not now:
"so God bless you."

Your loving Father *Charles R.*

Though the intimations in this Letter were strong for a present remove, yet they not being Positive, and the time of the year being such, as that the Prince could not be blocked up by Sea, and so could chuse his own time, and having one County entire, and *Exeter* and *Barnstable* in the other well Garrisoned, besides the Blockade before *Plymouth*, and the reputation of an Army, the Council were of opinion, that the time was not yet ripe; and so pursued the former design of joining the *Cornish* to the Horse, and to endeavour the relief of *Exeter*; for which purpose, the Prince undertook the Journey before mentioned to *Tavistock*, the day after Christ-mas-day; and, at his coming thither, received this other Letter from the King.

Oxford,

Oxford, *the* 7th *of December* 1645.

Charles,

Another Letter from his Majesty.

"I writ to you this day Month; of which, few days after, I sent you a Duplicate. The causes of my Commands to You in that Letter, are now multiplied. I will name but one, which I am sure is sufficient for what I shall now add to my former: it is This; I have resolved to propose a Personal Treaty to the Rebels at *London;* in order to which a Trumpet is by this time there, to demand a Pass for my Messengers, who are to carry my Propositions; which if admitted, as I believe it will, then my real security will be, your being in another Country, as also a chief Argument (which speaks itself without an Orator) to make the Rebels hearken, and yield to Reason: whereas therefore I left you by my last to judge of the time, I absolutely command you to seek for carefully, and take the first opportunity of Transporting yourself into *Denmark,* if conveniently you can; but rather than not go out of this Kingdom, immediately after the receipt of this, I permit, and command you to repair to any other Country, as *France, Holland, &c.* whereto you may arrive with most convenient security as to your passage; for nothing else is to be feared: I need not recommend to you the leaving the Country in the best posture you may, it so speaks itself, as I shall always do to be,

Your loving Father *Charles R.*

His Highness, as he used to do, as soon as he had perused the Letter, which, as the rest, was written in

BOOK IX.

the Lord *Colepepper*'s Cipher, and by him Deciphered, delivered it again to his Lordship, "to be secretly "kept, and Communicated to the other three;" for it was by no means yet safe to trust it farther. They were much troubled at the receipt of this Letter; for, besides that it found them in the Article of the most probable design had been on foot since the late disasters, to preserve the West; if they should have attempted to have given Obedience to that Command, the sudden, unexpected, and unreasonable leaving the Army, would visibly have declared what the intent had been, and would probably have engaged the People, and the Soldiers (who would have wanted neither Intelligence, nor Instigation from the Prince's own Servants; of whom the Lords could not rely upon three Men) they being full of hope in the Enterprise they were upon, and full of dislike of the other they were to chuse, to have prevented it; in which, they might reasonably have expected assistance from the Garrison of *Pendennis;* from which place his Highness was necessarily to remove Himself. So that if the Prince should attempt to go, and succeed, the Army, upon that discountenance, must dissolve; and if he succeeded not, there might be a fatal consequence of the endeavour and disappointment. Then, though they had long kept a Ship in the Harbour in readiness, and had at that time another Frigate of Mr. *Hasdunks*, yet by it's having been carried with so much secrecy that very few had taken notice of it, they could not be provided for so long a Voyage as to *Denmark*, which, with so important a Charge, would require two Months Victual at least.

But that which troubled them most, was the very Argument which his Majesty was pleased to use for his so positive Command; which, to their understanding, seemed to conclude rather, that his Highness' Transportation (at least without an immediate absolute necessity) was at that time most unseasonable: for if, in expectation of a Treaty, his Majesty should venture his Royal Person in *London,* and should be received there, and at the same time his Highness' Person should be Transported out of the Kingdom, by his Majesty's own Commands (which could not then have been concealed) it was reasonable to believe, that not only the Rebels would make great advantage of it, as an Argument against his Majesty's sincere intentions, and thereby draw unspeakable and irreparable prejudice upon him; but that his own Council, by which he was disposed to that Overture, and whose Assistance he must constantly use, would take themselves to be highly disobliged by that Act; and they would lose all confidence in their future Counsels.

Upon the whole Matter, the Lords were unanimously of opinion, "that the Relief of *Exeter* was "to proceed in the manner formerly agreed, and that "the Prince's Person was to be present at it:" and thereupon they sent an Express to the King, with a despatch signed by the Four who were trusted, a Duplicate whereof was sent by another Express the next day, in which they presented a clear state to his Majesty of his Forces, and the hopes they then had of improving their condition by the Prince's Presence; of the condition of *Exeter,* and of the Strength,

as they conceived, of the Enemy; and of the inconveniency, if not the impoſſibility of obeying his Majeſty at that time. They farther informed his Majeſty of "the great indiſpoſition, that they perceived
" in all the Servants towards his Highneſs' leaving the
" Kingdom; and that the jealouſy was ſo great of his
" going into *France*, that they had reaſon to believe
" that many who were very faithful, and tender of
" his Safety, would rather wiſh him in the hands of
" the Enemy, than in that Kingdom; and therefore,
" when the time of Neceſſity ſhould come (which
" they aſſured his Majeſty they would with any
" hazard watch and obſerve) they muſt prefer the
" continuing Him ſtill within his Majeſty's own
" Dominions, and ſo to waſt him to *Scilly*, or *Jerſey*,
" and from thence conclude what was to be done
" farther. They preſented likewiſe their humble
" opinion to him, that in caſe he ſhould be engaged
" in a Perſonal Treaty at *London* (which they con-
" ceived the Rebels would never admit, without
" ſuch Acts firſt obtained from his Majeſty, as might
" invalidate His power, and confirm Theirs) how in-
" convenient it might be, without the Privity of
" thoſe Counſellors, whom he was then to truſt, to
" Tranſport the Prince, except in danger of Sur-
" priſal, before the iſſue of that Treaty might be diſ-
" cerned:" Aſſuring his Majeſty, " that nothing
" ſhould put his Highneſs' Perſon into the hands of
" the Parliament, but his Majeſty's own Commands;
" which they ſhould not reſiſt in his own Domi-
" nions. nor, they conceived, any body elſe, if he
" were out of them.

The appearance at *Tavistock* answered the expectation; there being full two thousand four hundred of the Trained-bands, very cheerful, and ready to march; at *Okington* were eight hundred old Soldiers, under Major-General *Molesworth*; the Foot with the Lord *Wentworth* were given out to be eight hundred, with the Lord *Goring*'s Guards which were in *Dartmouth*; and to be drawn thence, upon the advance to the Army: from *Barnstable*, the Governor had promised to send five hundred Men; and out of *Exeter*, at the least, a thousand five hundred Men were promised: all which, with his Highness' Guards, might well be depended upon for six thousand Foot. The Horse was very little fewer than five thousand; whereof his Highness's Guards made near seven hundred; so that, if all these could have been brought to Fight, the day seemed not desperate. The Foot were appointed to have marched the morrow, when the News came, "that the Enemy was ad-
"vanced, and had beaten up the Lord *Wentworth*'s
"Quarters in two several places," and shortly after the News, the Lord *Wentworth* himself came in, in great disorder, not informed of the particular of his loss, but conceived it to be greater than in truth it was, though many Men, and more Horses, were taken in both places. The Prince was very desirous to pursue the former resolution, and to have advanced with the whole Body to *Totnefs*; but the Lord *Wentworth* did not only alledge, "that probably the Enemy was
"possessed by that time of *Totnefs*, but that he had
"in truth no hope to rally his Horse together, in
"any Numbers, till they might be allowed three or

"four days reft." Whereas all that Rout had been occafioned by fmall Parties of the Enemy, who, at day-time, came into their Quarters, and found no Guards, but all the Horfe in the Stables; and their whole Body moved not in two or three days after; encouraged, it was thought, by the great diforder they found thofe Troops to be in. Matters ftanding thus, and it being abfolutely neceffary, by reafon of this diforderly retreat of the Horfe, to draw off the Blockade from *Plymouth*, *Taviftock* was no longer thought a place for the Prince's Refidence; his Highnefs by the Advice of a Council of War removed to *Launcefton*; whither all the Foot were drawn, and the Horfe appointed to keep the *Devonfhire* fide of the River; and from thence he hoped he fhould be fpeedily able to advance towards *Exeter*.

The King had ftaid at *Hereford*, as hath been faid, in great perplexity, and irrefolution; not knowing which way to take, but moft inclined to go to *Worcefter*; till he was affured, "that the whole ftrength "of the Parliament in the North was gathered to-"gether under the Command of *Pointz*; and that "he was already come between *Hereford* and *Wor-*"*cefter*, with a Body of above three thoufand Horfe "and Dragoons; with which he was appointed "always to attend the King's motion:" fo that it would be very hard for his Majefty to get to *Worcefter*, whither his purpofe of going was, upon the new refolution he had taken again to march into *Scotland* to join with *Mountrofe*, who was yet underftood to be profperous. This being the only defign, it was not thought reafonable " to profecute that

"march by *Worcester*, and thereby to run the hazard
"of an Engagement with *Pointz*; but rather to take
"a more secure passage through North-*Wales* to
"*Chester*; and thence, through *Lancashire*, and
"*Cumberland*, to find a way into *Scotland*, unob-
"structed by any Enemy that could oppose them."
This Counsel pleased; and within four days, though
through very unpleasant ways, the King came within half a day's Journey of *Chester*; which he found in
more danger than he suspected; for within three
days before, the Enemy, out of their Neighbour-
Garrisons, had surprised both the Out-works, and
Suburbs of *Chester*; and had made some attempt
upon the City, to the great Terror, and Consterna-
tion of those within; who had no apprehension of
such a surprise. So that this unexpected coming of
his Majesty, looked like a designation of Providence
for the preservation of so important a place: and the
Besiegers were no less amazed, looking upon themselves as lost, and the King's Troops believed them
to be in their power.

The King marches to Chester, where his Horse are Routed by Pointz.

Sir *Marmaduke Langdale* was sent with most of the
Horse over *Holt*-Bridge, that he might be on the
East-side of the River *Dee*; and the King, with his
Guards, the Lord *Gerrard*, and the rest of the Horse,
marched directly into *Chester*, with a resolution,
"that, early the day following, Sir *Marmaduke Lang-
"dale* should have fallen upon the back of the Ene-
"my, when all the force of the Town should have
"Sallied out, and so inclosed them." But Sir *Marmaduke Langdale*, being that Night drawn on a Heath
two Miles from *Chester*, had intercepted a Letter

from *Pointz* (who had marched a much shorter way, after he was informed which way the King was bound) to the Commander that was before *Chester*, telling him, "that he was come to their rescue, and "desiring to have some Foot sent to him, to assist "him against the King's Horse:" and the next Morning he appeared, and was Charged by Sir *Marmaduke Langdale*, and forced to retire with loss; but kept still at such a distance, that the Foot from before *Chester* might come to him. The Besiegers begun to draw out of the Suburbs in such haste, that it was believed in *Chester*, they were upon their Flight; and so most of the Horse and Foot in the Town, had order to pursue them. But the others haste was to join with *Pointz*; which they quickly did; and then they Charged Sir *Marmaduke Langdale*; who, being overpowered, was Routed, and put to Flight; and pursued by *Pointz* even to the Walls of *Chester*. There the Earl of *Lichfield* with the King's Guards, and the Lord *Gerrard* with the rest of the Horse, were drawn up, and Charged *Pointz*, and forced him to retire. But the disorder of those Horse which first fled, had so filled the narrow ways, which were unfit for Horse to Fight in, that at last the Enemies Musqueteers compelled the King's Horse to turn, and to Rout one another, and to overbear their own Officers, who would have restrained them. Here fell many Gentlemen, and Officers of Name, with the brave Earl of *Lichfield*; who was the third Brother of that Illustrious Family, that Sacrificed their Lives in this Quarrel. He was a very faultless young Man, of a most gentle, courteous, and affable Nature, and of a Spirit and Courage invincible; whose loss all Men exceedingly lamented, and the King bore it with extraordinary grief. There were many Persons of Quality taken Prisoners, amongst whom Sir *Philip Musgrave*, a Gentleman of a noble Extraction, and ample Fortune in *Cumberland* and *Westmoreland*; who lived to engage himself again in the same Service, and with the same Affection, and after very great Sufferings, to see the King Restored. This Defeat broke all the Body of Horse, which had attended the King from the Battle of *Naseby*, and which now fled over all the Country to save themselves; and were as much dispersed, as the greatest Rout could produce.

The design of marching Northward, was now at an end; and it was well it was so; for about this very time *Mountrose* was Defeated by *David Lesley*; so that if the King had advanced farther, as he resolved to have done, the very next day after he came to *Chester*, he could never have been able to have retreated. He staid in *Chester* only one Night after this blow, but returned, by the same way by which he had come, to *Denbigh*-Castle in North-*Wales*, being attended only with five hundred Horse; and there he staid three days to refresh himself, and to rally such of his Troops as had stopped within any distance. So that, in a short time, he had in view four-and-twenty hundred Horse; but whither to go with them was still the difficult question. Some proposed " the Isle of *Anglesey*, as a place of Safety, and an " Island Fruitful enough to support his Forces; " which would defend itself against any Winter-

The King retires to Denbigh to rally his Horse.

BOOK IX.

"attempt, and from whence he might be eafily
"Tranfported into *Ireland* or *Scotland*." They who
objected againft this, as very many objections might
well be made, propofed "that his Majefty might Com-
"modioufly make his Winter-Quarters at *Worcefter*,
"and by Quartering his Troops upon the *Severn*,
"between *Bridgenorth* and *Worcefter*, ftand there
"upon his Guard; and by the accefs of fome other
"Forces, might be able to Fight with *Pointz*;" who,
by this time, that he might both be able the more to
ftraiten *Chefter*, and to watch the King's motion,
had drawn his Troops over the River *Dee* into *Den-
bighſhire*; fo that he was now nearer the King, and
made the march laft propofed, much the more difficult; but there was fo little choice, that is was profecuted, and with good Succefs; and there being
another Bridge to pafs the *Dee* fome Miles further,
and through as ill ways as any thofe Countries have,
his Majefty went over without any oppofition; and
had, by this means, left *Pointz* a full day's Journey behind. Here Prince *Maurice* waited on his Majefty with
eight hundred Horfe, part whereof was of Prince
Rupert's Regiment that came out of *Briſtol*. And now
being thus ftrengthened, they lefs apprehended the
Enemy; yet continued, their march without refting,
till, by Fording the *Severn* they came to *Bridgenorth*,

Thence to Bridgenorth.

the place defigned. Now every body expected, that
they fhould forthwith go to *Worcefter*, and take up
their Winter-Quarters; but upon the News of the
Surrender of *Berkeley* Caftle in *Glocefterſhire*, and of
the *Devizes* in *Wiltſhire*, two ftrong Garrifons of the
King's, it was urged, "that *Worcefter* would not be a

"good place for the King's Winter-Refidence, and
"*Newark* was propofed as a place of more fecurity."
This advice was the more like to be embraced, becaufe it was vehemently purfued upon a private, and
particular Intereft.

Though Prince *Rupert* had fubmitted to the King's
pleafure, in refigning his Commiffion, yet he refolved
not to make ufe of his Pafs, and to quit the Kingdom,
till he might firft fee his Majefty, and give an account
of the Reafons which obliged him to deliver up
Briftol, and was ready to begin his Journey towards
him as foon as he could be informed where the King
intended to reft. The Lord *Digby*, who had then the
chief influence upon his Majefty's Councils, and was
generally believed to be the fole caufe of revoking
the Prince's Commiffion, and of the Order fent to
him to leave the Kingdom, without being heard
what He could fay for himfelf, found that the odium
of all this proceeding fell upon Him; and therefore,
to prevent the breaking of that Cloud upon Him,
which threatened his Ruin (for he had not only the
indignation of Prince *Rupert*, and all his Party to contend with, but the extreme Malice of the Lord
Gerrard; who ufed to hate heartily upon a fudden
accident, without knowing why; over and above
this, as Prince *Rupert* would have an eafy Journey to
Worcefter, fo Prince *Maurice* was Governor there, who
had a very tender fenfe of the feverity his Brother
had undergone, and was ready to revenge it; whereas if the King went to *Newark*, the Journey from
Oxford thither would be much more difficult, and
Prince *Maurice* would be without any Authority

BOOK IX.

Thence to Newark.

The condition of the Garrison of Newark at this time.

there) thefe Reafons were Motives euough to the Lord *Digby*, to be very folicitous to divert the King from *Worcefter*, and to incline him to *Newark;* and his Credit was fo great, that againft the opinion of every other Man, the King refolved to take that courfe; fo having ftayed only one day at *Bridgenorth*, and from thence fent Sir *Thomas Glemham* to receive the Government of *Oxford*, he made hafte to *Lichfield;* and then paffed with that fpeed to *Newark* that he was there as foon as the Governor had notice of his purpofe. In this manner, in the greateft perplexity of his own Affairs, was his Majefty compelled to condefcend to the particular, and private Paffions of other Men.

When the King came to *Newark*, he betook himfelf to the regulating the diforders of that Garrifon; which, by their great Luxury and Exceffes, in a time of fo general Calamity, had given juft fcandal to the Commiffioners, and to all the Country. The Garrifon confifted of about two thoufand Horfe and Foot; and to thofe there were about four and twenty Colonels and General-Officers, who had all liberal Affignments out of the Contributions, according to their Qualities; fo that though that fmall County paid more Contribution than any other of that bignefs in *England*, there was very little to pay the Common-Soldiers, or to provide for any other Expenfes. This made fo great a noife, that the King found it abfolutely neceffary to reform it; and reduced fome of the Officers entirely, and leffened the Pay of others; which added to the number of the Difcontented; which was very much too numerous before. Now reports were fpread abroad with great confidence, and the advertisement sent from several places, though no Author named " that *Mountrose*, after his Defeat " by an access of those Troops which were then " absent, had Fought again with *David Lesley*; and " totally Defeated him; and that he was marched " towards the Borders with a strong Army." This News, how groundless soever, was so very good that it was easily believed, and believed to that degree, that the King himself declared a Resolution, the third time, " to advance, and join with *Mount-* " *rose*;" and the Lord *Digby* (who knew that Prince *Rupert* was already upon his way from *Oxford*, and that Prince *Maurice* had met him at *Banbury*) prevailed so far, that the King resolved, without delay, or expecting any Confirmation of the Report, " to " move Northward to meet the News, and, if it " fell not out to his Wish, he would return to " *Newark*." In this Resolution, after a Week's stay at *Newark*, he marched to *Tuxford*; and the next day to *Wellbeck*, having, in his way, met with the same general Reports of *Mountrose*'s Victories; which were interpreted as so many Confirmations; and therefore, though the King assembled his Council to consult at *Wellbeck*, he declared " that he would not have it " Debated, whether he should advance or retire; " but concerning the manner of his advancing; since " he was resolved not to retire; which he was sure " would be attended with more mischief than could " accompany his advancing."

This Declaration, how disagreeable soever it was to the sense of much the Major part, left very little to be consulted upon; for since they must advance, it was easily agreed " that they should march the next day to *Rotherham*; and that the Troops should be drawn to a Rendezvous, the next Morning, at such an Hour;" and so the Officers were rising to give Orders out for the execution of what was resolved; when, in the instant, one knocked at the door; who, being called in was found to be the Trumpeter formerly sent from *Cardiff* to the *Scottish* Army, with a Letter to the Earl of *Leven*, General thereof; who had taken him with him as far as *Berwick*, before he would suffer him to be discharged. The King asked him, "what he had heard of " the Marquis of *Mountrose*?" He answered, " that " the last News he had heard of him, was that he " was about *Sterling*, retiring farther North; and " that *David Lesley* was in *Lothian*, on this side *Edinborough*; and that the *Scottish* Army lay between " North-*Allerton* and *New-Castle*." This so unexpected Relation, dashed the former purpose; and the Lord *Digby* himself declared, " that it was by no " means fit for his Majesty to advance; but to retire " presently to *Newark*; which was, by every body, agreed to; and the Rendezvous of the Army for the next Morning to continue. When they were at the Rendezvous, the King declared, " that though it " was not judged fit for Himself to advance Northward, yet he thought it very necessary, that Sir " *Marmaduke Langdale* should, with the Horse under " his Command, march that way; and endeavour " to join with *Mountrose*. And having said so, his Majesty looked upon Sir *Marmaduke*; who very cheerfully submitted to his Majesty's pleasure; and said, "he had only one Suit to make to his Majesty; which was that the Lord *Digby* might Command in Chief, and He under him." All who were present, stood amazed at what was now said; of which, no word had passed in Council; but when the Lord *Digby* as frankly accepted of the Command, they concluded, that it had been concerted before between the King and the other Two.

No Man contradicted any thing that had been proposed; and so immediately, upon the place, a short Commission was prepared, and Signed by the King, to constitute the Lord *Digby* Lieutenant-General of all the Forces raised, or to be raised for the King on the other side of *Trent*; and with this Commission he immediately departed from the King, taking with him from the Rendezvous all the Northern Horse, with Sir *Marmaduke Langdale*, and Sir *Richard Hutton*, High-Sheriff of *Yorkshire*, together with the Earls of *Carnewarth*, and *Niddisdale*, and several other *Scottish* Gentlemen: He marched in the head of fifteen hundred Horse; and so in a moment became a General, as well as a Secretary of State; and marched presently to *Doncaster*.

Because this Expedition was in a short time at an end, it will not be amiss to finish the relation in this place; there being no occasion to resume it hereafter. The Lord *Digby* was informed at his being at *Doncaster*, "that there was, in a Town two or three Miles distant, and little out of the way of the next day's march, one thousand Foot newly raised for the Parliament;" which he resolved, the next Morning, to fall upon; and did it so well, that they all threw down their Arms, and difperfed; whereupon he profecuted his march to a Town called *Sherborne*, where he ftayed to refrefh his Troops; and whilft he ftayed there, he had notice of the advance of fome Troops of Horfe towards him, under the Command of Colonel *Copley*: *Digby* prefently Sounded to Horfe, and having gotten fome few Troops ready, marched with them out of the Town; and finding *Copley* ftanding upon a convenient ground, he would not ftay for his other Companies, but immediately Charged them with that Courage, that he routed moft of their Bodies; which, after a fhort refiftance, Fled, and were purfued by his Horfe through *Sherborn*; where the other Troops were refrefhing themfelves; who difcerning the Flight of Horfe, in great Confternation, concluded, that they were their own Fellows, who had been Routed by the Enemy; and fo with equal confufion they mounted their Horfes, and Fled as faft as the other, fuch ways, as they feverally conceived to be moft for their fafety. By this means, a Troop that remained upon the Field unbroken, fell upon the Lord *Digby*, and thofe Officers, and Gentlemen, who remained about him; who were compelled to make their retreat to *Skipton*; which they did with the lofs of Sir *Richard Hutton* (a gallant and worthy Gentleman, and the Son and Heir of a very Venerable Judge, a Man famous in his Generation) and two or three other Perfons; and with the lofs of the Lord *Digby*'s Baggage; in which was his Cabinet of Papers; which, being publifhed by the Parliament, adminiftered afterwards fo much occafion of difcourfe.

The Lord Digby Routed at Sherborne in Yorkshire.

At

At *Skipton*, most of the scattered Troops came together again, with which he marched, without any other misadventures, through *Cumberland* and *Westmoreland*, as far as *Dumfries* in *Scotland*; and then, neither receiving directions which way to march, nor where *Mountrose* was, and less knowing how to retire without falling into the hands of the *Scottish* Army upon the Borders; in the highest despair, that Lord, Sir *Marmaduke Langdale*, the two Earls, and most of the other Officers, Embarked themselves for the Isle of *Man;* and, shortly after, for *Ireland*; where we shall leave them, all the Troops being left by them, to shift for themselves. Thus those fifteen hundred Horse which marched Northward, within very few days were brought to nothing; and the Generalship of the Lord *Digby*, to an end. But if it had not been for that extraordinary accident of the flying of his own Troops, because the Enemy fled (as the greatest misfortunes which befel that Noble Person, throughout the whole course of his Life, usually fell out in a conjuncture when he had near attained to what he could wish) he had without doubt been Master of *York*, and of the whole North; the Parliament having no other Forces in all those parts, their Garrisons excepted, than those Foot which he first defeated, and those Horse which he had so near broken. The temper, and composition of his Mind was so admirable, that he was always more pleased and delighted that he had advanced so far, which he imputed to his own Virtue and Conduct, than broken or dejected that his Success was not answerable, which he still

BOOK IX.

charged upon second Causes, for which he thought himself not accountable.

When the Lord *Digby* and Sir *Marmaduke Langdale* left the King, his Majesty marched back to *Newark* with eight hundred Horse of his own Guards, and the Troops belonging to the Lord *Gerrard*; and quickly heard of the misfortune that befel the Northern Adventurers; upon which He concluded that it would not be safe for him to stay longer in the place where he was, for by this time *Pointz* was come with all his Troops to *Nottingham*, and *Rossiter* with all the Force of *Lincolnshire* to *Grantham*; and all the power his Majesty had, was not in any degree strong enough to oppose either of them; so that he was only to watch an opportunity by the Darkness of the Nights, and good Guides, to steal from thence to *Worcester*, or *Oxford*; in either of which he could only expect a little more time, and leisure to consider what was next to be done.

An account of the Discontents of some of his Chief Commanders against the King at Newark.

But before his Majesty can leave *Newark*, he must undergo a new kind of Mortification from his Friends, much sharper than any he had undergone from his Enemies; which, without doubt, he suffered with much more grief, and perplexity of mind. Prince *Rupert* was now come to *Belvoir*-Castle, with his Brother Prince *Maurice*, and about one hundred and twenty Officers who attended him; with which he had sustained a charge from *Rossiter*, and broke through without any considerable loss. When the King heard of his being so near, he writ a Letter to him, by which " he required him to stay at *Belvoir* " till further Order; and reprehended him for not

" having given obedience to his former Commands." Notwithstanding this Command, he came the next day to *Newark*, and was met by the Lord *Gerrard*, and Sir *Richard Willis*, Governor of the Town, with one hundred Horse, two miles in his way. About an hour after, with this Train, he came to the Court; and found the King in the presence; and, without Ceremony, told his Majesty, " that he was come to " render an account of the loss of *Bristol*, and to clear " himself from those imputations which had been " cast upon him." The King said very little to him; but, meat being brought up, went to Supper; and, during that time, asked some Questions of Prince *Maurice*, without saying any thing to the other. After he had Supped, he retired to his Chamber, without admitting any farther discourse; and the Prince returned to the Governor's House, where he was well treated and lodged. The King, how displeased soever, thought it necessary to hear what Prince *Rupert* would say, that he might with the more ease provide for his own escape from thence; which it was high time to make. So he appointed the next day to hear his defence, which the Prince made with many protestations of " his innocence, and how impossible it " was long to defend the Fort, after the Line was " entered." His Majesty did not suspect his Nephew to have any Malicious design against his Service, and had no mind to aggravate any circumstances which had accompanied that Action; and therefore, after a day or two's debate, caused a short Declaration to be drawn up, by which Prince *Rupert* was absolved and cleared from any Disloyalty, or

Treason in the rendering of *Bristol*, but not of Indiscretion. So that matter was settled; upon which the King expected the Prince should have departed, as himself resolved to prosecute the means for his own escape, without communicating it to him.

The change of the posture of the Enemy, and *Pointz*'s coming to the North-side of *Trent*, made his Majesty resolve to begin his march on the Sunday-Night, being the twentieth of *October*; which he imparted to none but two or three of the nearest trust. But the differences were grown so high between the Governor and the Commissioners (who were all the principal Gentlemen of the Country, and Who had with Courage and Fidelity adhered to the King from the beginning, and whose interest alone had preserved that place) and had been so much increased by the mutual Contests which had been between them in the presence of the King, that there was no possibility of reconciling them, and very little of preserving the Garrison, but by the removal of the Governor; which was so evident to the King, that he resolved on that expedient; and, on the Sunday-Morning, sent for Sir *Richard Willis* into his Bed-Chamber; and after many gracious expressions of "the Satisfaction "he had received in his Service, and of the great " abilities he had to serve him," he told him, " his " own design to be gone that Night; and that he " resolved to take him with him, and to make him " Captain of his Horse-Guards, in the place of the " Earl of *Lichfield*, who had been lately killed before " *Chester*" (which was a Command fit for any Subject) "and that he would leave the Lord *Bellasis*

" Governor of *Newark*, who being Allied to moſt
" of the Gentlemen of the adjacent Counties, and
" having a good Eſtate there, would be more accept-
" able to them." His Majeſty condeſcended ſo far,
as to tell him, " that he did not hereby give a judge-
" ment on the Commiſſioners ſide, who he declared
" had been to blame in many particulars; and that
" he himſelf could not have an ampler vindication,
" than by the honor and truſt he now conferred upon
" him; but he found it would be much eaſier to
" remove Him, than to reform the Commiſſioners;
" who, being many, could not be any other way
" united in his Service."

Sir *Richard Willis* appeared very much troubled;
and excuſed the not taking the other command, " as
" a place of too great Honor, and that his Fortune
" could not maintain him in that employment: he
" ſaid, that his Enemies would triumph at his remo-
" val, and he ſhould be looked upon as caſt out, and
" diſgraced." The King replied, " that he would
" take care, and provide for his Support; and that
" a man could not be looked upon as diſgraced, who
" was placed ſo near his Perſon; which, he told him,
" he would find to be true, when he had thought a
" little of it." So his Majeſty went out of his Chamber, and preſently to the Church. When he returned
from thence, he ſat down to dinner; the Lords, and
other of his Servants, retiring likewiſe to their
Lodgings. Before the King had dined, Sir *Richard
Willis*, with both the Princes, the Lord *Gerrard*, and
about twenty Officers of the Grrriſon, entered into
the preſence-Chamber: *Willis* addreſſed himſelf to the

King, and told him, "that what his Majesty had "said to him in private, was now the public Talk "of the Town, and very much to his Dishonor:" Prince *Rupert* said "that Sir *Richard Willis* was to "be removed from his Government, for no Fault "that he had committed, but for being His Friend:" the Lord *Gerrard* added, "that it was the Plot of the "Lord *Digby*, who was a Traytor, and he would "prove him to be so." The King was so surprised with this manner of behaviour, that he rose in some disorder from the Table, and would have gone into his Bed-Chamber; calling Sir *Richard Willis* to follow him; who answered aloud, "that he had received a "Public injury, and therefore that he expected a "Public satisfaction." This, with what had passed before, so provoked his Majesty, that, with greater indignation than he was ever seen possessed with, he commanded them "to depart from his Presence, and "to come no more into it;" and this with such circumstances in his looks and gesture, as well as words, that They appeared no less confounded; and departed the Room, ashamed of what they had done; yet as soon as they came to the Governor's House, they Sounded to Horse, intending to be presently gone.

The noise of this unheard of insolence, quickly brought the Lords who were absent, and all the Gentlemen in the Town, to the King, with expressions full of Duty, and a very tender sense of the usage he had endured. There is no doubt, he could have proceeded in what manner he would against the Offenders. But his Majesty thought it best, on

many confiderations, to leave them to themfelves, and to be punifhed by their own reflections; and prefently declared the Lord *Bellafis* to be Governor; who immediately betook himfelf to his Charge, and placed the Guards in fuch a manner as he thought reafonable. In the Afternoon, a Petition and Remonftrance was brought to the King, figned by the two Princes, and about four-and-twenty Officers; in which they defired, "that Sir *Richard Willis* might
" receive a Trial by a Court of War; and if they
" found him faulty, then to be difmiffed from his
" Charge; and that, if this might not be granted,
" they defired Paffes for themfelves, and as many
" Horfe as defired to go with them." Withal, they faid, "they hoped, that his Majefty would not look
" upon this Action of theirs as a Mutiny." To the laft, the King faid, " he would not now Chriften
" it; but it looked very like one: As for the Court
" of War, he would not make that a judge of His
" Actions; but for the Paffes, they fhould be imme-
" diately prepared for as many as defired to have
" them." The next Morning the Paffes were fent to them; and in the Afternoon they left the Town; being in all about two hundred Horfe; and went to *Wyverton*, a fmall Garrifon depending upon *Newark*; where they ftayed fome days; and from thence went to *Belvoir*-Caftle; from whence they fent one of their Number to the Parliament, "to defire leave, and
" Paffes, to go beyond the Seas."

Befides the exceeding trouble and vexation that this Action of his Nephews, towards whom he had always expreffed fuch tendernefs and indulgence, gave the King, it had well nigh broke the design he had for his present escape; which was not possible to be executed in that time; and *Pointz* and *Rossiter* drew every day nearer, believing they had so encompassed him round, that it was not possible for him to get out of their hands. They had now Besieged *Shetford*-House, a Garrison belonging to *Newark*, and kept strong Guards between them and *Belvoir*, and stronger towards *Lichfield*; which was the way they most suspected his Majesty would incline to take; so that the truth is, nothing but Providence could conduct him out of that Labyrinth; but the King gave not himself over. He had fixed now his Resolution for *Oxford*, and sent a trusty Messenger thither with directions, that the Horse of that Garrison should be ready, upon a day he appointed, between *Banbury* and *Daventry*. Then, upon *Monday*, the third of *November*, early in the Morning, he sent a Gentleman to *Belvoir*-Castle, to be informed of the true State of the Rebels-Quarters, and to advertise Sir *Gervas Lucas*, the Governor of that Garrison, of his Majesty's design to march thither that Night, with order that his Troops and Guides should be ready at such an hour; but with an express charge, "that he should not acquaint the Princes, or any of "their Company, with it." That Gentleman being returned with very particular information, the resolution was taken "to march that very night," but not published till an hour after the shutting the Ports. Then order was given, "that all should be ready in "the Market-place, at ten of the Clock;" and by that time the Horse were all there, and were in number between four and five hundred, of the Guards and of other loose Regiments; they were all there put in order; and every Man was placed in some Troop; which done, about eleven of the Clock, they began to march; the King himself in the head of his own Troop, marched in the middle of the whole Body. By three of the Clock in the Morning, they were at *Belvoir*; without the least interruption or alarm given. There Sir *Gervas Lucas*, and his Troops with good Guides were ready; and attended his Majesty till the break of day; by which time he was past those Quarters he most apprehended; but he was still to march between their Garrisons; and therefore made no delay, but marched all that day; passing near *Burleigh* upon the Hill, a Garrison of the Enemy, from whence some Horse waited upon the Rear, and took and killed some Men, who either negligently staid behind, or whose Horses were tired. Towards the Evening the King was so very weary, that he was even compelled to rest and sleep for the space of four hours, in a Village within eight miles of *Northampton*. At ten of the Clock that Night, they begun to march again; and were, before Day, the next Morning, past *Daventry*; and before Noon, came to *Banbury*, where the *Oxford*-Horse were ready, and waited upon his Majesty, and conducted him safe to *Oxford* that Day; so he finished the most tedious and grievous march that ever King was exercised in, having been almost in perpetual motion from the loss of the Battle of *Naseby* to this hour, with such a variety of dismal accidents as must have broken the Spirits of any Man who had not been truly magnanimous. At

BOOK IX.

The King retreats towards Oxford:

And arrives there.

BOOK IX.

Oxford, the King found himself at rest, and ease to revolve, and reflect upon what was past, and to advise and consult of what was to be done, with Persons of entire devotion to him, and of steady Judgments; and presently after his coming thither, he writ that Letter of the seventh of *November*; and, shortly after, the other of the seventh of *December*; both which are mentioned before, and set down at large.

The King's Affairs in the West about this time.

The Prince of *Wales* did not enjoy so much rest and ease in His Quarters; for, upon the hurry of the Retreat of the Horse, which is mentioned before, and which indeed was full of confusion, very many of the Trained-bands of *Cornwal* broke loose, and run to their Houses, pretending " they feared that " the Horse would go into that County, and plunder " them;" for which fear they had the greater pretence, because, upon the Retreat, many Regiments had Orders from the Lord *Wentworth* to Quarter in *Cornwal*; of which his Highness was no sooner advertised, than he sent his Orders positive, " that no one " Regiment of Horse should be there, but that they " should be all Quartered on the *Devon*-side." Upon that, they were dispersed about the County, for the space of thirty miles breadth, as if no Enemy had been within two days march of them. There were now drawn together, and to be engaged together in one Action against the Enemy, all the Horse and Foot of the Lord *Goring*; the Command whereof, the Lord *Wentworth* challenged to himself by deputation; the Horse and Foot of Sir *Richard Greenvil*; and the Horse and Foot of General *Digby*, neither of which acknowledged a superiority in the other, besides the Guards; which no body pretended to Command but the Lord *Capel*. When the Prince removed from *Tavistock*, the raising the Blockade from *Plymouth* was absolutely necessary, and it was concluded, as hath been said, at a Council of War, "that it "would be fit for his Highness to remove to *Launceston*; whither the Trained-bands, and the rest "of the Foot should likewise come, and the Horse "march on the *Devonshire*-side, and Quarter most "conveniently in that County." The care of the Retreat, and bringing the Provisions from *Tavistock*, was committed to Sir *Richard Greenvil*; which was performed by him so negligently, that besides the disorders he suffered in *Tavistock*, by the Soldiers, a great part of the Magazine of Victuals, and three or four hundred pair of Shoes, were left there; and so lost. The day after the Prince came to *Launceston*, Sir *Richard Greenvil* writ a Letter to him, wherein he represented "the impossibility of keeping that Army "together, or fighting with it in the condition it "was then in:" told him, "that he had, the night "before, sent directions to Major-General *Harris*" (who Commanded the Foot that came from about *Plymouth*) "to guard such a Bridge; but that he "returned him word, that he would receive Orders "from none but General *Digby*; that General *Digby* "said, that he would receive Orders from none but "his Highness; that a Party of the Lord *Wentworth's* "Horse had the same Night come into his Quarters, "where his Troop of Guards, and his Firelocks "were; that neither submitting to the Command of "the other, they had fallen foul, and two or three Men had been killed; that they continued still in the same place, drawn up one against another; that it was absolutely necessary, his Highness should constitute one Superior Officer, from whom all those independent Officers might receive Orders; without which, it would not be possible for that Army to be kept together, or do Service; that for His own part, he knew his Severity and Discipline had rendered him so odious to the Lord *Goring*'s Horse, that they would sooner chuse to serve the Enemy, than receive Orders from Him; therefore he desired his Highness to constitute the Earl of *Brentford*, or the Lord *Hopton*, to Command in Chief, and then he hoped, some good might be done against the Enemy."

The mischief was more visible by much than a remedy; it was evident some Action must be with the Enemy within few days, and what inconvenience would flow from any alteration, at such a conjuncture of time, was not hard to guess, when both Officer and Soldier were desirous to take any occasion, and to find any excuse to lay down their Arms; and it was plain, though there were very few who could do good, there were enough that could do hurt; besides, whoever was fit to undertake so great a trust and charge, would be very hardly entreated to take upon him the Command of a dissolute, undisciplined, wicked, beaten Army, upon which he must engage his Honor, and the hope of what was left, without having time to reform, or instruct them. That which made the resolution necessary, was, that though there was little hope of doing good by any alteration in Command, there was evident and demonstrable ruin attended No-alteration; and they who were trusted might be accountable to the World, for not advising the Prince to do that, which, how hopeless soever, only remained to be done.

Thereupon, on the fifteenth of *January*, his Highness made an Order, "that the Lord *Hopton* should take the Charge of the whole Army upon him; and that the Lord *Wentworth* should Command all the Horse, and Sir *Richard Greenvil* the Foot." It was a heavy imposition, I confess, upon the Lord *Hopton* (to the which nothing but the most abstracted Duty and Obedience could have Submitted) to take charge of those Horse whom only their Friends feared, and their Enemies laughed at; being only terrible in Plunder, and resolute in Running away. Of all the Trained-bands of *Cornwal*, there were not three hundred left; and those, by some infusions from *Greenvil* and others, not so devoted to him as might have been expected. The rest of the Foot (besides those who belonged to the Lord *Goring*, which were two Regiments of about four hundred) were the three Regiments of about six hundred, which belonged to Sir *Richard Greenvil*, and the Officers of them entirely His Creatures; and those belonging to General *Digby*, which were not above five hundred;. To these were added (and were indeed the only Men, but a small Troop of his own of Horse and some Foot, upon whose affection, courage, and duty he could Rely; except some particular Gentlemen,

The Lord Hopton made General of the remains of the western Army. Lord Wentworth to Command the Horse, Greenvil the Foot.

who could only undertake for themselves) about two hundred and fifty Foot, and eight hundred Horse of the Guards; who were Commanded by the Lord *Capel*, and entirely to receive Orders from his Lordship.

The Lord *Hopton* very generously told the Prince, "that it was a custom now, when Men were not "willing to submit to what they were enjoined, to "say, that it was against their Honor; that their "Honor would not suffer them to do this or that; "for His part, he could not obey his Highness at this "time, without resolving to lose his Honor, which "he knew he must, but since his Highness thought "it necessary to Command him, he was ready to "obey him with the loss of his Honor." Since the making of this Order was concluded an Act of absolute necessity, and the Lord *Hopton* had so worthily Submitted to it, it was positively resolved by his Highness, "that it should be dutifully Submitted "to by all other Men; or that the Refusers should "be exemplarily punished." There was not the least suspicion that Sir *Richard Greenvil* would not willingly have Submitted to it, but it was believed that the Lord *Wentworth*, who had carried himself so high, and more insolently since his disorderly retreat than before, would have refused; which if he had done, it was resolved by the Prince presently to have committed him, and to have desired the Lord *Capel* to have taken the charge of the Horse.

His Highness sent Sir *Richard Greenvil* a Letter of thanks, "for the advice which he had given; and "which, he said, he had followed, as by the inclosed

" Order he might perceive ; by which his Highnefs
" had committed the care and charge of the whole
" Army to the Lord *Hopton*, appointing that the
" Lord *Wentworth* fhould Command all the Horfe,
" and Sir *Richard Greenvil* all the Foot, and both to
" receive Orders from the Lord *Hopton :*" no Man
imagining it poffible that, befides that he had given
the advice, he could have refufed that Charge, by
which he was to have a greater Command than
ever he had before, and was to be commanded by
none but by whom he had often been formerly commanded. But the next day after he received that
Letter and Order, contrary to all expectation, he
writ to his Highnefs "to defire to be excufed, in
" refpect of his indifpofition of health ; expreffing,
" that he could do him better fervice in getting up
" the Soldiers who ftraggled in the Country, and in
" fuppreffing Malignants ;" and at the fame time,
writ to the Lord *Colepepper,* " that he could not con-
" fent to be commanded by the Lord *Hopton*." It
plainly appeared now, that his drift was to ftay
behind, and Command *Cornwal*; with which, confidering the premifes, the Prince thought he had no
reafon to truft him. He fent for him therefore, and
told him " the extreme ill confequence that would
" attend the public Service, if he fhould Then, and
" in fuch a manner, quit the Charge his Highnefs
" had committed to him; that more fhould not be
" expected from him than was agreeable to his
" health ; and that if he took the Command upon
" him, he fhould take what Adjudants he pleafed
" to affift him." But notwithftanding all that the

Prince could say to him, or such of his Friends who thought they had Interest in him, he continued obstinate; and positively refused to take the Charge, or to receive Orders from the Lord *Hopton*.

What should the Prince have done? for besides the ill consequence of suffering himself to be in that manner contemned, at a time when that Army was so indisposed, it was very evident, if *Greenvil* were at liberty, and the Army once marched out of *Cornwal*, he would have put himself in the head of all the discontented Party, and at least endeavoured to have hindered their retreat back into *Cornwal*, upon what occasion soever; and for the present that he would under-hand have kept many from marching with the Army, upon the senseless pretence of defending their own Country. So that, upon full consideration, his Highness thought fit to commit him to Prison to the Governor of *Launceston*; and within two or three days after, sent him to the Mount; where he remained till the Enemy was possessed of the County; when his Highness, that he might by no means fall into their hands, gave him leave to Transport himself beyond the Sea.

Sir R. Greenvil refusing the Command, the Prince commits him to Prison.

The Lord *Wentworth*, though he seemed much surprised with the Order when he heard it read at the Board, and desired "time to consider of it till the
" next day, that he might confer with his Officers;
" yet, when the Prince told him, that he would not
" refer his Acts to be scanned by the Officers; but
" that he should give his positive Answer, whether
" he would submit to it, or no; and then his High-
" ness knew what he had to do;" he only desired
" to

"to consider till the Afternoon; when he submitted;" and went that Night out of Town to his Quarters; of which most Men were not glad, but rather wished (since they knew he would never obey cheerfully) that he would have put the Prince to have made further alterations; which yet would have been accompanied with hazard enough. By this time the Intelligence was certain of the loss of *Dartmouth*, which added neither Courage, nor Numbers to our Men; and the importunity was such from *Exeter* for present relief, that there seemed even a necessity of attempting somewhat towards it, upon how great disadvantage soever; and therefore the Lord *Hopton* resolved to march by the way of *Chimley*; that so, being between the Enemy and *Barnstable*, he might borrow as many Men out of the Garrison, as could be spared; and by strong Parties at least to attempt upon their Quarters. But it was likewise resolved, "that in respect of the smallness of the numbers, and "the general indisposition, to say no worse, both "in Officer and Soldier, it would not be fit for his "Highness to venture his own Person with the "Army; but that he should retire to *Truro*, and "reside there;" against which there were objections enough in view, which were however weighed down by greater.

Whoever had observed the temper of the Gentry of that County towards Sir *Richard Greenvil*, or the Clamor of the Common-People against his Oppression, and Tyranny, would not have believed, that such a necessary proceeding against him, at that time, could have been any Unpopular Act; there being scarce a day, in which some Petition was not presented against him. As the Prince passed through *Bodmin*, he received Petitions from the Wives of many substantial, and honest Men; amongst the rest, of the Mayor of *Liflithiel*; who was very eminently well affected and useful to the King's Service; all whom *Greenvil* had committed to the Common-Goal, for presuming to Fish in that River; the Royalty of which he pretended belonged to him, by Virtue of the Sequestration, granted him by the King, of the Lord *Roberts*' Estate at *Lamhetherick*; whereas they who were committed, pretended a Title, and had always used the liberty of Fishing in those Waters, as Tenants to the Prince of his Highness' Manor of *Liflithiel*; there having been long Suits between the Lord *Roberts* and the Tenants of that Manor, for that Royalty. And when his Highness came to *Tavistock*, he was again Petitioned by many Women for the liberty of their Husbands, whom Sir *Richard* had committed to Prison, for refusing to grind at his Mill, " which, he said, they were bound by the Custom to " do." So by his Martial Power he had Asserted whatever Civil-Interest he thought fit to lay claim to; and never discharged any Man out of Prison, till he absolutely submitted to his Pleasure.

There were in the Goal at *Launceston*, at this time when himself was committed, at least thirty Persons, Constables and other Men, whom he had committed, and imposed Fines upon, some of three, four, and five hundred pounds, upon pretence of Delinquency (of which he was in no case a proper Judge) for the payment whereof they were detained in Prison.

Amongst the rest, was the Mayor of St. *Ives*, one *Hammond*, who had then the reputation of an honest Man; and was certified to be such by Colonel *Robinson* the Governor, and by all the Neighbouring-Gentlemen. After the late Insurrection there, which is spoken of before, he had given his Bond to Sir *Richard Greenvil*, of five hundred pound, to produce a young Man, who was then absent, and accused to be a favorer of that Mutiny, within so many days. The time expired before the Man could be found; but within three days after the expiration of the term, the Mayor sent the Fellow to Sir *Richard Greenvil*; That would not satisfy; but he sent his Marshal for the Mayor himself, and required fifty pound of him for having forfeited his Bond, and upon his refusal forthwith to pay it, committed him to the Goal at *Launceston*. The Son of the Mayor presented a Petition to the Prince, at *Truro*, for his Father's liberty, setting forth the matter of fact as it was, and annexing a very ample testimony of the good Affection of the Man. The Petition was referred to Sir *Richard Greenvil*, with direction, " that " if the case were in truth such, he should discharge " him." As soon as the Son brought this Petition to him, he put it in his Pocket; told him, " the Prince " understood not the business;" and committed the Son to Goal, and caused Irons to be put upon him for his presumption. Upon a second Petition to the Prince, at *Launceston*, after the time that Sir *Richard* himself was committed, he directed the Lord *Hopton*, " upon examination of the truth of it, to discharge " the Man;" of which, when Sir *Richard* heard, he sent to the Goaler "to forbid him, at his peril, to "discharge *Hammond*; threatening him "to make "him pay the Money;" and, after that, caused an Action to be entered in the Town-Court at *Launceston* upon the forfeiture of the Bond. Yet, notwithstanding all this, he was no sooner committed by the Prince, than even those who had complained of him as much as any, expressed great trouble; and many Officers of those Forces which he had Commanded, in a Tumultuous manner, Petitioned for his release; and others took great pains to have the indisposition of the People, and the ill accidents that followed, imputed to that proceeding against Sir *Richard Greenvil*; in which none were more forward, than some of the Prince's own Household-Servants; who were so tender of Him, that they forgot their duty to their Master.

It was *Friday* the sixth of *February*, before the Lord *Hopton* could move from *Launceston*, for want of Carriages for their Ammunition, and Provision of Victual. Neither had he then Carriages for above half their little Store, but relied upon the Commissioners to send the remainder after; and so went to *Torrington*; where he resolved to fasten, till his Provisions could be brought up; and he might receive certain Intelligence of the Motion, and Condition of the Enemy. He had not continued there above four days, in which he had Barricadoed, and made some little Fastnesses about the Town, when Sir *Thomas Fairfax* advanced to *Chimley*, within eight Miles of *Torrington*, with six thousand Foot, three thousand five hundred Horse, and five hundred Dragoons; of which so near advance of the Enemy (notwithstanding all the strict Orders for keeping of Guards; whereof one Guard was, or was appointed to be, within two Miles of *Chimley*) he had not known but by a Lieutenant, who was accidentally plundering in those parts, and fell amongst them. So negligent, and unfaithful, were both Officers and Soldiers in their duty.

The Lord *Hopton* having this Intelligence of the Strength, and Neighbourhood of the Enemy, had his Election of two things, either to retire into *Cornwal*, or to abide them where he was; the first, besides the disheartening of his Men, seemed rather a deferring, than a preventing of any mischief that could befal him; for he foresaw, if he brought that great Body of Horse into *Cornwal*, the few that remained of the Traind-bands, would immediately dissolve, and run to their Houses; and the remainder of Horse and Foot, in a short time, be destroyed without an Enemy. Therefore he rather chose, notwithstanding the great disadvantage of Number in Foot, to abide them in that place; where, if the Enemy should attempt him in so fast a Quarter, he might defend himself with more advantage, than he could in any other place. So he placed his Guards, and appointed all Men to their Posts, having drawn as many Horse (such as on the sudden he could get) into the Town, as he thought necessary; the rest being ordered to stand on a Common, at the East-end of the Town. But the Enemy forced the Barricadoe in one place by the baseness of the Foot; with which the Horse in the Town more basely received

The Lord Hopton's Forces routed at Torrington by Sir Thomas Fairfax.

such a Fright, that they could neither be made to Charge, nor Stand; but, in perfect confusion, run away; whose example all the Foot upon the Line, and at their other Posts, followed; leaving their General (who was hurt in the Face with a Pike, and his Horse killed under him) with two or three Gentlemen, to shift for themselves; one of the Officers publicly reporting, lest the Soldiers should not make haste enough in running away, "that he "saw their General run through the Body with a "Pike." The Lord *Hopton* recovering a fresh Horse, was compelled (being thus deserted by his Men) to retire; which he did, to the Borders of *Cornwal*; and stayed at *Stratton* two or three days, till about a thousand or twelve hundred of his Foot came up to him. It was then in consultation, since there was no likelihood of making any stand against the Enemy with such Foot, and that it was visible that Body of Horse could not long subsist in *Cornwal*, whether the Horse might not break through to *Oxford*; which, in respect of their great weariness, having stood two or three Days and Nights in the Field, and the Enemies strength being drawn up within two Miles of them, was concluded to be impossible. Besides (that there was at that time a confident assurance, by an Express (Sir *D. Wyat*) out of *France*, "of four or "five thousand Foot to come from thence within "three Weeks, or a Month at farthest;" those Letters, and the Messenger, averring, "that most of "the Men were ready, when He came away."

The Enemy advanced to *Stratton*, and so to *Launceston*; where Mr. *Edgecomb*, who had always pretended to be of the King's Party, with his Regiment of Trained-bands, joined with them; and the Lord *Hopton* retired to *Bodmin*; the Horse, Officers and Soldiers, notwithstanding all the strict Orders, very negligently performing their duty; insomuch as the Lord *Hopton* protested, " that, from the time " he undertook the Charge, to the hour of their " dissolving, scarce a Party or Guard appeared with " half the Number appointed, or within two hours " of the time;" and *Goring*'s Brigade, having the Guard upon a Down near *Bodmin*, drew off without Orders, and without sending out a Scout; insomuch as the whole gross of the Rebels, were at day-time marched within three Miles, before the Foot in *Bodmin* had any notice. So that the Lord *Hopton* was instantly forced to draw off his Foot and Carriages Westward; and kept the Field that cold Night, being the first of *March*; but could not, by all his Orders diligently sent out, draw any considerable Body of Horse to him by the end of the next day; they having Quartered themselves at pleasure over the Country, many above twenty Miles from *Bodmin*, and many running to the Enemy; and others purposely staying in their Quarters, till the Enemy came to dispossess them.

When by the disorders and distractions of the Army, which are before set down, his Highness was persuaded to make his own Residence in *Cornwal*, he came to *Truro* on the 12th day of *February*; where he received a Letter from the King, directed to those four of the Council who had Signed that to his

Majesty at *Tavistock*. This Letter was dated at *Oxford* the fifth of *February*, and contained these words;

"Yours from *Tavistock* hath fully satisfied me, why my Commands concerning Prince *Charles* his going beyond Sea were not obeyed. And I likewise agree with you in opinion, that he is not to go until there be an evident necessity; also approving very much of the Steps whereby you mean to do it. But withal, I re-iterate my Commands to you for the Prince's going over, whensoever there shall be a visible hazard of his falling into the Rebels hands. In the mean time, I like very well that he should be at the head of the Army; and so much the rather, for what I shall now impart to you of my resolution, &c." And so proceeded in the Communication of his own design of taking the Field; which was afterwards frustrated by the defeat of my Lord *Astley*, and the ill success in the West.

The Prince goes to Pendennis.

The Prince having staid some days at *Truro*, went to *Pendennis*; intending only to recreate himself for two or three days; and to quicken the Works, which were well advanced; his Highness having issued all the Money he could procure, towards the finishing of them. But, in the very Morning that he meant to return to *Truro*, his Army being then retired, and *Fairfax* at the edge of *Cornwal*, the Lord *Hopton* and the Lord *Capel* sent Advertisements, "that they had severally received Intelligence of a design to seize the Person of the Prince; and that many Persons of Quality of the Country were privy to it." Hereupon the Prince thought it most convenient to stay where he was, and so returned no more to *Truro*. The time of apparent danger was now in view, and if there were in truth any design of seizing the Prince's Person, they had reason to believe that some of his own Servants were not strangers to it. The Lords *Capel* and *Hopton* being at the Army; only the Prince, the Lord *Colepepper*, and the Chancellor of the Exchequer, knew the King's Pleasure, and what was to be done. And they two had no confidence, that they should have Reputation enough to go through with it; the Earl of *Berkshire* continuing very jealous of the design of going into *France*, whatever they said to the contrary: The Governor of the Castle was Old and Fearful, and not resolute enough to be trusted; and his Son, though a gallant Gentleman, and worthy of any Trust, had little Credit with his Father.

There was no Letter from the King (though they had long before desired such a one, and proposed the Form) fit to be publicly showed, in which there were not some Clauses which would have been applied to his Majesty's disservice; especially if he should have been at *London*, which was then confidently averred by some, who swore "they met " him at *Uxbridge*. Therefore these two Counsellors concluded, " that the Prince's going away must seem " to be the effect of Counsel upon necessity, and " the appearance of danger to his Person, without " any mention of the King's Command." But how to procure this Resolution from the Council was the difficulty. They very well knew the Lords

minds who were absent, but durst not own that knowledge, lest the design might be more suspected: In the end, having advised *Baldwin Wake*, to cause the Frigate belonging to *Hasdunck*, and the other Ships, to be ready upon an hour's warning; they proposed in Council, when the Lords *Berkshire*, and *Brentford* were present, "to send Mr. *Fanshaw*
" to the Army, to receive the opinion and advice
" of the Lords that were there, what was best to
" be done with reference to the Person of the Prince,
" and whether it were fit to hazard him in *Penden-*
" *nis*;" which was accordingly done. Their Lordships, according to the former agreement between them, returned their advice, " that it was not fit to
" adventure his Highness in that Castle (which
" would not only not preserve his Person, but pro-
" bably, by his stay there, might be lost; but by
" his absence might defend itself) and that he should
" remove to *Jersey* or *Scilly*." This, upon Mr. *Fanshaw*'s report, was unanimously consented to by the whole Council.

But because *Jersey* was so near to *France*, and so might give the greater umbrage, and that *Scilly* was a part of *Cornwal*, and was by them all conceived a place of unquestionable strength, the public Resolution was for *Scilly*, it being in their power, when they were at Sea, to go for *Jersey*, if the Wind was fair for one, and cross to the other. So the Resolution being imparted to no more that Night, than was of absolute necessity (for we apprehended clamor from the Army, from the Country, and from that Garrison in whose Power the Prince was) the next Morning, being *Monday*, the second of *March*, after the News was come that the Army was retiring from *Bodmin*, and the Enemy marching furiously after, and thereby Men were sufficiently awakened with the apprehension of the Prince's Safety; the Governor and his Son were called into the Council, and made acquainted with the Prince's Resolution, " that Night to " Embark himself for *Scilly*, being a part of *Cornwal*; " from whence, by such aids and relief, as he hoped " he should procure from *France* and Foreign parts, " he should be best able to relieve them." And accordingly, that Night, about ten of the Clock, he put himself on Board; and on *Wednesday* in the Afternoon, arrived safe in *Scilly*; from whence, within two days, the Lord *Colepepper* was sent into *France*, to acquaint the Queen " with his Highness' being at " *Scilly*; with the Wants and Incommodities of that " place; and to defire supply of Men and Monies " for the Defence thereof, and the Support of his " own Person;" it being agreed in Council, before the Lord *Colepepper*'s going from *Scilly*, " that if, " upon advancement of the Parliament-Fleet, or " any other apparent danger, his Highness should " have cause to suspect the security of his Person " there" (the strength of the place in no degree answering expectation, or the same of it) " he would " immediately Embark himself in the same Frigate (which attended there) " and go to *Jersey*."

When the Lord *Hopton* found that he could put no restraint to the Licence of the Soldiers, he called a Council of War to consider what was to be done. The principal Officers of Horse were so far from con-

Thence by Sea to Scilly.

BOOK IX.

sidering any Means to put their Men in order, and heart to face the Enemy, that they declared in plain *English*, " that their Men would never be brought " to Fight; and therefore proposed positively, to " send for a Treaty:" From which not one Officer dissented, except only Major-General *Web*, who always professed against it. The Lord *Hopton* told them, " it was a thing he could not consent to with- " out express leave from the Prince (who was then " at *Pendennis*-Castle) to whom he would immedi- " ately despatch away an Express;" hoping, that, by that delay, he should be able to recover the Officers to a better Resolution; or that, by the advance of the Enemy, they would be compelled to Fight. But they continued their importunity, and at last (no doubt by the advice of our own Men; for many, both Officers and Soldiers, went every day in to them) a Trumpet arrived from Sir *Thomas Fairfax* with a Letter to the Lord *Hopton*, offering a Treaty, and making some Propositions to the Officers and Soldiers. His Lordship Communicated not this Letter to above one or two, of principal Trust; conceiving it not fit, in that disorder and dejectedness, to make it public. Hereupon, all the principal Officers assemble together (except the Major-General, *Web*) and expressing much discontent that they might not see the Letter, declare peremptorily to the Lord *Hopton*, " that if he would not consent to it, they " were resolved to Treat themselves." And from this time they neither kept Guards, nor performed any Duty; Their Horse every day mingling with those of the Enemy, without any Act of Hostility. In this ſtrait, the Lord *Hopton* having ſent his Ammunition and Foot into *Pendennis*, and the Mount, and declared, "that he would neither Treat for himſelf nor the Garriſons," he gave the Horſe leave to Treat; and thereupon thoſe Articles were concluded, by which that Body of Horſe was diſſolved; and Himſelf and the Lord *Capel*, with the firſt Wind, went from the Mount to *Scilly*, to attend his Highneſs; who, as is ſaid, was gone thither from *Pendennis*-Caſtle, after the Enemies whole Army was entered *Cornwal*.

The Lord Hopton's Army diſſolved.

Having left the Prince in *Scilly*, ſo near the end of that unproſperous year 1645 (for it was upon the three-and-twentieth of *March*) that there will be no more occaſion of mentioning him till the next year, and being now to leave *Cornwal*, it will be neceſſary to inform the Reader of one particular. It is at large ſet down, in a former Book, what proceedings had been at *Oxford* againſt Duke *Hamilton*; and how he had been firſt ſent Priſoner to *Briſtol*, and from thence to *Pendennis*-Caſtle in *Cornwal*. And ſince we ſhall hereafter find him acting a great part for the King, and General in the Head of a great Army, it would be very incongruous, after having ſpent ſo much time in *Cornwal* without ſo much as naming him, to leave Men ignorant what became of him, and how he obtained his Liberty; which he employed afterwards with ſo much Zeal for the King's Service to the loſs of his Life; by which he was not only vindicated, in the opinion of many Honeſt Men, from all thoſe Jealouſies and Aſperſions, he had long ſuffered under; but the proceeding that had been againſt

Touching Duke Hamilton Priſoner at Pendennis.

BOOK IX.

him at *Oxford*, was looked upon by many as void of that Justice and Policy, which had been requisite; and they concluded by what he did after a long Imprisonment, how much he might have done more Succesfully, if he had never been restrained. Without doubt, what he did afterwards, and what he Suffered, ought, in great measure, to free his Memory from any Reproaches for the Errors, or Weakness, of which he had before been guilty. What were the Motives, and Inducements of his Commitment, have been at large set down before in the proper place. It remains now, only to set down how he came at last to be possessed of his Liberty, and why he obtained it no sooner, by other more gracious ways from the King; which might have been an obligation upon him;' when it might easily have been foreseen, that he must be, in a short time, at Liberty, notwithstanding any opposition.

When the Prince first visited *Cornwal*, to settle his own Revenue of that Dutchy; which was the only support he had, and out of which he provided for the carrying on the King's Service, upon many emergent occasions; he spent some days at *Truro*, to settle his duty upon the Tin, by Virtue of his ancient Privilege of Pre-emption. And in that time, which was about the end of *July*, the Governor of *Pendennis* Castle invited him to dine there; which his Highness willingly accepted, that he might take a full View of the Situation and Strength thereof; having it then in his view, that he might probably be compelled to resort thither. Every Man knew well that Duke *Hamilton* was then a Prisoner there, and therefore it was to be confidered, what the Prince was to do, if the Duke fhould defire, as without doubt he would, to kifs his hand. And it was refolved without difpute, " that the Prince was not to admit fuch a Perfon into " his Prefence, who ftood fo much in his Father's " difpleafure, and was committed to Prifon by him; " and that none of the Council, or of his Highnefs' " Servants, fhould vifit, or enter into any kind of " correfpondence with him." Thereupon the Governor was advifed, in regard the Accommodations in the Caftle were narrow, " that during the time the " Prince was in the Caftle, the Duke fhould be re- " moved out of his Chamber into one of the Soldier's " Houfes;" which was done accordinly. This the Duke took very heavily, lamenting " that he might " not be admitted to fee the Prince;" and had a defire to have conferred with the Lord *Colepepper*, or the Chancellor, which they were not then at liberty to have fatisfied him in. He afterwards renewed the fame defire to them both by his Servant Mr. *Hamilton*. Hereupon, when the Chancellor was fhortly after fent to vifit the Ports of *Padftow*, the Mount, and *Pendennis*, which was about the middle of *Auguft* (the bufinefs being, under that difguife, to provide for the Prince's Tranfportation, when it fhould be neceffary) the Prince referred it to him " to fee the Duke, if he found it convenient." When he came to *Pendennis*, and was to ftay there neceffarily fome days, he was informed, " that the Duke " came always abroad to Meals, and that at that time " all Men fpoke freely with him:" So that, either he was to be made a clofe Prifoner by his being there, or they were to meet at Supper and Dinner. The Governor then asked him, "whether the Duke "should come abroad. The Chancellor had neither Authority nor Reason to make any alteration; therefore he told him, "he knew his own "course, which he presumed he would observe "whoever came; and that if the Duke pleased, he "would wait upon him in his Chamber, to kiss his "hands before Supper;" the which he did.

When the Duke, after some Civilities to him whom he had long known, and some Reproaches to the Governor, who was present, "of his very strict "usage and carriage towards him;" which, he said he believed he could not justify (whereas the Chancellor well knew, that the Governor was absolutely governed by him) spoke to him of his own condition, and of "his Misfortune to fall into his Majesty's dis- "pleasure, having giving him any Offence." He told him, "that he had very much desired to speak "with him, that he might make a Proposition to "him, which he thought for the King's Service; "and he desired, if it seemed so to Him, that he "would find means to recommend it to his Majesty, "and to procure his acceptance of it." Then he told him, "that he was an absolute Stranger to the Affairs "of both Kingdoms, having no other Intelligence, "than what he received from Gentlemen whom he "met in the next Room at Dinner; but he believed, "by his Majesty's late loss at *Naseby*, that his con- "dition in *England* was very much worse than his "Servants hoped it would have been; and therefore, "that it might concern him to transact his business in
Scotland

" *Scotland* as foon as might be: that he knew not in
" what ſtate the Lord *Mountroſe* was in that King-
" dom, but he was perſuaded that he was not with-
" out oppoſition." He ſaid, " he was confident that
" if he himſelf had his liberty, he could do the King
" conſiderable Service, and either incline that Nation
" powerfully to mediate a Peace in *England*, or po-
" ſitively to declare for the King, and join with
" *Mountroſe*." He ſaid, " he knew, it was believed
" by many, that the Animoſity was ſo great from
" him to *Mountroſe*, who indeed had done him very
" cauſeleſs injuries, that he would rather meditate
" Revenge than concur with him in any Action;
" but, he ſaid, he too well underſtood his own
" danger, if the King and Monarchy were deſtroyed
" in this Kingdom, to think of Private Contention
" and matters of Revenge, when the Public was ſo
" much at Stake. And he muſt acknowledge, how
" unjuſt ſoever the Lord *Mountroſe* had been to him,
" he had done the King great Service;" and therefore
proteſted with many Aſſeverations, " he ſhould join
" with him in the King's behalf, as with a Brother;
" and if he could not win his own Brother from the
" other Party, he would be as much againſt Him.
" He ſaid, he could not apprehend that his Liberty
" could be any way prejudicial to the King; for he
" would be a Priſoner ſtill upon his Parole; and
" would engage his Honor, that if he found he could
" not be able to do his Majeſty that acceptable Ser-
" vice, which he deſired (of which he had not the
" leaſt doubt) he would ſpeedily return, and render
" himſelf a Priſoner again in the place where he then

VOL. VIII. O

"was." In this discourse he made very great professions, and expressions of his Devotion to the King's Service, of his Obligations to him, and of the great confidence he had, in this particular, of being useful to his Majesty.

After he made some pause, in expectation of what the Chancellor would say, the Chancellor told him, " he doubted not but he was very able to serve the " King both in that and in this Kingdom; there being " very many in both who had a principal depend- " ance upon him: that he heard the King was making " some Propositions to the *Scottish* Army in *England*, " and that it would be a great instance of his Affec- " tion and Fidelity to the King, if by any Message " from him to his Friends, and Dependents in the " *Scottish* Army then before *Hereford*, or to his " Friends in *Scotland*, his Brother being the head or " prime Person of Power there that opposed *Moun-* " *trose*, they should declare for the King, or appear " willing to do him Service; and that he having free " liberty to send, through the Parliament's Army, " to *London*, or into *Scotland*, he might as soon do " the King this Service, as receive a Warrant for his " enlargement; which, he presumed, he knew could " not be granted but by the King himself."

The Duke replied, " that he expected that Answer, " but that it was not possible for him to do any thing " by Message or Letter, or any way but by his Pre- " sence: First, that they, in whom he had interest, " would look upon any thing he should write, or " any Message he should send, as the result of distress " and compulsion, not of his affection or judgment.

" Besides, he said, he looked upon himself as very
" odious to that Nation, which was irreconciled to
" him for his zeal to the King, and thought this a
" just judgment of God upon him for not adhering
" to them. And, he said, for his own Brother, who
" he heard indeed had the greatest influence upon
" their Counfels, he had no reason to be confident
" in him, at that diftance; for, besides the extreme
" injury he had done him, in making an escape from
" *Oxford*, by which both their innocencies were
" made to be fufpected, and for which he should
" never forgive him, he was the Heir of the House
" and Family; and he believed, would be content
" that himself should grow old and die in Prison:
" whereas, if he were at liberty, and amongst them,
" he was confident some for love, and others for fear,
" would stick to him; and he should easily make it
" appear to those who were fiercest against the King,
" that it concerned their own interest to support the
" King in his just power. However, he concluded,
" that the worst that could come was his returning to
" Prison, which he would not fail to do." So the
discourse ended for that Night.

The next day the Duke entered again into the same Argument, with much earneftness, that the Chancellor would interpose, upon that ground, for his liberty; who told him, " that he was so ill a
" Courtier, that he could not diffemble to him: that
" he was not satisfied with his Reasons, and could
" not but believe, he had interest enough, at that
" diftance, to make some real demonftration of his
" Affection to the King, by the impreffion he might

"make upon his Dependents and Allies: and there-
"fore that he could not offer any advice to the King,
"to the purpose he defired." He told him, "that
"he had been prefent at the Council-Table when
"the King Communicated that bufinefs, which con-
"cerned him, to the Board; and that he gave his
"opinion fully, and earneftly, for his Commitment;
"being fatisfied, upon the Information that was
"given concerning him, that his Affection to the
"King was very Queftionable; and that it appeared,
"that he had been earneftly preffed by thofe Perfons
"of Honor in that Kingdom, upon whom his Ma-
"jefty relied, to declare himfelf; and that if he could
"have been induced fo to do, having promifed the
"King he would, and having Authority to that pur-
"pofe from him, they might very eafily have fup-
"preffed that Rebellion in the bud: but that his
"Lordfhip and his Brother, were fo far from oppof-
"ing it, that the very Proclamation which had
"iffued out there for the general Infurrection (which
"Proclamation was perufed at Council-Table, when
"he was committed) was not only fet forth in his
"Majefty's own Name, but Sealed with his Signet;
"which was then in the Cuftody of the Earl of
"*Lanrick* his Brother, he being Secretary of State in
"that Kingdom. That thofe who were the principal
"Informers againft him, and who profeffed that they
"could do no Service, if he were at liberty, now
"fince his reftraint, being armed with no more Au-
"thority than he had, at his laft being there, when
"the Kingdom was in Peace, had, upon all difad-
"vantages imaginable, when that Kingdom was

"totally loſt to the King, reduced the greateſt part
"of it again to his obedience; and therefore, whe-
"ther it was his Lordſhip's Misfortune, or his Fault,
"ſince things proſpered ſo well in his abſence, he
"could not as a Counſellor, adviſe the King, without
"the privity and conſent of the Lord *Mountroſe*, or
"without ſome ſuch Teſtimony of his Service, as
"he had before propoſed, to give him his Liberty:
"and that any ill ſucceſs, which poſſibly might have
"no relation to that Act, would yet be imputed to
"that Counſel; and the Lord *Mountroſe* have at
"leaſt a juſt, or probable excuſe, for any thing that
"ſhould happen amiſs."

The Duke thanked him for the freedom he had
uſed towards him; and ſaid, "upon the Information
"which was given againſt him, he muſt acknowledge
"the proceedings to be very juſt; but he was con-
"fident, whenever he ſhould be admitted to a fair
"hearing, he ſhould appear very innocent from the
"Allegations which had been given. He ſaid, he
"had never made the leaſt promiſe to the King,
"which he had not exactly performed; that he had
"not Authority or Power to croſs any thing that
"was done to the prejudice of the King; and there-
"fore to have made any ſuch Attempt, or Declara-
"tion, as ſome Lords had deſired, in that conjunc-
"ture of time, had been to have deſtroyed themſel-
"ves to no purpoſe: and therefore, he made haſte to
"the King with ſuch Propoſitions, and Overtures,
"that he was confident, if he had been admitted to
"have ſpoken with his Majeſty, at his coming to
"*Oxford*, he ſhould have given good ſatisfaction in

"them; and then intended immediately to have re-
"turned into *Scotland*, with such Authority and
"Countenance, as the King could well have given
"him; and doubted not but to have prevented any
"inconveniences from that Kingdom: but that by
"his Imprisonment (which he could have prevented,
"for he had notice upon his Journey, what was in-
"tended, and trusted so much in his innocence, that
"he would not avoid it) all those designs failed.
"For his Brother he could say nothing; but he be-
"lieved him an honest Man; and for the proceed-
"ings of the Lord *Montrose*, though he had received
"good assistance from *Ireland*, which was a good
"Foundation, he could not but say, it had been little
"less than miraculous: However, he presumed the
"work was not so near done there, but that His
"Assistance might be very seasonable." After this
they spoke often together; but this was the substance
and result of all; he insisting upon his present Liberty,
and the other as pressing, that he would write to his
Friends. Yet the Chancellor promised him "to pre-
"sent, by the first convenience, his Suit and Pro-
"position to the King;" which he shortly after did
in a Letter to the Lord *Digby*.

Upon the first news of the loss of the Battle of
Naseby it was enough foreseen, that the Prince himself might be put to a retreat to *Pendennis*-Castle.
Therefore they wished, "that it might be in the
"Prince's power, upon an emergent occasion, to
"remove the Duke from that place." Which consideration the Lord *Colepepper* presented to the King,
at his being with him in *Wales*; and thereupon a

Warrant was sent from the King, for the removal of the Duke to *Scilly*; which was likewise foreseen that the Prince might repair to. As the Enemy drew nearer the West, many good Men were very solicitous, that the Duke should be removed from *Pendennis*, having a great jealousy of the interest he had in the Governor; of which there was so universal a suspicion, that many Letters were writ to the Council, "that if he were not speedily disposed to some "other place, they feared the Castle would be be- "trayed:" and Sir *Richard Greenvil* writ earnestly to the Prince about it, as did Sir *Harry Killigrew* (a Person of entire Affections to the King, and a true Friend of the Governor) very importunately. So that about the Month of *November*, the King's Warrant for his removal was sent to Sir *Arthur Bassel*, Governor of the Mount; who went to *Pendennis* in the Morning, and took him with him to the Mount, in order to remove him to *Scilly*, when the time should require it; the Duke expressing great trouble and discontent that he should be removed, and pretending, "that he could "not ride for the Stone" (of which he complained so much, that he had Petitioned the King for leave to go into *France* to be cut) and the Governor, and all that Family and Garrison, made show of no less grief to part with him, he having begotten a great opinion in that People of his Integrity and Innocence. But when the Duke saw there was no Remedy, he mounted a Horse that was provided for him, and passed the Journey very well.

After the loss of *Dartmouth*, some Persons of near trust about the Prince resumed the discourse again of

Duke Hamilton is removed to the Mount.

enlarging the Duke, and believed that he would be able to do the King great Service in the bufinefs of *Scotland*; and this prevailed fo far with one of the Lords of the Council, that, upon the confidence of Dr. *Frazier*, the Prince's Phyfician, he made a Journey with the Dr. to the Mount; and did think, that he had fo much prevailed with the Duke, that he had confented " to fend a Servant fpeedily to the *Scottifh*
" Army in *England* (who fhould likewife pafs by the
" King, and carry any Letters to his Majefty from
" the Prince) to perfuade them to comply with the
" King; and that he would likewife defpatch *Charles*
" *Murray* into *Scotland*, inftructed to his Brother
" *Lanrick*, and that Party, to oblige them to join
" with *Mountrofe.* But Dr. *Frazier* confeffed to thofe
" he trufted, that the Duke rather confented to it to
" fatisfy that Lord's vehemence and importunity,
" than that he had any great hope of fuccefs by it;
" infifting ftill, that nothing but his own Liberty
" would do it:" for which he gave a reafon, that before had never been heard of, and was very contrary to what the Duke had faid to the Chancellor, which was, " that the State of *Scotland* was fo fenfible of the
" injury done to the Duke by his imprifonment
" (which he had faid before that they were very glad
" of) that they had made an Order, that there fhould
" never be a Treaty with the King, or agreeing with
" *Mountrofe*, till he was at Liberty, or brought to a
" legal Trial." And when *Charles Murray* went to him for his inftructions, though he faid much for him to fay again to his Friends, and his Brother, towards their declaring for the King, he difcouraged him much

as to the Journey, reprefenting to him "his own
"danger, and the ftrict Orders that were in *Scotland*
"againft divifive Motions; of which, he faid, he
"feared this would be taken for one."

This made the Council to have no mind to be engaged in any Treaty with him, and lefs in propofing or confenting to his Liberty; not only upon the former knowledge they had of his difpofition and nature, but alfo that they believed, if he were not fincere, he would do much mifchief; and the more for being in any degree trufted; if he were fincere, that he would be able to do more good for the King, by being redeemed out of Prifon by the Enemy, than by being releafed by the King or Prince. And therefore, when the Prince removed in that hafte and diforder from *Pendennis* to *Scilly*, there was no poffibility of removing him; fo that, at the furrender of the Mount, which was, by his advice, much fooner than they had reafon to do it, when they were able to defend themfelves for many Months, he was enlarged, and removed himfelf to *London* by fpeedy Journies on Horfeback; and did never after complain of the Stone; which he before protefted "would "kill him, if he were not cut within a year."

Upon the Surrender of the Mount he obtained his Liberty.

We left the King in *Oxford*, free from the trouble and uneafinefs of thofe perpetual and wandering Marches, in which he had been fo many Months exercifed; and quiet from all rude and infolent provocations. He was now amongft his true and faithful Counfellors and Servants, whofe Affection and Loyalty had fiift engaged them in his Service, and made them ftick to him to the end; and who, if they

The King's tranfactions at Oxford.

were not able to give him aſſiſtance, to ſtem that mighty Torrent that overbore both Him and Them, paid him ſtill the Duty that was due to him, and gave him no vexation when they could not give him comfort. There were yet ſome Garriſons remaining in his Obedience, which were like, during the Winter-Seaſon, to be preſerved from any attempt of the Enemy. But upon the Approach of Spring, if the King ſhould be without an Army in the Field, the Fate of thoſe few places was eaſier to be diſcerned. And which way an Army could poſſibly be brought together, or where it ſhould be raiſed, was not within the compaſs of the wiſeſt Man's comprehenſion. However, the more difficult it was, the more vigor was to be applied in the attempt. *Worceſter*, as it was Neighbouring to *Wales*, had the greateſt Outlet and Elbow-room; and the Parliament-party that had gotten any Footing there, behaved themſelves with that Inſolence and Tyranny, that even they who had called them thither, were weary of them, and ready to enter into any combination to deſtroy them. Upon which proſpect, and ſome invitation, the King ſent the Lord *Aſtley* (whom he had before, at his being at *Cardiff*, conſtituted Governor of thoſe Parts, in the place of the Lord *Gerrard*) to *Worceſter*, with order "to proceed, as he ſhould find himſelf "able, towards the gathering a Body of Horſe to- "gether, againſt the Spring, from thoſe Garriſons "which were left, and from *Wales*:" and what progreſs he made towards it will be ſoon known.

When a full proſpect, upon the moſt mature deliberation, was taken of all the hopes which might

with any color of reason be entertained; all that occurred, appeared so hopeless and desperate, that it was thought fit to resort to an old expedient, that had been found as desperate as any; which was a new Overture for a Treaty of Peace: for which, they who advised it, had no other reason, but that they could not tell what else to do. *Cromwell* had left *Fairfax* in the West, and with a Party Selected had set down before *Basing*, and his imperious Summons having been rejected, he Stormed the Place and took it, and put most of the Garrison to the Sword: and a little before *Winchester* had surrendered upon easy conditions. The lesser Garrisons in the North, which had stood out till now, were rendered every day; and the *Scottish* Army, which had marched as far as their own Borders, was called back, and required to Besiege *Newark*. So that whoever thought the sending to the Parliament (puffed up and swoln with so many Successes) for a Peace, would prove to no purpose, was not yet able to tell, what was like to prove to better purpose. This reflection alone prevailed with the King, who had enough experimented those inclinations, to refer entirely to the Council, " to chuse any expedient, they thought most pro-
" bable to succeed, and to prepare any Message they
" would advise his Majesty to send to the Parlia-
" ment." And when they had considered it, the Overtures he had already made, by two several Messages, to which he had received no Answer, were so ample, that they knew not what addition to make to them; but concluded, "that this Message
" should contain nothing but a resentment of That,

BOOK IX.

The King sends another Message for Peace, which was laid aside by the Houses.

" and a demand of an Answer to the Messages his
" Majesty had formerly sent for a Treaty of Peace."
This Message had the same entertainment which the former had received. It was received, read, and then laid aside without any Debate; which they who wished well to it, had not credit or courage to advance; yet still found means to convey their advice to *Oxford*, " that the King should not give over that
" importunity:" and they who had little hopes of better effects from it, were yet of opinion, " that the
" neglecting those gracious invitations, made by
" his Majesty for Peace, would shortly make the
" Parliament so odious, that they would not dare
" long to continue in the same obstinacy." The *Scots* were grieved and enraged, to see their Idol Presbytery so undervalued, and slighted, that besides, the Independents power in the City, their very Assembly of Divines every day lost Credit and Authority to support it; and desired nothing more than a Treaty for Peace: and many others who had contributed most to the suppression of the King's Power, were now much more afraid of their own Army, than ever they had been of His Authority; and believed, that if a Treaty were once set on foot, it would not be in the power of the most violent to render it ineffectual: or whatever they believed themselves, they conveyed this to some about the King, as the concurrent advice of all who pretended to wish well: And some Men took upon them to send the subject of what Message the King should send, and clothed in such expressions, as they conceived were like to gain ground; which his Majesty

could not but graciously accept; though he very seldom imitated their Style.

His Majesty finds again for a Safe-Conduct for the Duke of Richmond and others.

After the King had long expected an Answer to his last Message, induced by those and the like reasons above mentioned, he sent again to the Parliament, " that they would send a Safe-Conduct for the Duke " of *Richmond*, and the Earl of *Southampton*, Mr. " *John Aſburnham*, and Mr. *Geoffrey Palmer*; by " whom he would make such particular Propoſi- " tions to them as he hoped would produce a Peace." To this they returned an Answer, such as it was, " that it would be inconvenient, and might be of " dangerous conſequence, to admit thoſe Lords and " Gentlemen to come into their Quarters; but that " they were preparing ſome Propoſitions, which, " when finiſhed, ſhould be ſent to his Majeſty in " Bills, to be Signed by him; which would be the " only way to produce a Peace." The King underſtood well what ſuch Bills would contain, and which when he had granted, he ſhould have nothing left to deny; and therefore liked not, that ſuch concluſions ſhould be made without a Treaty. He reſolved once more to try another way, which having been never yet tried, he believed they could not deny; and if granted, what hazard ſoever his Perſon ſhould be in, he ſhould diſcover, whether he had ſo many Friends in the Parliament, and the City, as many Men would perſuade him to conclude; and whether the *Scots* had ever a thought of doing him Service. He ſent to them, towards the end of *December*, " that ſince all other Overtures had proved ineffec- " tual, He deſired to enter into a Perſonal Treaty

Their Anſwer.

The King ſends to deſire a Perſonal Treaty at Weſtminſter.

BOOK IX.

"with the two Houses of Parliament at *Westminster*,
"and the Commissioners of the Parliament of *Scot-*
"*land*, upon all matters which might conduce to
"the Peace and Happiness of the distracted King-
"doms; and to that purpose his Majesty would
"come to *London*, or *Westminster*, with such of his
"Servants as now attended him, and their followers,
"not exceeding in the whole the Number of three
"hundred Persons, if he might have the engagement
"of the two Houses of Parliament, the Commis-
"sioners of the Parliament of *Scotland*, of the Chief-
"Commanders in Sir *Thomas Fairfax*'s Army, and of
"those of the *Scottish* Army, for his Free and Safe
"coming to, and abode in *London*, or *Westminster*,
"for the space of forty days; and after that time,
"for his Free and Safe repair to *Oxford*, *Worcester*,
"or *Newark*, if a Peace should not be concluded:
"For their better encouragement to hope well from
"this Treaty, his Majesty offered to settle the Mili-
"tia in such Persons as should be acceptable to them."

Their Answer.
This Message indeed awakened them, and made them believe that the Gamesters who were to play this Game, looked into their hands, and hoped to find a Party in their own Quarters; and that if they should neglect to send an Answer to this Message, their Silence might be taken for consent, and that they should quickly hear the King was in *London*; which they did not wish. They made thereupon more than ordinary haste, to let his Majesty know, "that
"there had been no delay on their parts; but for
"the Personal Treaty desired by his Majesty, after
"so much Innocent Blood shed in the War by his

"Commands, and Commiffions" (with the mention of many other odious particulars) "they conceived, that until Satisfaction and Security were firft given to both Kingdoms, his Majefty's coming thither could not be convenient, nor by them affented to; nor did they apprehend it a means conducing to Peace, to accept of a Treaty for few days, with any thoughts or intentions of returning to Hoftility again." They obferved, "that his Majefty defired the engagement, not only of the Parliament, but of the Chief-Commanders in Sir *Thomas Fairfax*'s Army, and thofe of the *Scottifh* Army; which, they faid, was againft the Privilege and Honor of Parliament, to have thofe joined with them, who were Subject and Subordinate to their Authority." They renewed what they had faid in their laft Anfwer, "that they would fhortly fend fome Bills to his Majefty, the figning of which would be the beft way to procure a good, and a fafe Peace."

Though the King was not willing to acquiefce with this ftubborn rejection, but fent Meffage upon Meffage ftill to them for a better Anfwer, and at laft offered "to difmantle all his Garrifons, and fo come to and refide with his Parliament, if all they who had adhered to him, might be at liberty to live in their own Houfes, and to enjoy their own Eftates, without being obliged to take any Oaths, but what were enjoined by the Law;" he could never procure any other Anfwer from them. And left all this fhould not appear Affront enough, they publifhed an Ordinance, as they called it, "that if

"the King should, contrary to the advice of the
Parliament already given to him, come, or attempt
to come, within the Lines of Communication,
the Committee of the Militia should raise such
Forces as they should think fit, to prevent any
Tumult that might arise by his coming, and to
suppress any that should happen; and to apprehend any who should come with him, or resort
to him; and to secure his Person from Danger:"
which was an expression they were not ashamed
always to use, when there was no Danger that threatened him, but what themselves contrived, and
designed against him. To this their Ordinance, they
added another Injunction, "that all who had ever
borne Arms for his Majesty" (whereof very many
upon the Surrender of Garrisons, and liberty granted
to them, by their Articles upon those Surrenders,
were come thither) "should immediately depart,
and go out of *London*, upon penalty of being
proceeded against as Spies." So that all doors being,
in this obstinate manner, shut against a Treaty, all
thoughts of That, at least with reference to the Parliament, were laid aside; and all endeavours used to
get such a power together, as might make them see
that his Majesty was not out of all possibility of
being yet able to defend himself.

The King tries to deal with the In- dependents:

When all hopes, as I said, were desperate of any
Treaty with the Parliament, and consequently many
hazards were to be run, in the contriving a Peace
any other way; the sustaining the War, with any
probability of Success, was the next desirable thing
to a Peace, and preferable before any such Peace,

as

as was probably to be hoped for from the Party that governed the Army, which governed the Parliament. The King therefore used all the means which occurred to him, or which were advised and proposed by others, to divide the Independent Party; and to prevail with some principal Persons of them, to find their Content and Satisfaction in advancing his Interest. That Party comprehended many who were not so much Enemies to the State, or to the Church, as not to desire heartily that a Peace might be established upon the foundations of Both, so their own particular Ambitions might be complied with. To them the King thought he might be able to propose very valuable Compensations for any Service they could do Him; and the power of the Presbyterians, as they were in conjunction with the *Scots*, seemed no unnatural Argument to work upon those, who professed to be swayed by matter of Liberty of Conscience in Religion: since it was out of all question, that they should never find the least satisfaction to their Scruples, and their Principles in Church Government, from those who pretended to Erect the Kingdom of *Jesus-Christ*. And it was thought to be no ill Presage towards the repairing of the Fabric of the Church of *England*, that it's two Mortal Enemies, who had exposed it to so much Persecution and Oppression, hated each other as mortally, and labored each other's Destruction, with the same Fury and Zeal they had both practised towards Her. This reasonable imagination very much disposed the King, who was well acquainted with the unruly Spirit and Malice of the Presbyterians, to think it

BOOK IX.

possible that he might receive some benefit from the Independents; a Faction newly grown up, and with which he was utterly unacquainted: and his Majesty's extraordinary Affection for the Church made him the less weigh and consider the incompatibility, and irreconcileableness of that Faction with the Government of the State; of which, it may be, he was the less sensible, because he thought nothing more impossible, than that the *English* Nation should submit to any other than Monarchical Government. There were besides an over-active and busy kind of Men, who still undertook to make Overtures as agreeable to the wish of some principal Leaders of that Party, and as with their Authority, and so prevailed with the King, to suffer some Persons of Credit near him, to make some Propositions, in his Name, to particular Persons. And it is very probable, that as the same Men, made the expectations of those People appear to the King much more reasonable and moderate, than in truth they were, so they persuaded the others to believe, that his Majesty would yield to many more important Concessions, than he would ever be induced to grant. So either side had, in a short time, a clear view into each other's intentions, and quickly gave over any expectation of benefit that way; save that the Independents were willing, that the King should cherish the hopes of their compliance, and the King as willing that they should believe that his Majesty might be prevailed with to grant more, than at first he appeared resolved to do.

But in vain.

The truth is, though that Party was most prevalent in the Parliament; and comprehended all the Superior Officers of the Army (the General only excepted; who thought himself a Presbyterian) yet there were only three Men, *Vane, Cromwell*, and *Ireton*, who governed and disposed all the rest according to their Sentiments; and without doubt they had not yet published their dark designs to many of their own Party, nor would their Party, at that time, have been so numerous and considerable, if they had known, or but imagined, that they had entertained those thoughts of Heart, which they grew every day less tender to conceal, and forward enough to discover.

There was another Intrigue now set on foot, with much more probability of Success, both in respect of the thing itself, and the circumstances with which it came accompanied; and that was a Treaty with the *Scots*, by the Interposition and Mediation of the Crown of *France*; which, to that purpose at this time, sent an Envoy, one *Montrevil*, to *London*, with some formal Address to the Parliament, but intentionally to Negotiate between the King and the *Scots*; whose Agent at *Paris* had given encouragement to the Queen of *England*, then there, to hope that That Nation would return to their Duty; and the Queen-Regent, in the great generosity of her Heart, did really desire to contribute all that was in Her Power to the King's recovery. To that purpose, she sent *Montrevil* at this time with Credentials to the King, as well as to the Parliament; by which the Queen had opportunity to Communicate her Advice to the King her Husband; and the Envoy had

BOOK IX.

A Treaty between the King and the Scots, set on foot by the Interposition of France: And Montrevil is sent for that purpose.

P 2

BOOK IX.

Authority " to engage the Faith of *France*, for " the performance of whatsoever the King should promise to the *Scots.*"

This was the first instance, and it will appear a very sorry one, that a Foreign Sovereign Prince gave, of wishing a Reconciliation, or to put a period to the Civil War in his Majesty's Dominions; towards the contrivance whereof, and the frequent fomenting it, too many of them contributed too much. The old Maxim, " that the Crown of *England* " could Balance the Differences which fell out be- " tween the Princes of *Europe*," by it's inclining to either Party, had made the Ministers of our State too negligent in cultivating the Affections of their Neighbours by any real Obligations; as if they were to be Arbiters only in the Differences which fell out between others, without being themselves liable to any impression of adverse Fortune. This made the unexpected Calamity that befel this Kingdom not ungrateful to it's Neighbours on all sides; who were willing to see it weakened and chastised by it's own strokes.

Cardinal *Richelieu*, out of the haughtiness of his own nature, and immoderate appetite of revenge, under the disguise of being jealous of the Honor of his Master, had discovered an implacable hatred against the *English*, ever since that unhappy provocation by the Invasion of the Isle of *Re*, and the declared Protection of *Rochelle*; and took the first opportunity, from the indisposition and murmurs of *Scotland*, to warm that People into Rebellion, and saw the Poison thereof prosper, and spread to his own wish; which he fomented by the *French* Ambassador in the Parliament, with all the Venom of his Heart; as hath been mentioned before. As he had not unwisely driven the Queen-Mother out of *France*, or rather kept her from returning, when she had unadvisedly withdrawn herself from thence, so he was as vigilant to keep her Daughter, the Queen of *England*, from coming thither; which she resolved to have done, when she carried the Princess-Royal into *Holland*; in hope to work upon the King her Brother, to make such a seasonable Declaration against the Rebels of *England*, and *Scotland*, as might terrify them from the farther prosecution of their wicked purposes. But it was made known to her, " that her Presence would not be acceptable in " *France*;" and so, for the present, that enterprise was declined.

But that great Cardinal being now dead, and the King himself dying within a short time after, the Administration of the Affairs of that Kingdom, in the Infancy of the King, and under his Mother, the Queen-Regent, was committed to Cardinal *Mazarin*, an *Italian* by Birth, and raised by *Richelieu* to the degree of a Cardinal, for his great dexterity in putting *Casal* into the hands of *France*, when the *Spaniard* had given it up to him, as the Nuntio of the Pope, and in trust that it should remain in the Possession of his Holiness, till the Title of the Duke of *Mantua* should be determined. This Cardinal was a Man rather of different, than contrary Parts from his Predecessor; and fitter to built upon the Foundations which he had laid, than to have laid those Foundations; and to cultivate, by Artifice, Dexterity, and Diffimulation (in which his Nature and Parts excelled) what the other had begun with great Refolution and Vigor, and even gone through with invincible Conftancy and Courage. So that, the one having broken the heart of all oppofition and contradiction to the Crown, by the cutting off the Head of the Duke of *Montmorency*, and reducing Monfieur, the Brother of the King, to the moft tame fubmiffion, and incapacity of fomenting another Rebellion, it was very eafy for the other, to find a compliance from all Men, now fufficiently terrified from any contradiction. And how great things foever this laft Minifter performed for the Service of that Crown, during the Minority of the King, they may all, in juftice, be imputed to the prudence and providence of Cardinal *Richelieu*; who had reduced and difpofed the whole Nation to an entire Subjection and Submiffion to what fhould be impofed upon them.

Cardinal *Mazarin*, when he came firft to that great Miniftry, was without any Perfonal Animofity againft our King, or the *English* Nation; and was no otherwife delighted with the diftraction and confufion they were both involved in, than as it difabled the whole People from making fuch a conjunction with the *Spaniard*, as might make the profecution of that War (upon which his whole Heart was fet) the more difficult to him: which he had the more reafon to apprehend by the Refidence of *Don Alonfo de Cardenas*, Ambaffador from the King of *Spain*, ftill at *London*, making all Addreffes to the Parliament.

When the Queen had been compelled in the last year, upon the advance of the Earl of *Essex* into the West to Transport herself out of *Cornwall* into *France*, she had found there as good a reception, as she could expect; and received as many expressions of kindness from the Queen-Regent, and as ample promises from the Cardinal, as she could wish. So that she promised herself a very good effect from her Journey; and did procure from him such a present supply of Arms and Ammunition, as, though of no great value in itself, she was willing to interpret, as a good evidence of the reality of his intentions. But the Cardinal did not yet think the King's Condition low enough; and rather desired, by administering little ordinary Supplies, to enable him to continue the struggle, than to see him Victorious over his Enemies; when he might more remember, how slender Aid he had received, than That he had been assisted; and might hereafter make himself Arbiter of the Peace between the two Crowns. Wherefore he was more solicitous to keep a good correspondence with the Parliament, and to profess a Neutrality between the King and them, than inclined to give them any jealousy, by appearing much concerned for the King.

But after the Battle of *Naseby* was lost, and that the King seemed so totally defeated, that he had very little hope of appearing again in the head of an Army, that might be able to resist the Enemy, the Cardinal was Awakened to new Apprehensions; and saw more cause to fear the Monstrous power of the Parliament, after they had totally subdued the King, than ever he had to apprehend the excefs of greatnefs in the Crown: and therefore, befides the frequent incitements he received from the generofity of the Queen-Regent, who really defired to fupply fome Subftantial relief to the King, he was himfelf willing to receive any Propofitions from the Queen of *England*, by which She thought that the King her Hufband's Service might be advanced; and had always the Dexterity and Artifice, by letting things fall in difcourfe, in the prefence of thofe, who, he knew, would obferve and report what they heard or conceived, to caufe that to be propofed to him, which he had moft mind to do, or to engage himfelf in. So he had Application enough from the Covenanting-Party of *Scotland* (who from the beginning had depended upon *France*, by the encouragement and promifes of Cardinal *Richelieu*) to know how to direct them, to apply themfelves to the Queen of *England*, that they might come recommended by her Majefty to him, as a good Expedient for the King's Service. For they were not now referved in their Complaints of the Treatment they received from the Parliament, and of the terrible apprehenfion they had of being difappointed of all their hopes, by the prevalence of the Independent Army, and of their Faction in both Houfes; and therefore wifhed nothing more, than a good opportunity to make a firm conjunction with the King; towards which they had all encouragement from the Cardinal, if they made their addrefs to the Queen, and if her Majefty would defire the Cardinal to conduct it. And becaufe many things muft be promifed, on the King's

behalf, to the *Scots* upon their engagement, "the
"Crown of *France* should give credit and engage,
"as well that the *Scots* should perform all that they
"should promise, as that the King should make good
"whatsoever should be undertaken by Him, or by
"the Queen on his behalf.

This was the occasion and ground of sending *Montrevil's* Monsieur *Montrevil* into *England*, as is mentioned *Negotiation* with the King. before. He arrived there in *January*, with as much credit as the Queen-Regent could give him to the *Scots*, and as the Queen of *England* could give him to the King; who likewise persuaded his Majesty, to believe, "that *France* was now become really
"kind to him, and would engage all it's power to
"serve him; and that the Cardinal was well assured,
"that the *Scots* would behave themselves hencefor-
wards very honestly:" which his Majesty was willing to believe, when all other hopes had failed; and all the Overtures made by him for a Treaty had been rejected. But it was not long before he was undeceived; and discerned that this Treaty was not like to produce better fruit, than his former Overtures had done. For the first Information he received from *Montrevil*, after his arrival in *England*, and after he had conferred with the *Scottish*-Commissioners, was,
"that they peremptorily insisted upon his Majesty's
"Condescension, and Promise, for the Establishment
"of the Presbyterian Government in *England*, as it
"was in *Scotland*; without which, he said, there was
"no hope, that they would ever join with his Ma-
"jesty;" and therefore the Envoy pressed his Majesty "to give them satisfaction therein, as the advice

"of the Queen-Regent and the Cardinal, and like-
"wife of the Queen his Wife; which exceedingly
"troubled the King." And the *Scots* alledged confidently, "that the Queen had exprefsly promifed to
"Sir *Robert Moray* (a cunning and a dexterous Man,
who had been employed by them to her Majefty)
"that his Majefty fhould confent thereunto." They
produced a Writing Signed by the Queen, and delivered to Sir *Robert Moray*, wherein there were fuch expreffions concerning Religion, as nothing pleafed the King; and made him look upon that Negotiation, as rather a Confpiracy againft the Church between the Roman Catholics and Prefbyterians, than as an Expedient for his Reftoration, or Prefervation: and he was very much difpleafed with fome Perfons, of near truft about the Queen, to whofe mifinformation, and advice, he imputed what her Majefty had done in that particular.

Thereupon he deferred not to let Monfieur *Montrevil* know, "that the alteration of the Government
"in the Church was exprefsly againft his Con-
"fcience; and that he would never confent to it;
"that what the Queen his Wife had feemed to pro-
"mife, proceeded from her not being well informed
"of the conftitution of the Government of *England*;
"which could not confift with the change that was
"propofed." But his Majefty offered, "to give all
"the affurance imaginable, and hoped that the
"Queen-Regent would engage her Royal word on
"his behalf in that particular, that the Maintenance
"and Support of the Epifcopal Government in *England*, fhould not in any degree fhake, or bring the

"least prejudice to that Government that was then settled in *Scotland*;" and, farther he offered, "that, if the *Scots* should desire to have the free exercise of their Religion, according to their own practice and custom, whilst they should be at any time in *England*, he would assign them convenient places to that purpose in *London*, or any other part of the Kingdom, were they should desire it." Nor could all the Importunity or Arguments, used by *Montrevil*, prevail with his Majesty to enlarge those Concessions, or in the least to recede from the constancy of his resolution; though he informed him of "the dissatisfaction both the *Scottish* Commissioners, and the Presbyterians in *London* had in his Majesty's resolution, and averseness from gratifying them in that, which they always had, and always would insist upon; and that the *Scots* were resolved to have no more to do with his Majesty; but to agree with the Independents; from whom they could have better conditions than from Him; and he feared such an Agreement was too far advanced already."

Many Answers and Replies passed between the King and *Montrevil* in Cipher, and with all imaginable Secrecy; in which, whatever reproaches were cast upon him afterwards, he always gave the King very clear and impartial information of the temper, and of the discourses of those People with whom he was to Transact. And though he did, upon all occasions, with much earnestness, advise his Majesty to consent to the unreasonable demands of the *Scots*, which, he did believe, he would be at last compelled to do, yet it is as certain, that he did use all the Arguments the Talent of his Understanding, which was a very good one, could suggest to him, to persuade the *Scots* to be contented with what the King had so frankly offered and granted to them; and did all he could to persuade and convince them, that their own preservation, and that of their Nation depended upon the preservation of the King, and the support of his Regal Authority. And it is very memorable, that, in Answer to a Letter which *Montrevil* writ to the King, and in which he persuaded his Majesty to agree with the *Scots* upon their own demands, and amongst other Arguments, assured his Majesty, " that the *English* Presbyterians were fully agreed " with the *Scots*" (which his Majesty believed they would never be) the *Scots* having declared, " that " they would never insist upon the settling any other " Government than was at that time practised in " *London*;" urging many other successes, which they had at that time obtained; the King, after some expressions of his adhering to what he had formerly declared, used these words in his Letter of the 21st of *January* to Monsieur *Montrevil*, " Let them never " flatter themselves so with their good successes; " without pretending to Prophecy, I will foretel " their ruin; except they agree with Me; however " it shall please God to dispose of Me;" which they had great reason to remember after.

But because, though this Treaty was begun, and proceeded so far as is recited, before the end of the present Year, yet it was carried on, and did not conclude, till some Months after the next Year was begun, we shall put an end to our Relation of it at present, and resume what remains, in it's place of the Year ensuing: Only, before we finish our Account of the Actions of this unfortunate Year forty-five, we must mention one more, which happened on the two- and twentieth of *March* just as the Year was expiring.

The King had hoped to draw out of the few Garrisons still in his possession, such a Body of Horse and Foot, as might enable Him to take the Field early in the Spring, though without any fixed design. But this was dashed in the very beginning, by the total Rout and Defeat the Lord *Astley* underwent; who being upon his March from *Worcester* towards *Oxford*, with two thousand Horse and Foot, and the King having appointed to meet him, with another Body of fifteen hundred Horse and Foot, Letters and Orders miscarried, and were intercepted; whereby the Enemy came to have notice of the Resolution, and drew a much greater strength from their several Garrisons of *Glocester*, *Warwick*, *Coventry*, and *Evesham*. So that the Lord *Astley* was no sooner upon his March, but they followed him; and the second day, after he had marched all night, when he thought he had escaped all their Quarters, they fell upon his wearied Troops; which, though a bold and stout Resistance was made, were at last totally Defeated; and the Lord *Astley* himself, Sir *Charles Lucas*, who was Lieutenant-General of the Horse, and most of the other Officers, who were not killed, were taken Prisoners. The few who escaped, were so scattered and dispersed, that they never came together again; nor did there remain, from that time, any possibility for the King to draw any other Troops together in the Field.

THE

History of the Rebellion, etc.

BOOK X.

***

Jer. xxx. 6.

Wherefore do I see every Man with his hands on his loins, as a Woman in travail, and all faces are turned into paleness?

Jer. xlvii. 6.

O thou sword of the Lord, how long will it be ere thou be quiet? put up thyself into thy scabbard, rest, and be still.

Ezek. xxxiv. 2.

Wo be to the Shepherds of Israel, that do feed themselves; should not the Shepherds feed the Flocks?

***

THE Actions of the last Year were attended with so many dismal Accidents and Events, that there were no seeds of hope left to spring up in this ensuing ill year; for it was enough discerned how little success the Treaty with the *Scots* would produce; which yet the King did not desire to put a period to, otherwise than by positively declaring, " that he would never consent to the alteration of "the Church-Government," but was willing enough that they should entertain any other hopes, and was not himself without hope, that by satisfying the Ambition, and Interest of particular Men, he might mitigate the rigor of the Presbyterian Faction; and to that purpose Monsieur *Montrevil* was gone from *London* to the *Scottish* Army, then before *Newark*, having taken *Oxford* in his way, and so given an Account to the King of his observations, and received from him such Information and Instruction as was necessary for the work in hand.

In the mean time no ways were left untried to draw such a Body of an Army together, as might enable his Majesty to make some attempt upon the Enemy; and if he could, by all possible endeavours, have drawn out of all his Garrisons left, a force of five thousand Horse and Foot (which at that time seemed a thing not to be despaired of) he did more desire to have lost his life, in some signal attempt upon any part of the Enemies Army, than to have enjoyed any conditions which he foresaw he was ever like to obtain by Treaty; and he was not out of hope of a Body of five thousand Foot to be landed in *Cornwall*, which his Letters from *France* confidently promised, and which had been so much expected, and depended upon by the Prince, that it kept him from transporting himself into *Scilly*, till *Fairfax* was marched (as hath been said before) within little more than twenty Miles of *Pendennis*. For Sir *Dudley Wyat* had been sent expresly from the Lord *Jermyn*, to assure the Prince, that such a Body of five thousand Foot were actually raised under the Command of *Ruvignie*, and

BOOK X.

should be Embarked for *Pendennis* within less than a month; and the Lord *Jermyn*, in a Postscript to that Letter which he writ to the Chancellor of the Exchequer by Sir *Dudley Wyat*, wished him not to be too strict in the computation of the Month from the date of the Letter, because there might be accidents of Winds at that Season; but he desired him to be confident, that they should be all landed within the expiration of six Weeks, and by that Measure to conduct the resolutions, and to decline fighting upon that Account: After all this, it is as true, that there was never a Man at this time levied, or designed for that Expedition, only the Name of *Ruvignie* (because he was of the Religion, and known to be a good Officer) had been mentioned, in some loose discourse by the Cardinal, as one who would be very fit to Command any Troops which might be sent into *England* for the relief of the King; which the other, according to his natural credulity, thought to be Warrant enough to give both the King and the Prince that unreasonable Expectation; the which and many other of that great Lord's Negotiations and Transactions, the succeeding, and long continuing Misfortunes, kept from being ever after examined, or considered and reflected upon.

The Prince stayed in the Isle of *Scilly* from *Wednesday* the 4th of *March* till *Thursday* the 16th of *April*, the Wind having continued so contrary, that the Lords *Capel* and *Hopton* came not to him from *Cornwall* till the *Saturday* before; at which time likewise arrived a Trumpeter from Sir *Thomas Fairfax*, with such a Message from the Parliament to the Prince

as

as might well be called a Summons, rather than an Invitation; yet it was well it came not to *Pendennis*, where it would have found a Party among the Prince's Servants. The next Morning, being *Sunday*, a Fleet of about twenty-seven, or twenty-eight Sail of Ships, encompassed the Island; but within three or four hours, by a very notable Tempest, which continued two days, they were dispersed. Upon this, and a clear determination of the weakness of the Place, if it should be attacked by any considerable strength (which both by the Message and the Attendants of it they had reason to apprehend) together with the extreme scarcity of Provisions in that Island, which had not been, in the six weeks the Prince staid there, supplied with Victual for two days out of *Cornwal*, neither had there been any returns from *France* upon the Lord *Colepepper*'s Application to the Queen, which returns would every day grow more difficult by the Season of the Year, his Highness inclined to remove to *Jersey*; against which nothing could be objected of Weight, but the consideration of the King's being at *London* (which was strongly reported still) in a Treaty; and then, that his Highness' remove, especially if by distress of Weather he should be forced into *France*, might be prejudicial to the King; and therefore it would be reasonable, first to expect some Advertisement from his Majesty in what condition he was. Hereupon his Highness produced in Council this ensuing Letter from the King, which was writ shortly after the Battle of *Naseby*, and which he had concealed till that Morning from all

A Letter from the King to the Prince, written from Hereford; June 23. 1645.

the Lords, and which truly, I think, was the only secret he had ever kept from the four he had trusted.

Hereford the 23ᵈ of June 1645.

Charles,

"My late misfortunes remember me to command you that which I hope you shall never have occasion to obey; it is this; If I should at any time be taken Prisoner by the Rebels, I command you (upon my blessing) never to yield to any conditions, that are dishonorable, unsafe for your Person, or Derogatory to Regal Authority, upon any considerations whatsoever, though it were for the saving of my Life; which in such a Case, I am most confident, is in greatest security by your constant resolution, and not a whit the more in danger for their threatening, unless thereby you should yield to their desires. But let their Resolutions be never so Barbarous, the saving of my Life by complying with them would make me end my days with torture, and disquiet of mind, not giving you my Blessing, and Cursing all the rest who are consenting to it. But your constancy will make me die cheerfully, praising God for giving me so gallant a Son, and heaping my blessings on you; which you may be confident (in such a case) will light on you. I charge you to keep this Letter still safe by you, until you shall have cause to use it; and then, and not till then, to show it to all your Council; it being my command to them, as well as you; whom I pray God to make as prosperously glorious as any of the Predecessors ever were of   Your loving Father *Charles* R."

After the reading this Letter, and a confideration of the probability that the Rebels would make fome attempt upon his Highnefs there, and the impoffibility of refifting fuch an attempt in the condition the Ifland then ftood, it was by his Highnefs with great earneftnefs propofed, and by the whole Council (except the Earl of *Berkfhire*) unanimoufly advifed, that the opportunity fhould be then laid hold on, whilft the Rebels Ships were fcattered; and that his Highnefs fhould Embark for *Jerfey*; which he did accordingly on *Thurfday*; and on the next day, being the 17th of *April*, with a profperous wind landed at *Jerfey*; from whence, the fame Night, they fent an Exprefs to the Queen, of the Prince's fafe arrival in that Ifland; and likewife Letters to St. *Maloes*, and *Havre de Grace*, to advertife the Lord *Colepepper* of the fame; who received the Information very feafonably, lying then at *Havre* with two Frigates in expectation of a Wind for *Scilly*, and with Command to the Prince from the Queen, immediately to remove from thence. After the Prince had taken an Account of this Ifland, both himfelf, and all their Lordfhips were of opinion, that it was a place of the greateft fecurity, benefit, and conveniency to repofe in, that could have been defired, and wifhed for; till upon a clear information; and obfervation of the King's condition, and the ftate of *England*, he fhould find a fit opportunity to Act; and the Prince himfelf feemed to have the greateft averfion, and refolution againft going into *France*, except in cafe of danger of furprifal by the Rebels, that could be imagined. In few days Mr. *Progers*,

BOOK X.

The Prince of Wales Embarks from Scilly, lands at Jerfey Apr. 17.

Q 2

A Letter from the Queen to the Chancellor of the Exchequer concerning the Prince's removal into France.

who had been despatched before (presently upon the Lord *Colepepper*'s coming) from *Paris* for *Scilly*, being hindered by contrary Winds till he received the News of the Prince's being at *Jersey*, came thither, and brought this following Letter from her Majesty to the Chancellor of the Exchequer in Cipher.

Paris the 5th of April 1645.

"My Lord *Colepepper* must witness for me that I have patiently and at large, heard all that he could say concerning the condition of *Scilly*, and all that has been proposed for rendering of the Prince of *Wales* his abode there safe; yet I must confess to you, that I am so far from being satisfied in that point, that I shall not sleep in quiet until I shall hear that the Prince of *Wales* shall be removed from thence. It is confessed, it is not sufficiently Fortified, and is accessible in divers places; and the Manning the Works will require a thousand Men more than you have, or, for ought I see, can procure; neither can you be confident, that the loss of *Cornwal* may not suddenly have a dangerous influence upon that Garrison; most of your Soldiers being of that Country. The power of the Parliament at Sea is so great, that you cannot rely upon the seasonable and safe conveyance of such proportions of Provisions, as so great a Garrison will require: I need not remember you of what Importance to the King, and all his Party, the safety of the Prince's Person is; If he should fall into the Rebels hands, the whole would thereby become desperate; therefore I must importun-

" ately conjure you to intend this work, as the prin-
" cipal service you can do to the King, Me, or the
" Prince. *Colepepper* will tell you how I have strained
" to assist you with present Provisions, Shipping,
" and Money, necessary for the Prince's Remove to
" *Jersey*; where, be confident of it, he shall want
" nothing. Besides, for satisfaction of others, I have
" moved the Queen-Regent to give assurance, that
" if the Prince, in his way to *Jersey*, should be ne-
" cessitated, by contrary Winds, or the danger of
" the Parliament-Shipping, to touch in *France*, he
" should have all freedom, and assistance from hence,
" in his immediate passage thither; which is granted
" with great Cheerfulness, and Civility, and will be
" Subscribed under the hand of the *French* King and
" Queen, my Brother, and Cardinal *Mazarin*: there-
" fore I hope all scruples are now satisfied. *Colepepper*
" is hastening to you with good Frigates; but if you
" shall find any danger before their Arrival, I shall
" rely upon your care not to omit any opportunity
" to prevent the danger, according to the resolution
" in Council, which *Colepepper* hath acquainted me
" with; for wich I thank you. I need not tell you
" how acceptable this service will be to the King,
" who in every Letter presses me to write to you
" concerning my Son's safety; nor that I am, and
" always will be, most constantly,
 " Your assured Friend *Henriette Marie R.*

The Prince and Council were very glad at the receipt of this Letter, conceiving that they had now
done all that could be required at their hands; though
they wer adveertised at their first landing there, that

230 THE HISTORY

BOOK X.
there was still an expectation of the Prince in *France*; and that he would be speedily importuned from thence; which they could not believe; but as soon as the Lord *Colepepper* came, they plainly discerned that Letter had been written upon advice to *Scilly*, and upon foreseeing that an immediate Journey into *France* would not have been submitted to; and that the Instrument mentioned for his Highness' quiet and uninterrupted Passage through *France* to *Jersey*, was only a color, the sooner to have invited the Prince to have landed there, if there had been any accidents in his passage; but that the resolution was, that he should not then have come to *Jersey*, as it was now, that he should quickly come from thence; to which purpose shortly after, came most importunate Letters from the Queen; and it seems, howsoever all the late Letters from the King to the Prince before his coming out of *England*, were for his repair into *Denmark*, his Majesty, upon what reasons I know not, conceived his Highness to be in *France*; for after his coming to *Jersey*, this following Letter was sent to him, by the Lord *Jermyn*, in whose Cipher it was writ, and deciphered by his Lordship.

Oxford the 22^d *of March.*

Charles,

A Letter from the King to the Prince.

"Hoping that this will find you safe with your
" Mother, I think fit to write this short but neces-
" sary Letter to you: Then know, that your being
" where you are, safe from the Power of the Re-
" bels, is under God, either my greatest security,
" or my certain ruin. For your constancy to Reli-

" gion, Obedience to me, and to the Rules of
" honor, will make thefe infolent Men begin to
" hearken to reafon, when they fhall fee their In-
" juftice not like to be crowned with quiet; but,
" if you depart from thofe grounds for which I have
" all this time fought, then your leaving this King-
" dom will be (with too much probability) called
" fufficient proof for many of the flanders heretofore
" laid upon me: wherefore, once again, I command
" you upon my blefling to be conftant to your Re-
" ligion, neither hearkening to Roman Superftitions,
" nor the feditious and fchifmatical Doctrines of the
" Prefbyterians and Independents; for, know that
" a perfecuted Church is not thereby lefs pure,
" though lefs fortunate. For all other things, I com-
" mand you to be totally directed by your Mother,
" and (as fubordinate to her) by the remainder of
" that Council which I put to you, at your parting
" from hence: and fo God blefs you."

Charles R.

This Letter, and the very paffionate Commands from the Queen, together with what was privately faid to his Highnefs by the Lord *Colepepper*, who from his being at *Paris* had changed his former opinions, and was (though he expreffed it tenderly; finding a general averfion) pofitive for his going, wrought fo far on the Prince, that he difcovered an Inclination to the Journey; whereupon the Council prefented at large to him, the Inconveniences and Dangers that naturally might be fuppofed would attend fuch a refolution: They remembered, the Carriage of the *French* since the beginning of this Rebellion; how it had been originally fomented, and afterwards countenanced by them; and that they had never, in the least degree, assisted the King; that there was no Evidence that, at that time, they were more inclined to him than to the Rebels; that it would be necessary they should make some public Declaration on his Majesty's behalf, before the Heir apparent of the Crown should put himself into their hands. There was nothing omitted that could be thought of, to render that resolution at least to be of that importance that it ought to be thoroughly weighed, and considered, before executed; and so, in the end they prevailed with the Prince (since at that time it was not known where the King was) to send the Lords *Capel* and *Colepepper* again to the Queen, to present the weightiness of the matter to her Majesty. One of their Instructions was as follows.

"You shall inform her Majesty, that We have, with all duty and submission, considered her Letters to Us concerning our speedy repair into the Kingdom of *France*; the which direction, We conceive to be grounded upon her Majesty's apprehension of danger to our Person by any residence here; the contrary whereof, We believe, her Majesty will be no sooner advertised of, than she will hold Us excused for not giving that present obedience which We desire always to yield to the least Intimation of her Majesty; and therefore, you shall humbly acquaint her Majesty, that We have great reason to believe this Island, to be defensible against a greater Force, than We suppose "probable to be brought against it. That the Inhabitants of the Island express as much cheerfulness, unanimity, and resolution, for the defence of our Person, by their whole carriage, and particularly by a Protestation voluntarily undertaken by them, as can be desired; and that, if, contrary to expectation, the Rebels should take the Island, We can from the Castle (a place in itself of very great strength) with the least hazard remove ourself to *France*; which in case of imminent danger We resolve to do. That our security being thus stated, We beseech her Majesty to consider, whether it be not absolutely necessary, before any thought of our remove from hence be entertained, that We have as clear an information as may be got, of the condition of our Royal Father, and the Affections of *England*; of the resolutions of the *Scots* in *England*, and the strength of the Lord *Mountrose* in *Scotland*; of the Affairs in *Ireland*, and the conclusion of the Treaty there; that so, upon a full and mature prospect upon the whole, We may so dispose of our Person as may be most for the benefit and advantage of our Royal Father; or patiently attend such an alteration and conjuncture, as may administer a greater advantage than is yet offered; and whether our remove out of the Dominions of our Royal Father (except upon such a necessity, or apparent visible conveniency) may not have an Influence upon the Affections of the three Kingdoms to the disadvantage of his Majesty."

Within two days after the two Lords were gone

for *Paris*, Sir *Dudley Wyat* arrived with the News of the King's being gone out of *Oxford*, before the break of day, only with two Servants, and to what place uncertain; it was believed by the Queen, as she said in her Letter to the Prince, that he was gone for *Ireland*, or to the *Scots*; and therefore her Majesty renewed her Command for the Prince's immediate repair into *France*; whereas the chief reason before was, that he would put himself into the *Scots* hands; and therefore it was necessary that his Highness should be in *France*, to go in the head of those Forces which should be immediately sent out of that Kingdom to assist his Majesty.

The two Lords found the Queen much troubled, that the Prince himself came not; she declared herself " not to be moved with any reasons that were, or " could be, given for his stay; and that her resolu- " tion was positive and unalterable:" yet they prevailed with her, to respite any positive Declaration till she might receive full advertisement of the King's condition; who was by this time known to be in the *Scottish* Army.

It is remembered before, that the Prince, upon his arrival at *Scilly*, sent a Gentleman to *Ireland* to the Marquis of *Ormond*, as well that he might be punctually informed of the State of that Kingdom (of which there were several reports) as that he might receive from thence a Company or two of Foot, for the better Guard of that Island; which he foresaw would be necessary, whether he should remain there or not. The Gentleman had a very quick passage to *Dublin*, and came thither very quickly after the

Peace was agreed upon with the *Irish* Roman-Catholics, and found the Lord *Digby* there; who, after his Enterprise, and disbanding in *Scotland*, had first transported himself into the Isle of *Man*, and from thence into *Ireland*; where he had been received, with great kindness and generosity, by the Marquis of *Ormond*, as a Man who had been in so eminent a Post in the King's Council and Affairs. He was a Person of so rare a composition by Nature and by Art (for Nature alone could never have reached to it) that he was so far from being ever dismayed upon any Misfortune (and greater variety of Misfortunes never befel any Man) that he quickly recollected himself so vigorously, that he did really believe his condition to be improved by that ill accident; and that he had an opportunity thereby to gain a new stock of Reputation, and Honor; and so he no sooner heard of the Prince's being in the Isle of *Scilly*, and of his condition, and the condition of that place, than he presently concluded, that the Prince's presence in *Ireland* would settle and compose all the factions there; reduce the Kingdom to his Majesty's Service; and oblige the Pope's Nuntio, who was an Enemy to the Peace, to quit his ambitious designs. The Lord Lieutenant had so good an opinion of the Expedient, that he could have been very well contented, that when his Highness had been forced to leave *England* he had rather chosen to have made *Ireland* than *Scilly* his retreat; but, being a Wise Man, and having many difficulties before him in view, and the apprehension of many contingencies which might increase those difficulties, he would

BOOK X.

The Lord Digby arrives at Jersey from Ireland.

not take upon him to give advice in a point of so great importance; but, forthwith, having a Couple of Frigates ready, he caused a hundred Men with their Officers to be presently put on board, according to his Highness' desire; and the Lord *Digby* (who always concluded, that That was fit to be done which his first thoughts suggested to him, and never doubted the Execution of any thing which he once thought fit to be attempted) put himself on board those Vessels; resolving, that upon the strength of his own reason, he should be able to persuade the Prince, and the Council which attended him, forthwith to quit *Scilly*, and to repair to *Dublin*; which, he did not doubt, if brought to pass in that way, would have been grateful to the Lord Lieutenant. But, by the sudden remove of the Prince from *Scilly*, the two Frigates from *Dublin* missed finding him there; and that Lord, whose order they were obliged to observe, made all the haste he could to *Jersey*; where he found the Prince, with many other of his Friends who attended his Highness, the two Lords being gone but the day before to attend the Queen; he lost no time in informing his Highness of the happy state and condition of *Ireland*; that the Peace was concluded; and an Army of twelve thousand Men ready to be transported into *England*; of the great Zeal, and Affection the Lord Lieutenant had for his Service; and that if his Highness would repair thither, he should find the whole Kingdom devoted to him; and thereupon, positively advised him, without farther deliberation, to put himself aboard those Frigates; which were excellent Sailers, and fit for his secure transportation.

The Prince told him, "that it was a matter of greater importance, than was fit to be executed upon so short deliberation; that he was no sooner arrived at *Jersey* than he received Letters from the Queen his Mother, requiring him forthwith to come to *Paris*,—where all things were provided for his reception; that he had sent two of the Lords of the Council to the Queen, to excuse him for not giving ready obedience to her Commands; and to assure her that he was in a place of unquestionable Security; in which he might safely expect, to hear from the King his Father before he took any other resolution: That it would be very incongruous now to remove from thence, and to go into *Ireland*, before his Messengers return from *Paris;* in which time, he might reasonably hope to hear from the King himself; and so wished him to have patience till the matter was more ripe for a determination." This reasonable Answer gave him no satisfaction; he commended the Prince's averseness from going into *France;* "which, he said, was the most pernicious Counsel that ever could be given; that it was a thing the King his Father abhorred, and never would consent to; and that he would take upon himself to write to the Queen, and to give her such solid advice, and reasons, that should infallibly convert Her from that desire, and that should abundantly satisfy Her that his going into *Ireland* was absolutely necessary; but that a little delay in the execution of it, might deprive Him of all the Fruit which was to be expected from that Journey; and therefore, renewed his advice, and "importunity, for losing no more time, but immediately to Embark;" which when he saw was not like to prevail with his Highness, he repaired to one of those of the Privy-Council, who attended the Prince, with whom he had a particular Friendship, and Lamented to him, the loss of such an occasion, which would inevitably restore the King; who would be equally ruined if the Prince went into *France*; of which he spoke with all the detestation imaginable; and said, "he was so far satisfied in his Conscience of "the benefit that would redound from the one, and "the ruin which would inevitably fall out by the "other, that, he said, if the Person with whom he "held this conference, would concur with him, he "would carry the Prince into *Ireland*, even without "and against his consent." The other Person answered, "that it was not to be attempted without "his consent; nor could he imagine it possible to "bring it to pass if they should both endeavour it." He replied, "that he would invite the Prince on "Board the Frigates to a Collation; and that he knew "well he could so commend the Vessels to him, "that his own curiosity would easily invite him to "a view of them; and that as soon as he was on "Board, he would cause the Sails to be hoisted up, "and make no stay till he came into *Ireland*."

The other was very angry with him for entertaining such imaginations; and told him, "they neither "agreed with his Wisdom nor his Duty;" and left him in despair of his Conjunction, and, at the same time, of being able to compass it. He had no sooner discharged himself of this imagination, but in the

OF THE REBELLION. 239

Inftant (as he had a moft pregnant fancy) he entertained another with the fame vigor; and refolved, with all poffible expedition, to find himfelf at *Paris*, not making the leaft Queftion but that he fhould convert the Queen from any farther thought of fending for the Prince into *France*, and as eafily obtain Her confent and approbation for his repairing into *Ireland*; and he made as little doubt, with the Queen's help, and by his own dexterity, to prevail with *France* to fend a good fupply of Money by him into *Ireland*; by which he fhould acquire a moft univerfal Reputation, and be the moft welcome Man alive to the Lord Lieutenant: and Tranfported with this happy Auguration, he left *Jerfey*; leaving at the fame time his two Ships, and his Soldiers, and half a dozen Gentlemen of Quality (who, upon his defire, and many promifes, had kept him Company from *Ireland*) without one penny of Money to fubfift on during his abfence.

BOOK X.

Thence he goes into France.

As foon as he came to *Paris*, and had feen the Queen (whom he found very well inclined to do all fhe could for the relief of *Ireland*, but refolute to have the Prince her Son immediately with Her, notwithftanding all the Reafons preffed againft it, by the Lords of the King's Council, who had been fent from *Jerfey*) He attended the Cardinal; who underftood him very well, and knew his foible; and received him with all the Ceremony, and Demonftration of refpect, he could poffible exprefs; entered upon the Difcourfe of *England*; celebrated the part which he had Acted upon that Stage, in fo many Actions of Courage, and Sagacity, of the higheft Prudence and

His Tranfactions there with the Queen of England and Cardinal Mazarin.

Circumspection, with an indefatigable Industry and Fidelity. He told him, "that *France* found too late "their own error; that they had been very well "content to see the King's great puissance weakened "by his Domestic Troubles, which they wished "only should keep him from being able to hurt his "Neighbours; but that they never had desired to "see him at the Mercy of his own Rebels, which "they saw now was like to be the Case; and they "were therefore resolved to wed his Interest in such "a way and manner, as the Queen of *England* should "desire; in which he well knew how much her Ma- "jesty would depend upon his Lordship's Counsel.

The Cardinal said, "it was absolutely necessary, "since the Crown of *France* resolved to wed the "King's Interest, that the Person of the Prince of "*Wales* should reside in *France*; that the method he "had thought of proceeding in, was that the Queen "of *England* should make choice of such a Person, "whom she thought best affected, and best qualified "for such an employment, whom the King of *France* "would immediately send as his Extraordinary Am- "bassador to the King and to the Parliament; that "he should govern himself wholly by such Instruc- "tions as the Queen should give him; which, he "knew, would be his Lordship's work to prepare; "that all things should be made ready as soon as the "Queen would nominate the Ambassador; and that, "upon the arrival of the Prince of *Wales* in any part "of *France*, as soon as notice should be sent to the "Court of it (for which due preparation should be "made) the Ambassador should be in the same manner

" manner defpatched for *England*, with one only
" Inftruction from *France;* which fhould be, That he
" fhould demand a fpeedy anfwer from the Parlia-
" ment, whether they would fatisfy the demands
" the *French* Court had made? which if they
" fhould refufe to do, he fhould forthwith, in the
" King his Mafter's name, declare War againft them,
" and immediately leave the Kingdom, and return
" Home; and then there fhould be quickly fuch an
" Army ready, as was worthy for the Prince of
" *Wales* to venture his own Perfon in; and that he
" fhould have the honor to redeem and reftore his
" Father."

This difcourfe ended, the Lord *Digby* wanted not Language to extol the Generofity and the Magnanimity of the refolution, and to pay the Cardinal all his Compliments in his own Coin, and, from thence, to enter upon the Condition of *Ireland*; in which the Cardinal prefently interrupted him, and told him, " he knew well he was come from thence, and " meant to return thither, and likewife the Carriage " of the Nuntio. That the Marquis of *Ormond* was " too brave a Gentleman, and had merited too much " of his Mafter to be deferted; and *France* was re-
" folved not to do its bufinefs by halves, but to give " the King's Affairs an entire relief in all Places; that " he fhould carry a good Supply of Money with " him into *Ireland*, and that Arms and Ammunition " fhould be fpeedily fent after him, and fuch direc-
" tion to their Agent there, as fhould draw off all " the *Irifh* from the Nuntio, who had not entirely " given themfelves up to the *Spanifh* Intereft.

The noble Person had that which he most desired; he was presently converted, and undertook to the Queen, that he would presently convert all at *Jersey*; and that the Prince should obey all her Commands; and entered into consultation with her upon the Election of an Amdassador, and what Instructions should be given him; which he took upon himself to prepare. Monsieur *Bellievre* was named by the Queen, whom the Cardinal had designed for that Office. The Cardinal approved the Instructions, and caused six thousand Pistoles to be paid to him, who was to go to *Ireland*; and though it was a much less Sum than he had promised himself, from the magnificent Expressions the Cardinal had used to him, yet it provided well for his own occasions; so he left the Queen with his usual professions, and confidence, and accompanied those Lords to *Jersey*, who were to attend upon his Highness with her Majesty's Orders for the Prince's repair into *France*; for the Advancement whereof the Cardinal was so solicitous, that he writ a Letter to the old Prince of *Conde* (which he knew he would forthwith send to the Queen; as he did) in which he said, "that he had "received very certain Advertisement out of *England*, that there were some Persons about the Prince "of *Wales* in *Jersey*, who had undertaken to deli-"ver his Highness up into the hands of the Parlia-"ment for twenty thousand Pistoles;" and this Letter was forthwith sent by the Queen to overtake the Lords, that it might be showed to the Prince; and that they who attended upon him, might discern, what would be thought of them, if they dissuaded

his Highness from giving a present obedience to his
Mother's Commands.

As soon as they came to *Jersey*, the Lord *Digby*
used all the means he could to persuade his Friend to
concur in his advice for the Prince's immediate
repair into *France*. He told him all that had passed
between the Cardinal and him, not leaving out any
of the Expressions of the high value his Eminence
had of his particular Person: "That an Ambassador
" was chosen by his advice, and his Instructions
" drawn by him, from no part of which the Ambas-
" sador durst swerve" (and, which is very wonderful,
he did really believe for that time, that he himself had
nominated the Ambassador, and that his Instructions
would be exactly observed by him; so great a Power
he had always over himself, that he could believe
any thing which was grateful to him) "That a War
" would be presently proclaimed upon their refusal
" to do what the Ambassador required, and that
" there wanted nothing to the expediting this great
" Affair, but the Prince's repairing into *France*
" without farther delay; there being no other ques-
" tion concerning that matter, than whether his
" Highness should stay in *Jersey?* where there could
" be no question of his Security, until he could re-
" ceive express direction from the King his Father;
" and therefore he conjured his Friend to concur in
" that advice;" which would be very grateful to the
Queen, and be attended with much benefit to himself; telling him "how kind her Majesty was to
" him, and how confident she was of his Service, and
" that if he should be of another opinion, it would

"not hinder the Prince from going;" who, he knew, was refolved to obey his Mother; and fo concluded his Difcourfe, with thofe Arguments which he thought were like to make moſt impreſſion on him; and gave him the Inſtructions by which the Ambaſſador was to be guided.

His Friend, who in truth loved him very heartily, though no Man better knew his Infirmities, told him, "whatever the Prince would be difpofed to do, "he could not change his opinion in point of Coun- "fel, until the King's pleafure might be known:" he put him in mind, "how he had been before de- "ceived at *Oxford* by the *Comte de Harcourt*, who "was an Ambaſſador likewife, as We then thought, "named by ourfelves, and whofe Inſtructions he "had likewife drawn; and yet, he could not but "well remember how foully that bufinefs had been "managed, and how difobligingly He himfelf had "been treated by that Ambaſſador; and therefore "he could not but wonder, that the fame Artifices "fhould again prevail with him; and that he could "imagine that the Inſtructions he had drawn, would "be at all confidered, or purfued, farther than they "might contribute to what the Cardinal for the pre- "fent defigned; of the integrity whereof, they had "no Evidence, but had reafon enough to fufpect it.

The Lord *Capel*, and the Lord *Colepepper*, ſtayed at *Paris* with the Queen full three Weeks; having only prevailed with her to fufpend her prefent Commands for the Prince's remove from *Jerfey*, until fhe fhould have clear Intelligence where the King was, and how he was treated, though fhe declared a positive resolution that his Highness should come to Paris, let the Intelligence be what it could be; and, in the end, they were well assured that his Majesty had put himself into the *Scottish* Army as it lay before *Newark*; and that, as soon as he came thither, he had caused that Garrison to deliver the Town into the hands of the *Scots*; and that thereupon the *Scots* marched presently away to *New-Castle:* That they had pressed the King to do many things, which he had absolutely refused to do; and that thereupon they had put very strict Guards upon his Majesty, and would not permit any Man to repair to him, or to speak with him; so that his Majesty looked upon himself as a Prisoner, and resolved to make another Escape from them as soon as he could. Mr. *Ashburnham*, who attended upon him in his Journey from *Oxford* as his sole Servant, was forbid to come any more near him; and if he had not put himself on board a Vessel, then at *New-Castle,* and bound for *France,* the *Scots* would have delivered him up to the Parliament. Monsieur *Montrevil*, the *French* Envoy pretended that they were so incensed against him for briskly expostulating with them for their ill Treatment of the King, that it was no longer safe for him to remain in their Quarters, and more dangerous to return to *London*; and therefore, he had likewise procured a *Dutch* Ship to land him in *France,* and was come to *Paris* before the Lords returned to *Jersey*.

The Queen thought now she had more reason to be confirmed in her former resolution for the speedy remove of the Prince, as it was pretended that he had brought a Letter from the King, which was Deciphered by the Lord *Jermyn*; in which, he said, "that he did believe that the Prince could not be "safe any where but with the Queen; and therefore "wished, that if he were not there already, he should "be speedily sent for; and *Montrevil* professed to have a Message by word of mouth to the same purpose; whereas Mr. *Ashburnham*, who left the King but the day before *Montrevil*, and was as entirely trusted by the King as any Man in *England*, brought no such Message; and confessed to the Lord *Capel*, "that he thought it very pernicious to the King that "the Prince should come into *France* in that con- "juncture, and before it was known how the *Scots* "would deal with him; and that the King's opinion "of the convenience of his coming into *France*, "could proceed from nothing but the thought of "his insecurity in *Jersey*." The Lord *Capel* offered to undertake a Journey himself to *New-Castle*, and to receive the King's positive Commands, which he was confident would be submitted to, and obeyed by all the Council as well as by himself; but the Queen was positive, that, without any more delay, the Prince should immediately repair to Her; and, to that purpose, She sent the Lord *Jermyn* (who was Governor of *Jersey*) together with the Lord *Digby*, the Lord *Wentworth*, the Lord *Wilmot*, and other Lords and Gentlemen, who, with the two Lords who had been sent to her by the Prince, should make haste to *Jersey* to see her Commands executed. Whilst they are upon their Journey thither, it will be seasonable to inquire how the King came to involve himself in that perplexity, out of which he was never able afterwards to recover his Liberty and Freedom.

A farther Account of Monsieur Montrevil's Negotiation with the Scots.

Monsieur *Montrevil* was a Person utterly unknown to me, nor had I ever intercourse or correspondence with him; so that what I shall say of him cannot proceed from affection or prejudice, nor if I shall say any thing for his vindication from those reproaches which he did, and does lie under, both with the *English* and *Scottish* Nation, countenanced enough by the discountenance he received from the Cardinal after his return, when he was, after the first account he had given of his Negotiation, restrained from coming to the Court, and forbid to remain in *Paris*, and lay under a formed, declared dislike till his death, which with grief of mind shortly ensued. But as it is no unusual hard-heartedness in such chief Ministers, to sacrifice such Instruments, how innocent soever, to their own dark purposes, so it is probable, that temporary Cloud would soon have vanished, and that it was only cast over him, that he might be thereby secluded from the conversation of the *English* Court; which must have been reasonably very inquisitive, and might thereby have discovered somewhat which the other Court was carefully to conceal: I say if what I here set down of that Transaction, shall appear some vindication of that Gentleman from those imputations under which his memory remains blasted, it can be imputed only to the love of truth, which ought, in common honesty, to be preserved in History as the very Soul of it, towards all Persons who come to be mentioned in it; and since I have in my hands all the original Letters which passed from him to the King, and the King's Answers and Directions thereupon, or such Authentic Copies thereof, as have been by myself examined with the Originals, I take it to be a duty incumbent on me to clear him from any guilt with which his memory lies unjustly charged, and to make a candid interpretation of those Actions, which appear to have resulted from ingenuity, and upright Intentions, how unsuccessful soever.

He was then a young Gentleman of parts very equal to the Trust the Cardinal reposed in him, and to the Employment he gave him; and of a Nature not inclined to be made use of in ordinary dissimulation and cozenage. Whilst he took his Measures only from the *Scottish* Commissioners at *London*, and from those Presbyterians whom he had opportunity to converse with there, he did not give the King the least Encouragement to expect a conjunction, or any compliance from the one or the other, upon any Cheaper price or condition than the whole alteration of the Government of the Church by Bishops, and an entire Conformity to the Covenant; and he used all the Arguments which occurred to him, to persuade his Majesty that all other hopes of Agreement with them were desperate; and when he saw his Majesty unmoveable in that particular, and resolute to undergo the utmost event of War, before he would wound his Peace of Mind, and Conscience, with such an odious concession, he undertook that Journey we mentioned in the end of the last Year, to discover whether the same rude and rigid

Spirit, which Governed those Commissioners at *Westminster*, possessed also the Chief Officers of the *Scottish* Army, and that Committee of State that always remained with the Army.

The *Scottish* Army was then before *Newark*; and, in his passage thither, he waited upon the King at *Oxford*; and was confirmed in what he had reason before to be confident of, that it was absolutely impossible ever to prevail with his Majesty to give up the Church to the most impetuous Demands they could make, or to the greatest necessity himself could be environed with; but as to any other concessions which might satisfy their Ambition or their Profit, which were always Powerful and Irresistible Spells upon that Party, he had ample Authority and Commission to comply with the most extravagant Demands from Persons like to make good what they undertook, except such Propositions as might be mischievous to the Marquis of *Mountrose*; whom the King resolved never to desert, nor any who had joined with and assisted him; all which, he desired to unite to those who might now be persuaded to serve him. His Majesty, for his better information, recommended him to some Persons who had then Command in the *Scottish* Army; of whose Affections and Inclinations to his Service, he had as much confidence, at least, as he ought to have; and of their Credit, and Courage, and Interest, a greater than was due to them.

When *Montrevil* came to the Army, and after he had endeavoured to undeceive those who had been persuaded to believe, that a peremptory and obstinate insisting upon the alteration of the Church-Government (the expectation, and assurance whereof, had indeed first enabled them to make that Expedition) would at last prevail over the King's Spirit, as it had done in *Scotland*, he found those in whom the Power, at least the Command of the Army was, much more moderate than he expected, and the Committee which presided in the Counsels, rather devising and projecting Expedients how they might recede from the rigor of their former Demands, than peremptory to adhere to them, and willing he should believe that they stayed for the coming of the Lord Chancellor out of *Scotland*, who was daily expected, before they would declare their Resolution; not that they were, for the present, without one. They were very much pleased that the King offered, and desired to come to them, and remain in the Army with them, if he might be secured of a good reception for Himself, and for his Servants who should attend him, and his Friends who should resort to him; and the principal Officers of the Army spoke of that, as a thing they so much wished, that it could be in no body's Power to hinder it, if there were any who would attempt it; and they who had the greatest Power in the Conduct of the most secret Counsels, took pains to be thought to have much franker Resolutions in that particular, than they thought yet seasonable to express in direct Undertakings; and employed those who were known to be most entirely trusted by them, and some of those who had been recommended to him by the King, to assure him that he might confidently advise his

Majesty to repair to the Army, upon the Terms himself had proposed; and that they would send a good Body of their Horse, to meet his Majesty at any place he should appoint to Conduct him in Safety to them. Upon which encouragement *Montrevil* prepared a Paper to be signed by himself, and sent to the King as his Engagement; and showed it to those who had been most clear to him in their Expressions of duty to the King, which, being approved by them, he sent by the other who had appeared to him to be trusted by those who were in the highest Trust to be communicated to them, who had in a manner excused themselves for being so reserved towards him, as being necessary in that conjuncture of their Affairs, when there evidently appeared to be the most Hostile jealousy between the Independent Army and them. When the Paper was likewise returned to him with approbation after their perusal, he sent it to the King; which Paper is here faithfully Translated out of the Original.

The Paper Montrevil sent to the King, being a promise for the Scots receiving the King, Apr. 1.

" I do promise in the Name of the King and Queen
" Regent (my Master and Mistress) and by virtue
" of the Powers that I have from their Majesties,
" That if the King of Great Britain shall put himself
" into the *Scottish* Army, he shall be there received
" as their Natural Sovereign; and that he shall be
" with them in all freedom of his Conscience and
" Honor; and that all such of his Subjects and Ser-
" vants as shall be there with him, shall be safely
" and honorably protected in their Persons; and
" that the said *Scots* shall really, and effectually
" join with the said King of Great Britain; and also

"receive all such Persons as shall come in unto him, and join with them for his Majesty's Preservation: And that they shall protect all his Majesty's Party to the utmost of their Power, as his Majesty will Command all those under his obedience to do the like to them; and that they shall employ their Armies and Forces, to assist his Majesty in the procuring of a happy and well grounded Peace, for the good of his Majesty and his said Kingdoms, and in recovery of his Majesty's just Rights. In witness whereof I have hereunto put my Hand and Seal, this first of *April* 1646."

De Montrevil, Résident pour sa Majesté très Chrétienne en Ecosse.

Many days had not passed after the sending that Express, when he found such Chagrin, and Tergiversation, in some of those he had treated with, one Man denying what he had said to himself, and another disclaiming the having given such a Man Authority to say that from him which the other still avowed he had done, that *Montrevil* thought himself obliged, with all speed, to advertise his Majesty of the foul change, and to dissuade him from venturing his Person in the Power of such Men; but the Express who carried that Letter, was taken Prisoner; and though he made his Escape, and preserved his Letter, he could not proceed in his Journey; and was compelled to return to him who sent him; and by that time, he having informed the Committee, what he had done to vindicate himself from being made a Property by them to betray the King, and expressed a deep resentment of the injury done to the King his Master, and to himself, in their receding from what they had promised, they appeared again to be of another Temper, and very much to desire his Majesty's Presence in the Army; and to that purpose, they promised, as an unanimous Resolution, "that they " would send a considerable party, of Horse to meet " his Majesty at *Burton* upon *Trent*; for that they " could not advance farther with the whole party; " but that some Horse should be sent to wait upon his " Majesty at *Bosworth*, which is the middle way " between *Burton* and *Harborough*, whither they " hoped his own Horse would be able to Convey him " securely;" they desired " the King to appoint the " day, and they would not fail to be there." They wished, " that when their Troops should meet his " Majesty, he would tell them that he was going " into *Scotland*; upon which, they would find them- " selves obliged to attend him into their Army, with- " out being able to discover any thing of a Treaty; " of which, the Parliament ought yet to receive no " Advertisement:" of all which *Montrevil* gave the King a very full and plain Narration, together with what he had written before, by his Letter of the 15th of the same *April*, to Secretary *Nicholas*; and, in the same Letter, he informed his Majesty, "that they " did not desire that any of those Forces which had " followed the King's Party, should join with them, " no nor so much as those Horse that should have " accompanied his Majesty, should remain in their " Army with him: That they had with much ado " agreed, that the two Princes" (for his Majesty, upon Prince *Rupert*'s humble submission, was reconciled to both his Nephews) "might follow the King, with such other of his Servants as were not excepted from pardon; and that they might stay with his Majesty until the Parliament of *England* should demand them; in which case they should not refuse to deliver them; but that they would first furnish them with some means of getting beyond Seas."

The King had proposed, "that there might be a Union between them and the Marquis of *Mountrose*; and that his Forces might be joined with their Army;" which they had said, "they could not consent to, with reference to the person of *Mountrose*; who, after so much blood spilt by him of many of the greatest Families, they thought could not be safe among them: whereupon the King had declared, that he would send him his Extraordinary Ambassador into *France*; which they appeared not to contradict, but had now changed their mind; of which *Montrevil* likewise gave an Account in the same Letter: That they could not give their consent that the Marquis of *Mountrose* should go Ambassador into *France*, but into any other place, he might; and that they again, without limiting the time, insisted upon settling the Presbyterian Government;" and he concluded his Letter with these words, "I will say no more but this, that his Majesty and You know the *Scots* better than I do; I represent these things nakedly to you, as I am obliged to do; I have not taken upon me the boldness to give any Counsel to his Majesty; yet if he hath any other refuge, or means

" to make better conditions, I think he ought not to
" accept of these; but if he sees all things desperate
" every where else, and that he and his Servants
" cannot be secure with his Parliament of *England*,
" I dare yet assure him, that though He and his Ser-
" vants may not be here with all that satisfaction per-
" haps which he might desire, yet He especially shall
" be as secure as possible."

In another Letter dated the next day after (the 16th of *April*) to the same Secretary, he hath these words; "I have Orders from the Deputies of *Scot-*
" *land* to assure you, that they will not herein fail" (which related to sending the Horse to meet his Majesty) " as soon as they shall know his day; and that
" the King shall be received into the Army as hath
" been promised;" and that his Conscience shall not be forced. And in the last Letter, which his Majesty or the Secretary received from him, and which was dated the 20th of *April* 1646, there are these words,
" They tell me that they will do more than can be
" expressed; but let not his Majesty hope for any
" more than I send him word of; that he may not be
" deceived; and let him take his Measures aright;
" for certainly the Enterprise is full of danger: yet,
" in the same Letter, he says the disposition of the
" Chiefs of the *Scottish* Army is such as the King can
" desire; they begin to draw off their Troops to-
" wards *Burton*, and the hindering his Majesty from
" falling into the hands of the *English* is of so great
" importance to them, that it cannot be believed
" but that they will do all that lies in their Power to
" hinder it."

This was the proceeding of Monsieur *Montrevil* in that whole Transaction; and if he were too Sanguine upon his first Conversation with the Officers of the *Scottish* Army, and some of the Committee, and when he signed that Engagement upon the first of *April*, he made haste to retract that confidence, and was in all his Despatches afterwards Phlegmatic enough; and, after his Majesty had put himself into their hands, he did honestly and stoutly charge all the particular Persons with the Promises and Engagements they had given to him, and did all he could to make the Cardinal sensible of the Indignity that was offered to that Crown in the violation of those Promises, and Engagements; which was the reason of his being Commanded to return Home, as soon as the King came to *New-Castle*; lest his too keen resentment might irritate the *Scots*, and make it appear to the Parliament how far *France* was engaged in that whole Negotiation; which the Cardinal had no mind should appear to the World; and there can be no doubt, but that the Cautions and Animadversions which the King received from *Montrevil* after his Engagement, would have diverted him from that Enterprise, if his Majesty had discerned any other course to take that had been preferable even to the hazard that he saw he must undergo with the *Scots*; but he was clearly destitute of any other Refuge. Every day brought the News of the loss of some Garrison; and as *Oxford* was already blocked up at a distance, by those Horse which *Fairfax* had sent out of the West to that purpose, or to wait upon the King, and follow him close, if he should remove out
of

of *Oxford*; so he had soon reduced *Exeter*, and some other Garrisons in *Devonshire*. The Governors then, when there was no visible and apparent hope of being Relieved, thought that they might deliver up their Garrisons before they were pressed with the last Extremities, that they might obtain the better Conditions; and yet it was observed that better and more honorable Conditions were not given to any, than to those who kept the Places they were trusted with, till they had not one day's Victual left; of which We shall observe more hereafter. By this means *Fairfax* was within three days of *Oxford* before the King left it, or fully resolved what to do.

His Majesty had before sent to two Eminent Commanders of Name, who had blocked up the Town at a distance, " that if they would pass their words" (how slender a security soever, from such Men who had broken so many Oaths, for the Safety of the King) " that they would immediately Conduct him to the " Parliament, he would have put himself into their " hands;" for he was yet persuaded to think so well of the City of *London*, that he would not have been unwilling to have found himself there; but those Officers would submit to no such Engagements; and great care was taken to have strict Guards round about *London*, that he might not get thither. What should the King do? There was one thing most formidable to him, which he was resolved to avoid, that was, to be inclosed in *Oxford*, and so to be given up, or taken, when the Town should be Surrendered, as a Prisoner to the Independents Army; which he was advertised from all hands, would treat him very Barbarously.

In this perplexity, he chose rather to commit himself to the *Scottish* Army; which yet he did not trust so far as to give them notice of his Journey, by sending for a Party of their Horse to meet him, as they had proffered; but early in the Morning upon the 27th day of *April*, he went out of *Oxford*, attended only by *John Ashburnham*, and a Divine (one *Hudson*) who understood the by-ways as well as the common, and was indeed a very skilful Guide. In this Equipage he left *Oxford* on a *Monday*, leaving those of his Council in *Oxford*, who were privy to his going out, not informed whether he would go to the *Scottish* Army, or get privately into *London*, and lie there concealed, till he might chuse that which was best; and it was generally believed, that he had not within himself at that time a fixed resolution what he would do; which was the more credited because it was nine days after his leaving *Oxford*, before it was known where the King was; insomuch as *Fairfax*, who came before it the fifth day after his Majesty was gone, was sat down, and had made his Circumvallation about *Oxford*, before he knew that the King was in the *Scottish* Army; but the King had wasted that time in several Places; whereof some were Gentlemen's Houses (where he was not unknown, though untaken notice of) purposely to be informed of the condition of the Marquis of *Mountrose*, and to find some secure passage that he might get to him; which he did exceedingly desire; but in the end, went into the *Scottish* Army before *Newark*, and sent for *Montevil* to come to him.

It was very early in the Morning when the King went to the General's Lodging, and difcovered himfelf to him; who either was, or feemed to be, exceedingly furprifed, and confounded at his Majefty's prefence; and knew not what to fay; but prefently gave notice of it to the Committee, who were no lefs perplexed. An Exprefs was prefently fent to the Parliament at *Weftminfter*, to inform them of the unexpected News, as a thing the *Scots* had not the leaft imagination of. The Parliament were fo difordered with the Intelligence, that at firft they refolved to command their General to raife the Siege before *Oxford*, and to march with all expedition to *Newark*; but the *Scottifh* Commiffioners at *London*, diverted them from that, by affuring them " that all their Or-
" ders would meet with an abfolute obedience in
" their Army:" fo they made a fhort defpatch to them, in which it was evident that they believed the King had gone to them by invitation, and not out of his own free choice; and implying, " that they fhould
" fhortly receive farther direction from them;" and in the mean time, " that they fhould carefully watch that
" his Majefty did not difpofe himfelf to fome whi-
" ther elfe." The great care in the Army, was, that there might be only refpect and good manners fhowed towards the King, without any thing of affection or dependence; and therefore the General never afked the Word of him, or any Orders, nor, willingly, fuffered the Officers of the Army to refort to, or to have any difcourfe with his Majefty. *Montrevil* was ill looked upon, as the Man who had brought this inconvenience upon them without their confent; but he was

Their manner of treating his Majefty.

not frighted from owning and declaring what had passed between them, what they had promised, and what they were engaged to do. However, though the King liked not the treatment he received, he was not without apprehension, that *Fairfax* might be forthwith appointed to decline all other Enterprises, and to bring himself near the *Scottish* Army, they being too near together already; and therefore he forthwith gave order to the Lord *Bellasis* to Surrender *Newark*, that the *Scots* might march Northward; which they resolved to do; and he giving up that place, which he could have defended for some Months longer from the Enemy, upon honorable conditions, that Army with great expedition marched towards *New-Castle*; which the King was glad of, though their behaviour to him was still the same; and great strictness used that he might not confer with any Man who was not well known to them, much less receive Letters from any.

The King orders Newark to be surrendered; whereupon the Scottish Army marches Northward with the King to New-castle.

It was an observation in that time, that the first publishing of extraordinary News was from the Pulpit; and by the Preacher's Text, and his manner of discourse upon it, the Auditors might judge, and commonly foresaw, what was like to be next done in the Parliament or Council of State. The first Sermon that was preached before the King, after the Army rose from *Newark* to march Northwards, was upon the 19. *chap.* of the 2 Book of *Samuel*, the 41, 42, and 43 *verses.*

> 41. *And behold, all the men of Israel came to the King, and said unto the King, Why have our brethren the men of Judah stolen thee away, and have brought*

the King and his houshold, and all David's men with him over Jordan?

42. *And all the men of Judah answered the men of Israel, Because the King is near of kin to us: wherefore then be ye angry for this matter? have we eaten at all of the King's cost? or hath he given us any gift?*

43. *And the men of Israel answered the men of Judah, and said, We have ten parts in the King, and we have also more right in David than ye: why then did ye despise us that our advice should not be first had in bringing back our King? And the words of the men of Judah were fiercer than the words of the men of Israel.*

Upon which words, the Preacher gave Men cause to believe, that now they had gotten their King they resolved to keep him, and to adhere to him. But his Majesty came no sooner to *New-Castle*, than both Monsieur *Montrevil* was restrained from having any conference with him, and Mr. *Ashburnham* was advised " to shift for himself, or else that he should be " delivered up to the Parliament;" and both the one, and the other, were come to *Paris* when the Queen sent those Lords to hasten the Prince's remove from *Jersey*.

When those Lords, with their great Train, came to *Jersey*, which was towards the end of *June*, they brought with them a Letter from the Queen to the Prince; in which she told him, " that she was now " fully satisfied, from the Intelligence she had from " *New-Castle* and *London*, that he could not make

Where Montrevil was restrained from him.

The Lord Jermyn and other Lords arrive at Jersey, about the end of June, from the Queen, to

"any longer residence in *Jersey* without apparent danger of falling into the Enemies hands; and that if he should continue there, all possible attempts would be suddenly made, as well by Treachery as by Force, to get his Person into their Power; and therefore, her Majesty did positively require him, to give immediate obedience to the King's Commands, mentioned in the Letter which he had lately sent by Sir *Dudley Wyat*" (which is set out before) "and reiterated in a Letter which she had since received from the King by Monsieur *Montrevil*." Her Majesty said, "that she had the greatest assurance from the Crown of *France*, that possibly could be given, for his honorable reception, and full liberty to continue there, and to depart from thence, at his pleasure; and she engaged her own word, that whenever his Council should find it fit for him to go out of *France*, she would never oppose it; and that during his residence in that Kingdom, all matters of importance which might concern himself, or relate to his Majesty's affairs, should be debated and resolved by himself and the Council, in such manner as they ought to have been, if he had continued in *England*, or in *Jersey*:" and concluded, "that he should make all possible haste to her."

The Lords which arrived with this despatch from her Majesty, had no imagination that there would have been any question of his Highness' compliance with the Queen's command; and therefore, as soon as they had kissed the Prince's hand, which was in the Afternoon, they desired that the Council might

presently be called; and when they came together, the Lords *Jermyn, Digby,* and *Wentworth,* being likewise present, and sitting in the Council, they desired the Prince "that his Mother's Letter might be read;
" and then, since they conceived there could be no
" debate upon his Highness' yielding obedience to
" the Command of the King and Queen, that they
" might only consider of the day when he might
" begin his Journey, and of the order he would ob-
" serve in it. The Lords of the Council represented
" to the Prince, that they were the only Persons that
" were accountable to the King, and to the King-
" dom, for any resolution his Highness should take,
" and for the Consequence thereof; and that the
" other Lords who were present, had no Title to
" deliver their advice, or to be present at the debate,
" they being in no degree responsible for what his
" Highness should resolve to do; and therefore de-
" sired that the whole matter might be debated; the
" State of the King's present Condition understood
" as far as it might be; and the Reasons considered
" which made it Counsellable for his Highness to
" repair into *France,* and what might be said against
" it; and the rather, because it was very notorious
" that the King had given no positive direction in
" the Point, but upon a Supposition that the Prince
" could not remain secure in *Jersey;* which was
" likewise the ground of the Queen's last command;
" and which they believed had no Foundation of
" Reason; and that his Residence there might be very
" unquestionably safe." This begot some warmth, and contradiction between Persons; insomuch as

Debates in the Prince's Council concerning his going.

BOOK X.

the Prince thought it very neceſſary to ſuſpend the debate till the next day, to the end that by ſeveral and private Conferences together between the Lords who came from *Paris*, and thoſe who were in *Jerſey*, they might convert, or confirm each other in the ſame opinions; at leaſt that the next debate might be free from Paſſion and Unkindneſs; and ſo the Council roſe, and the ſeveral Lords betook themſelves to uſe the ſame Arguments, or ſuch as they thought more agreeable to the ſeveral Perſons, as the Lord *Digby* had before done to his Friend, and with the ſame ſucceſs.

The Lord Capel delivers his opinion againſt it.

The next day when they were called together, the Lord *Capel* gave an account of all that had paſſed with the Queen from the time that the Lord *Colepepper* and he came thither; and " that the reaſons they
" had carried from the Prince, had ſo far prevailed
" with the Queen, that her Majeſty reſolved to take
" no final reſolution till ſhe received farther Adver-
" tiſement of the King's pleaſure; and he did not think
" that the information ſhe had received from Mon-
" ſieur *Montrevil*, had weight enough to produce the
" quick reſolution it had done: that he thought it
" ſtill moſt abſolutely neceſſary, to receive the King's
" poſitive Command before the Prince ſhould re-
" move out of his Majeſty's own Dominions; there
" being no ſhadow of cauſe to ſuſpect his ſecurity
" there: That he had then offered to the Queen,
" that he would himſelf make a Journey to *New-*
" *Caſtle* to receive his Majeſty's Commands; and
" that he now made the ſame offer to the Prince; and
" becauſe it did appear that his Majeſty was very

OF THE REBELLION.

"strictly guarded, and that Persons did not easily
"find access to him, and that his own Person might
"be seized upon in his Journey thither, or his stay
"there, or his return back, and so his Highness might
"be disappointed of the Information he expected,
"and remain still in the same uncertainty as to a reso-
"lution, he did propose, and consent to, as his
"opinion, that if he did not return again to *Jersey*
"within the space of one Month, the Prince should
"resolve to remove into *France*, if in the mean time
"such preparatories were made there, as he thought
"were necessary, and were yet defective."

He said, "he had been lately at *Paris* by the
"Prince's Command; and had received many Gra-
"ces from the Queen, who had vouchsafed to im-
"part all her own Reasons for the Prince's remove,
"and the grounds for the confidence she had of the
"Affections of *France*; but, that he did still wonder,
"if the Court of *France* had so great a desire, as was
"pretended, that the Prince of *Wales* should repair
"thither, that in the two Months time his Highness
"had been in *Jersey*, they had never sent a Gentle-
"man to see him, and to invite him to come thither;
"nor had these who came now from the Queen,
"brought so much as a Pass for him to come into
"*France*: that he could not but observe, that all We
"had hitherto proposed to ourselves from *France*,
"had proved in no degree answerable to our expec-
"tations; as the five thousand Foot, which We had
"expected in the West before the Prince came from
"thence; and that We had more reason to be jealous
"now than ever, since it had been by the advice of

266 THE HISTORY

BOOK X.

"*France*, that the King had now put himself into the hands of the *Scots*; and therefore We ought to be the more watchful in the disposing the Person of the Prince by their advice likewise." He concluded, "that he could not give his advice, or consent, that the Prince should repair into *France*, till the King's pleasure might be known, or such other circumstances might be provided in *France*, as had been hitherto neglected."

The Arguments of the Lord Digby and Lord Jermyn for it.

The Lord *Digby* and the Lord *Jermyn* wondered very much, "that there should be any doubt of the affections of *France*, or that it should be believed that the Queen could be deceived, or not well enough informed in that particular:" They related many particulars which had passed between the Cardinal and them in private Conferences, and the great professions of affection he made to the King. They said, "that the Ambassador who was now appointed to go thither, was chosen by the Queen herself, and had no other Instructions but what she had given him; and that he was not to stay there above a Month; at the end of which he was to denounce War against the Parliament, if they did not comply with such Propositions as he made; and so to return; and then, that there should be an Army of thirty thousand Men immediately Transported into *England*, with the Prince of *Wales* in the head of them; that the Ambassador was already gone from *Paris*, but was not to Embark till he should first receive Advertisement that the Prince of *Wales* was landed in *France*; for that *France* had no reason to interest themselves so far

" in the King's Quarrel, if the Prince of *Wales* should
" refuse to venture his Person with them; or, it may
" be, engage against them upon another Interest.
 They therefore besought the Prince, and the Lords
" that they would consider well, whether he would
" disappoint his Father and himself of so great Fruit
" as they were even ready to Gather, and of which
" they could not be disappointed but by unseason-
" able jealousies of the Integrity of *France*, and by
" delaying to give them satisfaction in the remove
" of the Prince from *Jersey*.
 These Arguments pressed with all the assurance imaginable, by Persons of that near Trust and Confidence with the King, who were not like to be deceived Themselves, nor to have any purpose to deceive the Prince, wrought so far with his Highness, that he declared " he would comply with the Com-
" mands of the Queen, and forthwith remove into
" *France*;" which being resolved, he wished " there
" might be no more debate upon that point, but
" that they would all prepare to go with him, and
" that there might be as great an Unity in their Coun-
" sels, as had hitherto always been.
 This so positive Declaration of the Prince of his own Resolution, made all farther Arguments against it not only useless but indecent; and therefore they replied not to that Point, yet every Man of the Council, the Lord *Colepepper* only excepted, besought his Highness, " that he would give them his Pardon,
" if they did not farther wait upon him; for they
" conceived their Commission to be now at an end;
" and that they could not assume any Authority by

The Prince resolves to go into France.

All but one of his Council dissent, and stay behind.

"it to themselves, if they waited upon him into "France; nor expect that their Counsels there "should be hearkened unto, when they were now "rejected." And so, after some sharp replies between the Lords of different Judgments, which made the Council break up the sooner, they who resolved not to go into *France* took their leaves of the Prince, and kissed his hand; his Highness then declaring, "that "he would be gone the next day by five of the "Clock in the Morning." though the cross Winds, and want of some Provisions which were necessary for the Journey detained him there four or five days longer; during which time, the Dissenting Lords every day waited upon him, and were received by him very Graciously; his Highness well knowing and expressing to them a confidence in their Affections, and that they would be sure to wait upon him, whenever his occasions should be ready for their Service. But between them and the other Lords, there grew by degrees so great a strangeness, that, the last day, they did not so much as speak to each other; they who came from the Queen taking it very ill, that the others had presumed to dissent from what her Majesty had so positively Commanded. And though they neither loved their Persons, nor cared for their Company, and without doubt, if they had gone into *France*, would have made them quickly weary of theirs; yet, in that Conjuncture, they believed that the Dissent and Separation of all those Persons who were trusted by the King with the Person of the Prince, would blast their Counsel, and weigh down the single positive Determination of the Queen herself.

On the other side, the others did not think they were treated in that manner as was due to Persons so intrusted; but that in truth many ill consequences would result from that sudden departure of the Prince out of the King's Dominions, where his residence might have been secure in respect of the Affairs of *England*; where, besides the Garrisons of *Scilly* and *Pendennis* (which might always be relieved by Sea) there remained still within his Majesty's Obedience, *Oxford*, *Worcester*, *Wallingford*, *Ludlow*, and some other places of less name; which, upon any divisions among themselves, that were naturally to be expected, might have turned the Scale: Nor did they know, of what ill consequence it might be to the King, that in such a conjuncture the Prince should be removed, when it might be more Counsellable that he should appear in *Scotland*.

Moreover, Mr. *Ashburnham*'s opinion, which he had delivered to the Lord *Capel*, wrought very much upon them; for that a Man so entirely trusted by the King, who had seen him as lately as any Body, should bring no directions from his Majesty to his Son, and that he should believe, that it was fitter for the Prince to stay in *Jersey* than to remove into *France*, till his Majesty's pleasure was better understood, confirmed them in the judgment they had delivered.

But there was another reason that prevailed with those who had been made Privy to it, and which, out of Duty to the Queen, they thought not fit to publish, or insist upon; it was the Instructions given to *Bellievre* (and which too much manifested the irresolution her Majesty had) not to insist upon what they well knew the King would never depart from; for, though that Ambassador was required to do all he could to persuade the Presbyterians to join with the King's Party, and not to insist upon the destruction of the Church, yet if he found that could not be compassed, He was to press, as the advice of the King his Master, his Majesty to part with the Church, and to satisfy the Presbyterians in that point, as the advice of the Queen his Wife, and of his own Party; which method was afterwards observed and pursued by *Bellievre*; which those Lords perfectly abhorred; and thought not fit ever to concur in, or to be privy to those Counsels that had begun, and were to carry on that Confusion.

Within a day or two after the Prince's departure from *Jersey*, the Earl of *Berkshire* left it likewise, and went for *England*; the Lords *Capel, Hopton*, and the Chancellor of the Exchequer, remained together in *Jersey* to expect the King's pleasure, and to attend a conjuncture to appear again in his Majesty's Service; of all which they found an opportunity to inform his Majesty, who very well interpreted all that they had done according to the sincerity of their hearts; yet did believe, that if they had likewise waited upon the Prince into *France*, they might have been able to have prevented or diverted those violent Pressures, which were afterwards made upon him from thence, and gave him more disquiet than he suffered from all the Insolence of his Enemies.

In a word, if the King's Fortune had been farther to be conducted by any fixed Rules of policy and

OF THE REBELLION. 271

discretion, and if the current towards his destruction had not run with such a Torrent, as carried down all obstructions of Sobriety and Wisdom, and made the Confusion inevitable, it is very probable that this so sudden remove of the Prince from *Jersey* with all the Circumstances thereof, might have been looked upon, and Censured with Severity, as an Action that swerved from that prudence which by the fundamental Rules of policy had been long established; but by the Fatal and prodigious Calamities which followed, all Counsels of wise and unwise Men proving equally unsuccessful, the Memory of what had passed before, grew to be the less thought upon and considered.

Whilst these things were thus Transacted in other Parts, the King remained yet in the *Scottish* Army; that People behaving themselves in such a manner, that most Men believed they would never have parted with his Majesty till a full Peace had been made. The Parliament made many sharp Instances " that " the King might be delivered into their hands; " and that the *Scottish* Army would return into " their own Country, having done what they were " sent for, and the War being at an end." To which the Council of *Scotland* seemed to Answer with courage enough, and insisted most on those Arguments of the King's legal Rights, which had been, in all his Majesty's Declarations, urged against the Parliament's proceedings; and which indeed could never be Answered; and as much condemned Them, as the Parliament.

In the mean time, though the King received all

Transactions relating to the King in the Scottish Army.

outward Respect, he was in truth in the condition of a Prisoner; no Servant whom he could Trust suffered to come to him; and though many Persons of Quality who had served the King in the War, when they saw the resolute Answers made by the *Scots,* " that they neither would nor could compel " their King to return to the Parliament, if his Ma- " jesty had no mind to do so, repaired to *New-Castle,* " where his Majesty was," yet none of them were suffered to speak to him; nor could he receive from, or send any Letter to the Queen or Prince; and yet the *Scots* observed all distances, and performed all the Ceremonies as could have been expected if they had indeed treated him as their King; and made as great profession to him of their Duty and good pur- poses, " which they said they would manifest as soon " as it should be seasonable; and then his Servants, " and Friends should repair to him with all Liberty, " and be well received:" and as they endeavoured to persuade the King to expect this from them, so they prevailed with many Officers of that Army, and some of the Nobility, to believe that they meant well, but that it was not yet time to discover their Intentions.

The King sends to the Marquis of Mountrose to disband ; which he did.

Thus they prevailed with the King to send his po- sitive Orders to the Marquis of *Mountrose,* who had indeed done Wonders, to lay down his Arms, and to leave the Kingdom; till when, they pretended they could not declare for his Majesty; and this was done with so much earnestness, and by a parti- cular Messenger known and Trusted, that the Mar- quis obeyed, and Transported himself into *France.*

Then

Then they employed their *Alexander Henderson*, and their other Clergy, to perſuade the King to conſent to the Extirpation of Epiſcopacy in *England*, as he had in *Scotland*; and it was, and is ſtill believed, that if his Majeſty would have been induced to have ſatisfied them in that particular, they would either have had a Party in the Parliament at *Weſtminſter* to have been ſatisfied therewith, or that they would thereupon have declared for the King, and have preſently joined with the Loyal Party in all places for his Majeſty's defence. But the King was too Conſcientious to buy his Peace at ſo Prophane and Sacrilegious a price as was demanded, and he was ſo much too hard for Mr. *Henderſon* in the Argumentation (as appears by the Papers that paſſed between them, which were ſhortly after Communicated to the world) that the old Man himſelf was ſo far Convinced, and Converted, that he had a very deep ſenſe of the miſchief he had himſelf been the Author of, or too much contributed to, and lamented it to his neareſt Friends, and Confidents; and died of grief, and heart-broken, within a very ſhort time after he departed from his Majeſty.

BOOK X.

They employ Henderſon to diſpute with him concerning Church-Government.

Mr. Henderſon dies ſhortly after.

Whilſt the King ſtayed at *New-Caſtle*, *Bellievre* the *French* Ambaſſador, who was ſent from *Paris* after the Prince arrived there, and by whom the Cardinal had promiſed to preſs the Parliament ſo imperiouſly, and to denounce a War againſt them if they refuſed to yield to what was reaſonable towards an Agreement with the King, came to his Majeſty, after he had ſpent ſome time at *London* in all the low Application to the Parliament that can be imagined,

Bellievre's negotiations at London, and with the

BOOK X.

King afterwards at New-Castle.

without any mention of the King with any tenderness, as if his Interest were at all considered by the King his Master, and without any consultation with those of his Majesty's Party; who were then in *London*, and would have been very ready to have advised with him. But he chose rather to converse with the principal Leaders of the Presbyterian Party in the Parliament, and with the *Scottish* Commissioners; from whose Information he took all his Measures; and they assured him "that nothing could be done "for the King, except he would give up the Church; "extirpate Episcopacy; and grant all the Lands be- "longing to Cathedral-Churches to such Uses as the "Parliament should advise;" so that, when he came to the King, he pressed him very earnestly to that Condescension.

But, besides the matter proposed, in which his Majesty was unmoveable, he had no esteem of any thing the Ambassador said to him, having too late discovered the little affection the Cardinal had for him, and which he had too much relied upon. For, as hath been already said, by his advice, and upon his undertaking and assurance that his Majesty should be well received in the *Scottish* Army, and that they would be firm to his Interest, his Majesty had ventured to put himself into their hands; and he was no sooner there, than all they with whom *Montrevil* had Treated, disavowed their undertaking what the King had been informed of; and though the Envoy did avow, and justify, what he had informed the King, to the Faces of the Persons who had given their Engagements, the Cardinal chose rather to

Recal, and Difcountenance the Minifter of that Crown, than to enter into any Expoftulation with the Parliament, or the *Scots*.

The Ambaffador, by an Exprefs, quickly informed the Cardinal that the King was too referved in giving the Parliament fatisfaction; and therefore wifhed, " that fome Body might be fent over, who was like " to have fo much credit with his Majefty as to per- " fuade him to what was neceffary for his Service." Upon which, the Queen, who was never advifed by thofe who either underftood, or valued his true Intereft, confulted with thofe about her; and fent Sir *William Davenant*, an honeft Man, and a Witty, but in all refpects inferior to fuch a Truft, with a Letter of credit to the King (who knew the Perfon well enough under another Character than was like to give him much credit in the Argument in which he was inftructed) although her Majefty had likewife other ways declared her opinion to his Majefty, " that he fhould part with the Church for his Peace " and Security."

Sir *William Davenant* had, by the countenance of the *French* Ambaffador, eafy admiffion to the King; who heard him patiently all he had to fay, and anfwered him in that manner that made it evident he was not pleafed with the advice. When he found his Majefty unfatisfied, and that he was not like to confent to what was fo earneftly defired by them by whofe advice he was fent, who undervalued all thofe fcruples of Confcience which his Majefty himfelf was ftrongly poffeffed with, he took upon himfelf the confidence to offer fome Reafons to the King to

Sir William Davenant fent from the Queen to the King to perfuade him to give up the Church.

induce him to yield to what was propofed; and, among other things, faid, "it was the advice and opinion of all his Friends;" his Majefty afking, "what Friends?" and he anfwering, "that it was the opinion of the Lord *Jermyn*," the King faid, "that the Lord *Jermyn* did not underftand any thing of the Church. The other faid, the Lord *Colepepper* was of the fame mind." The King faid, *Colepepper* had no Religion: and afked, "whether the Chancellor of the Exchequer was of that mind?" to which he anfwered, "he did not know; for that he was not there, and had deferted the Prince:" and thereupon, faid fomewhat from the Queen of the difpleafure fhe had conceived againft the Chancellor; to which the King faid, "the Chancellor was an honeft Man, and would never defert Him, nor the Prince, nor the Church; and that he was forry he was not with his Son;" but that his Wife was miftaken. *Davenant* then offering fome reafons of his own, in which he mentioned the Church flightingly, as if it were not of Importance enough to weigh down the benefit that would attend the conceffion, his Majefty was tranfported with fo much indignation, that he gave him a fharper reprehenfion than was ufual for him to give to any other Man; and forbid him to prefume to come again into his Prefence. Whereupon the poor Man, who had in truth very good Affections, was exceedingly dejected and afflicted; and returned into *France*, to give an Account of his ill Succefs to thofe who fent him.

As all Men's expectations from the Courage and

Activity of the *French* Ambaſſador in *England*, were thus fruſtrated, by his mean and low Carriage both towards the Parliament and at *New-Caſtle*, ſo all the profeſſions which had been made of reſpect and tenderneſs towards the Prince of *Wales*, when his Perſon ſhould once appear in *France*, were as unworthily diſappointed. The Prince had been above two Months with the Queen his Mother, before any Notice was taken of his being in *France*, by the leaſt Meſſage ſent from the Court to Congratulate his arrival there; but that time was ſpent in debating the Formalities of his Reception; how the King ſhould treat him? and how he ſhould behave himſelf towards the King? whether he ſhould take place of Monſieur the King's Brother? and what kind of Ceremonies ſhould be obſerved between the Prince of *Wales*, and his Uncle the Duke of *Orleans*? and many ſuch other particulars; in all which they were reſolved to give the Law themſelves; and which had been fitter to have been adjuſted in *Jerſey*, before he put himſelf into their Power, than diſputed afterwards in the Court of *France*; from which there could be then no Appeal.

The Prince's treatment when He came into France.

There can be no doubt but that the Cardinal, who was the ſole Miniſter of State, and directed all that was to be done, and dictated all that was to be ſaid, did think the preſence of the Prince there of the higheſt importance to their affairs, and did all that was in his Power, to perſuade the Queen that it was as neceſſary for the affairs of the King her Huſband, and of her Majeſty: but now that work was over, and the Perſon of the Prince brought into their power, without the least public Act or Ceremony to invite him thither, it was no less his care that the Parliament in *England*, and the Officers of the Army, whom he feared more than the Parliament, should believe that the Prince came thither without their wish, and in truth against their will; that the Crown of *France* could not refuse to interpose, and mediate, to make up the difference between the Parliament and the *Scottish* Nation, and that the Kingdoms might be restored to Peace; but that when they had performed that Office of Mediation, they had performed their Function; and that they would no more presume to take upon them to judge between the Parliament and the *Scots*, than they had done between the King and the Parliament; and that since the Prince had come to the Queen his Mother, from which they could not reasonably restrain him, it should not be attended with any prejudice to the Peace of *England*; nor should he there find any means, or assistance, to disturb it. And it was believed by those who stood at no great distance from affairs, that the Cardinal then laid the Foundation for that Friendship which was shortly after built up between him and *Cromwell*, by promising "that they should "receive less inconvenience by the Prince's remain-"ing in *France*, than if he were in any other part of "*Europe*." And it can hardly be believed, with how little respect they treated him during the whole time of his stay there. They were very careful that he might not be looked upon as supported by them either according to his Dignity, or for the maintenance of his Family; but a mean addition to the Pen-sion, which the Queen had before, was made to her Majesty, without any mention of the Prince her Son; who was wholly to depend upon her Bounty, without power to gratify and oblige any of his own Servants; that they likewise might depend only upon the Queen's goodness and favor, and so behave themselves accordingly.

When the *Scots* had secured the peace and quiet of their own Country, by Disbanding the Forces under the Marquis of *Mountrose*, and by his Transporting himself beyond the Seas, and by putting to death several Persons of Name who had followed the Marquis, and had been taken Prisoners, among whom Sir *Robert Spotswood* was one, a worthy honest Loyal Gentleman, and as wise a Man as that Nation had at that time (whom the King had made Secretary of State of that Kingdom, in the place of the Earl of *Lanrick*, who was then in Arms against him; which, it may be, was a principal cause that the other was put to death) And when they had with such Solemnity and Resolution made it plain and evident, that they could not, without the most barefaced violation of their Faith and Allegiance, and of the fundamental principle of Christian Religion, ever deliver up their Native King, who had put himself into their hands, into the hands of the Parliament, against his own Will and Consent: And when the Earl of *Lowden* had publicly declared to the two Houses of Parliament in a Conference, "that an Eternal Infamy
" would lie upon them, and the whole Nation, if
" they should deliver the Person of the King; the
" securing of which was equally their Duty, as it

"was the Parliament's, and the difpofal of his Perfon
"in order to that fecurity did equally belong to
"Them as to the Parliament; however, they faid,
"they would ufe all the perfuafion, and all the im-
"portunity they could with the King that his Ma-
"jefty might yield, and confent to the propofitions
"the Parliament had fent to him."

The Parliament had, upon the firft notice of the King's being arrived in the *Scottifh* Army, fent a pofitive Command to the Committee of both Kingdoms refiding in the *Scottifh* Army, that the Perfon of the King fhould be forthwith fent to *Warwick*-Caftle; but the *Scots*, who apprehended they could not be long without fuch an Order, had, within two days after his Majefty's coming to them, and after he had caufed *Newark* to be delivered up, with wonderful expedition marched towards *New-Caftle*; and were arrived there before they received that Order for fending his Majefty to *Warwick*; which proceeding of theirs, pleafed his Majefty very well, among many other things which difpleafed him; and perfuaded him, that though they would obferve their own method, they would, in the end, do fomewhat for his Service.

Upon the receiving that Order, they renewed their profeffions to the Parliament of obferving punctually all that had been agreed between them; and befought them, "that fince they had promifed the King, before
"he left *Oxford*, to fend Propofitions to him, they
"would now do it; and faid, 'that if he refufed to
"comply with them, to which they fhould perfuade
"him, they knew what they were to do." Then

they advised the King, and prevailed with him, to send Orders to the Governor of *Oxford* to make conditions, and to surrender that place (where his Son the Duke of *York* was, and all the Council) into the hands of *Fairfax*, who with his Army then besieged them: and likewise to publish a general Order (which they caused to be printed) " that all Governors of
" any Garrisons for his Majesty, should immediately
" deliver them up to the Parliament upon fair and
" honorable Conditions, since his Majesty resolved in
" all things to be advised by his Parliament; and till
" this was done, they said, they could not declare
" themselves in that manner for his Majesty's Service,
" and Interest, as they resolved to do; for that they
" were, by their Treaty and Confederacy, to serve
" the Parliament in such manner as they should direct,
" until the War should be ended; but, that done they
" had no more obligations to the Parliament; and that,
" when his Majesty had no more Forces on foot, nor
" Garrisons which held out for him, it could not be
" denied but that the War was at an end; and then
" they could speak and expostulate with freedom."
By which arts, they prevailed with the King to send, and publish such Orders as aforesaid: and which indeed, as the case then stood, he could have received little benefit by not publishing.

BOOK X.

The King, upon the Scots desire sends Orders for the Surrender of Oxford, and all his other Garrisons.

The Parliament was contented, as the more expedite way (though they were much offended at the presumption of the *Scots* in neglecting to send the King to *Warwick*) to send their Propositions to the King (which they knew his Majesty would never grant) by Commissioners of both Houses, who

The Parliament, upon the Scots request, sends Propositions of Peace to the King at Newcastle; about the end of July.

had no other Authority, or Power, than " to demand a positive Answer from the King in ten days, and then to return." These Propositions were delivered about the end of *July;* and contained such an eradication of the Government of the Church and State, that the King told them, " he knew not " what Answer to make to them, till he should be " informed what Power or Authority they had left " to him, and his Heirs, when he had given all that " to them which they desired." He desired, "that he " might be removed to some of his own Houses, and " that he might reside there till, upon a Personal " Treaty with his Parliament, such an agreement " might be established as the Kingdom might enjoy " peace and happiness under it; which, he was sure, " it could never do by the concessions they pro- " posed."

The *Scots*, who were enough convinced that his Majesty could never be wrought upon to sacrifice the Church to their wild lusts and impiety, were as good as their words to the Parliament, and used all the rude importunity and Threats to his Majesty, to persuade him freely to consent to all: though they confessed " that the Propositions were higher in " many things than they approved of, yet they saw " no other means for him to close with his Parlia- " ment, than by granting what they required."

The Chancellor of *Scotland* told him, " that the " consequence of his Answer to the Propositions, " was as great, as the ruin, or preservation of his " Crown or Kingdoms: That the Parliament after " many bloody Battles, had got the strong-holds and

"Forts of the Kingdom into their hands: that they
"had his Revenue, Excise, Assessments, Sequestra-
"tions, and power to raise all the Men and Money
"of the Kingdom: that they had gained Victory
"over all, and that they had a strong Army to
"maintain it; so that they might do what they would
"with Church or State: that they desired neither
"Him, nor any of his Race, longer to Reign over
"them; and had sent these Propositions to his Ma-
"jesty, without the granting whereof, the Kingdom
"and his People could not be in safety: that if he
"refused to Assent, he would lose all his Friends in
"Parliament, lose the City, and lose the Country;
"and that all *England* would join against him as one
"Man to process, and depose him, and to set up
"another Government; and so, that both King-
"doms, for either's safety, would agree to settle
"Religion and Peace without him, to the ruin of his
"Majesty, and his Posterity: and concluded, that
"if he left *England*, he would not be admitted to
"come and Reign in *Scotland*."

And it is very true that the General Assembly of the Kirk, which was then sitting in *Scotland*, had petitioned the Conservators of the Peace of the Kingdom, "that if the King should refuse to give satisfac-
"tion to his Parliament, he might not be permitted
"to come into *Scotland*." This kind of Argumentation did more provoke than persuade the King; he told them, with great Resolution, and Magnanimity, "that no condition they could reduce him to, could
"be half so miserable, and grievous to him, as that
"which they would persuade him to reduce himself
"to; and therefore, bid them proceed their own

His Majesty's Answer to them.

BOOK X.

The Parliament require the Scots to quit the Kingdom and to deliver up the Person of the King.

"way; and that though They had all forsaken him, "God had not."

The Parliament had now received the Answer they expected; and, forthwith, required "the *Scots* "to quit the Kingdom, and to deliver the Person of "the King to such Persons as they should appoint to "receive him;" who should attend upon his Majesty from *New-Castle* to *Holmby*, a House of his at a small distance from *Northampton*, a Town and Country of very eminent disaffection to the King throughout the War; and declared "that his Majesty should be "treated with respect to the safety and preservation "of his Person, according to the Covenant: and "that after his coming to *Holmby*, he should be "attended by such as they should appoint; and "that when the *Scots* were removed out of *England*, "the Parliament would join with their Brethren of "*Scotland*, again to persuade the King to pass the "Propositions; which if he refused to do, the "House would do nothing that might break the "Union of the two Kingdoms, but would endeavour "to preserve the same."

The *Scots* now begun again to talk sturdily, and denied "that the Parliament of *England* had power ab- "solutely to dispose of the Person of the King without "their approbation;" and the Parliament as loudly replied, "that they had nothing to do in *England*, "but to observe their Orders;" and added such Threats to their Reasons, as might let them see they had a great contempt of their power, and would exact obedience from them, if they refused to yield it. But these discourses were only kept up till they could adjust all Accounts between them, and agree what price they should pay for the delivery of His Person whom one side was resolved to have, and the other as resolved not to keep; and so they agreed; and, upon the payment of two hundred thousand pounds in hand, and security for as much more upon days agreed upon, the *Scots* delivered the King up into such hands as the Parliament appointed to receive Him.

{BOOK X. *The Scots agree to deliver up the King.*}

In this infamous manner that excellent Prince was, in the end of *January*, given up, by his *Scottish* Subjects, to those of his *English* who were intrusted by the Parliament to receive Him; which had appointed a Committee of Lords and Commons to go to the place agreed upon with a Party of Horse and Foot of the Army, which were subject to the Orders of that Committee; and the Committee itself to go to *New-Castle* to receive that Town as well as the King; where, and to whom, his Majesty was delivered.

They received Him with the same formality of respect as he had been treated with by the *Scots*, and with the same strictness restrained all resort of those to his Majesty, who were of doubtful Affections to them, and their Cause. Servants were particularly appointed, and named by the Parliament, to attend upon his Person, and Service, in all relations; amongst which, in the first place, they preferred those who had faithfully adhered to them against their Master; and, where such were wanting, they found others who had manifested their Affection to them. And, in this distribution, the Presbyterian Party in the Houses did what they pleased, and were thought to govern all. The Independents craftily letting them enjoy that confidence of their power and interest, till

{*The Committee appointed by the Parliament receive the King at New-Castle in the end of January. Servants appointed by the Parliament to attend his Majesty.*}

they had difmiffed their Friends, the *Scots*, out of the Kingdom; and permitting them to put Men of their principles about the Perfon of the King, and to chufe fuch a Guard as they could confide in, to attend his Majefty.

Of the Committee employed to govern and direct all, Major-General *Brown* was one, who had a great Name and Intereft in the City, and with all the Perfbyterian Party, and had done great Service to the Parliament in the War under the Earl of *Effex*, and was a diligent and ftout Commander. In this manner, and with this attendance, his Majefty was brought to his own Houfe at *Holmby* in *Northamptonfhire*; a place he had taken much delight in: And there he was to ftay till the Parliament and the Army (for the Army now took upon them to have a fhare, and to give their opinion in the Settlement that fhould be made) fhould determine what fhould be farther done.

In the mean time, the Committee paid all refpects to his Majefty; and he enjoyed thofe Exercifes he moft delighted in; and feemed to have all liberty, but to confer with Perfons he moft defired, and to have fuch Servants about him as he could truft. That which moft difpleafed him, was, that they would not permit him to have his own Chaplains; but ordered Prefbyterian Minifters to attend for Divine Service; and his Majefty, utterly refufing to be prefent at their Devotions, was compelled at thofe hours to be his own Chaplain in his Bed-Chamber; where he conftantly ufed the Common-Prayer by himfelf. His Majefty bore this conftraint fo heavily that he writ a Letter to the House of Peers, in which he inclosed a List of the Names of thirteen of his Chaplains; any two of which he desired might have liberty to attend him for his Devotion. To which, after many days consideration, they returned this Answer; "that all those Chaplains were disaffected to the "Established Government of the Church, and had "not taken the Covenant; but that there were "others who had, who, if his Majesty pleased, "should be sent to him." After this Answer, his Majesty thought it to no purpose to importune them farther in that particular; but, next to the having his own Chaplains, he would have been best pleased to have been without any; they who were sent by them, being Men of mean Parts and of most impertinent and troublesome Confidence and Importunity.

The King desires certain of his Chaplains; is refused.

Whilst those Disputes continued between the Parliament and the *Scots* concerning the King's Person, the Army proceeded with great Success in reducing those Garrisons which still continued in his Majesty's Obedience; whereof though some Surrendered more easily and with less resistance than they might have made, satisfying themselves with the King's general Order, and that there was no reasonable expectation of Relief, and therefore that it would not be amiss, by an early submission, to obtain better Conditions for themselves; yet others defended themselves with notable Obstinacy to the last, to the great damage of the Enemy, and to the detaining the Army from Uniting together; without which they could not pursue the great designs they had. And this was one of the reasons that made the Treaty with the *Scots*

Divers Garrisons Surrendered to the Parliament.

depend so long, and that the Presbyterians continued their Authority and Credit so long; and We may observe again, that those Garrisons which were maintained, and defended with the greatest Courage and Virtue, in the end, obtained as good and as honorable Conditions, as any of those who Surrendered upon the first Summons.

This was the Case of *Ragland* and *Pendennis*-Castles; which endured the longest Sieges, and held out the last of any Forts or Castles in *England*; being bravely defended by two Persons of very great Age; but were at length delivered up within a day or two of each other. *Ragland* was maintained, with extraordinary Resolution and Courage, by the old Marquis of *Worcester*, against *Fairfax* himself, till it was reduced to the utmost Necessity. *Pendennis* refused all Summons; admitting no Treaty, till all their Provisions were so far consumed, that they had not Victual left for four-and-twenty hours; and then they treated, and carried themselves in the Treaty with such Resolution, and Unconcernedness, that the Enemy concluded they were in no straits; and so gave them the Conditions they proposed; which were as good as any Garrison in *England* had accepted. This Castle was defended by the Governor thereof, *John Arundel* of *Trerice* in *Cornwall*, an old Gentleman of near fourscore years of Age, and of one of the best Estates and Interest in that County; who, with the Assistance of his Son *Richard Arundel* (who was then a Colonel in the Army; a stout and diligent Officer; and was by the King after his Return made a Baron, Lord *Arundel* of *Trerice*, in memory

of

of his Father's Service, and his own eminent behaviour throughout the War) maintained, and defended the same to the last extremity.

There remained with him in that Service many Gentlemen of the Country of great Loyalty, amongst whom Sir *Henry Killigrew* was one; who, being an intimate Friend of the Chancellor of the Exchequer, resolved to go to *Jersey*; and, as soon as the Castle was surrendered, took the first opportunity of a Vessel then in the Harbour of *Falmouth*, to Transport himself with some Officers and Soldiers to St. *Maloes* in *Britany*; from whence he writ to the Chancellor in *Jersey*, that he would procure a Bark of that Island to go to St. *Maloes* to fetch him thither; which, by the kindness of Sir *George Carteret*, was presently sent, with a longing desire to receive him into that Island; the two Lords *Capel* and *Hopton*, and the Governor, having an extraordinary affection for him, as well as the Chancellor. Within two days after, upon view of the Vessel at Sea (which they well knew) they all made haste to the Harbour to receive their Friend; but, when they came thither, to their infinite regret they found his Body there in a Coffin, he having died at St. *Maloes* within a day after he had written his Letter.

After the Treaty was signed for delivering the Castle, he had walked out to discharge some Arms which were in his Chamber; among which, a Carabine that had been long charged, in the shooting off, broke; and a splinter of it struck him in the forehead; which, though it drew much Blood, was not apprehended by him to be of any danger;

so that his Friends could not perfuade him to ftay there till the wound was cured; but, the Blood being ftopped, and the Surgeon having bound it up, he profecuted his intended Voyage; and at his landing at St. *Maloes*, he writ that Letter; believing his wound would give him little trouble. But his Letter was no fooner gone than he fent for a Surgeon; who, opening the wound, found it was very deep and dangerous; and the next day he died, having defired that his dead Body might be fent to *Jerfey*; where he was decently buried. He was a very Gallant Gentleman, of a noble Extraction, and a fair Revenue in Land; of excellent Parts and Courage; he had one only Son, who was killed before him in a Party that fell upon the Enemies Quarters near *Bridgewater*; where he behaved himfelf with remarkable Courage, and was generally lamented.

Sir *Henry* was of the Houfe of Commons; and though he had no other relation to the Court than the having many Friends there, as wherever he was known he was exceedingly beloved, he was moft zealous and paffionate in oppofing all the extravagant proceedings of the Parliament. And when the Earl of *Effex* was chofen General, and the feveral Members of the Houfe ftood up, and declared, what Horfe they would raife, and maintain, and that they would live and die with the Earl their General, one faying he would raife ten Horfes, and another twenty, He ftood up and faid, " he would provide " a good Horfe, and a good Buff-Coat, and a good " pair of Piftols, and then he doubted not but he " fhould find a good Caufe;" and fo went out of the House, and rode Post into *Cornwall*, where his Estate and Interest lay; and there joined with those Gallant Gentlemen his Friends, who first received the Lord *Hopton*, and raised those Forces which did so many famous Actions in the West.

He would never take any Command in the Army; but they who had, consulted with no Man more. He was in all Actions, and in those places where was most danger, having great Courage and a pleasantness of humor in Danger that was very exemplary; and they who did not do their duty, took care not to be within his view; for he was a very sharp Speaker, and cared not for angering those who deserved to be reprehended. The *Arundels, Trelawnies, Slannings, Trevanions*, and all the signal Men of that County, infinitely loved his Spirit, and Sincerity, and his Credit and Interest had a great influence upon all but those who did not love the King; and to those, he was very terrible; and exceedingly hated by them; and not loved by Men of moderate Tempers; for he thought all such prepared to Rebel, when a little Success should encourage them; and was many times too much offended with Men who wished well, and whose Constitutions and Complections would not permit them to express the same franknefs, which his Nature and keenness of Spirit could not suppress. His loss was much lamented by all good Men.

From the time that the King was brought to *Holmby*, and whilst he stayed there, he was afflicted with the same pressures concerning the Church, which had disquieted him at *New-Castle*; the Parli-

BOOK X.

ament not remitting any of their Infolencies in their Demands: all which was imputed to the Prefbyterians, who were thought to exercife the whole Power, and begun to give Orders for the leffening their great Charge by difbanding fome Troops of their Army, and fending others for *Ireland*; which they made no doubt fpeedily to Reduce; and declared, "that they would then difband all Armies, "that the Kingdom might be governed by the "known Laws."

Differences arife between the Parliament and the Army.

This temper in the Houfes raifed another Spirit in the Army; which did neither like the Prefbyterian Government that they faw ready to be fettled in the Church, nor that the Parliament fhould fo abfolutely difpofe of them, by whom they had gotten power to do all they had done; and *Cromwell*, who had the fole influence upon the Army, under hand, made them Petition the Houfes againft any thing that was done contrary to his opinion. He himfelf, and his Officers, took upon them to Preach and Pray publicly to their Troops; and admitted few or no Chaplains in the Army, but fuch as bitterly inveighed againft the Prefbyterian Government, as more Tyrannical than Epifcopacy; and the Common-Soldiers, as well as the Officers, did not only Pray, and Preach among themfelves, but went up into the Pulpits in all Churches, and Preached to the People; who quickly became infpired with the fame Spirit; Women as well as Men taking upon them to Pray and Preach; which made as great a noife and confufion in all opinions concerning Religion, as there was in the Civil Government of the State; fcarce

Divers Sects increafe in the Army.

any Man being suffered to be called in question for delivering any opinion in Religion, by speaking or writing, how Prophane, Heretical, or Blasphemous soever it was; " which," they said, " was to restrain " the Spirit."

Liberty of Conscience was now the Common Argument and Quarrel, whilst the Presbyterian Party proceeded with equal bitterness against the several Sects as Enemies to all Godliness, as they had done, and still continued to do, against the Prelatical Party; and finding themselves superior in the two Houses, little doubted, by their Authority and Power there, to be able to reform the Army, and to new-model it again; which they would, no doubt, have attempted, if it had not pleased God to have taken away the Earl of *Essex* some Months before this; who died without being sensible of sickness, in a time when he might have been able to have undone much of the mischief he had formerly wrought; to which he had great inclinations; and had indignation enough for the indignities himself had received from the ungrateful Parliament, and wonderful apprehension, and detestation of the ruin he saw like to befal the King, and the Kingdom. And it is very probable, considering the present temper of the City at that time, and of the two Houses, he might, if he had lived, have given some check to the rage and fury that then prevailed. But God would not suffer a Man, who, out of the pride and vanity of his nature, rather than the wickedness of his heart, had been made an Instrument of so much mischief, to have any share in so glorious a work: though his consti-

The Earl of Essex died in Sept. this year.

tution, and temper, might very well incline him to the Lethargic indisposition of which he died, yet it was loudly said by many of his Friends, " that " he was Poisoned."

Sure it is that *Cromwell*, and his Party (for he was now declared head of the Army, though *Fairfax* continued General in Name) were wonderfully exalted with his death; he being the only Person whose Credit and Interest they feared without any esteem of his Person.

And now, that they might more substantially enter into dispute, and competition with the Parliament, and go a share with them in settling the Kingdom (as they called it) the Army erected a kind of Parliament among themselves. They had from the time of the defeat of the King's Army, and when they had no more Enemy to contend with in the Field, and after they had purged their Army of all those inconvenient Officers, of whose entire submission, and obedience to all their dictates, they had not confidence, set aside, in effect, their self-denying Ordinance, and got their principal Officers of the Army, and others of their Friends, whose principles they well knew, to be elected Members of the House of Commons into their places who were dead, or who had been expelled by them for adhering to the King. By this means, *Fairfax* himself, *Ireton*, *Harrison*, and many other of the Independents, Officers and Gentlemen, of the several Counties, who were transported with new fancies in Religion, and were called by a new name *Fanatics*, sat in the House of Commons; notwithstanding all which, the Presbyterians still carried it.

But about this time, that they might be upon a nearer Level with the Parliament, the Army made choice of a number of such Officers as they liked; which they called the General's Council of Officers; who were to resemble the House of Peers; and the Common-Soldiers made choice of three or four of each Regiment, most Corporals or Serjeants, few or none above the degree of an Ensign, who were called Agitators, and were to be as a House of Commons to the Council of Officers. These two Representatives met severally, and considered of all the Acts and Orders made by the Parliament towards settling the Kingdom, and towards reforming, dividing, or disbanding of the Army: and, upon mutual Messages and Conferences between each other, they resolved in the first place, and declared, "that they " would not be divided, or disbanded, before their full " Arrears were paid, and before full Provision was " made for Liberty of Conscience; which, they said, " was the ground of the Quarrel, and for which so " many of their Friends lives had been lost, and so " much of their own Blood had been spilt; and that " hitherto there was so little security provided in that " point, that there was a greater persecution now " against Religious and Godly Men, than ever had " been in the King's Government, when the Bishops " were their Judges.

They said, "they did not look upon themselves as " a Band of *Janizaries*, hired and entertained only to " Fight their Battles; but that they had voluntarily " taken up Arms for the Liberty and Defence of the " Nation of which they were a part; and before they "laid down those Arms, they would see all those ends well provided for, that the People might not hereafter undergo those grievances which they had formerly suffered. They complained that some Members of the Army had been sent for by the Parliament, and committed to Prison, which was against their Privilege; since all Soldiers ought to be tried by a Council of War, and not by any other Judicatory; and therefore they desired redress in these, and many other particulars of as ungrateful a Nature; and that such as were Imprisoned and in Custody, might be forthwith set at liberty; without which they could not think themselves justly dealt with:" and with this Declaration and address, they sent three or four of their own Members to the House of Commons; who delivered it at the Bar with wonderful Confidence.

The Soldiers published a vindication, as they called it, of their Proceedings and Resolutions, and directed it to their General; in which they complained of a design to disband, and new-model the Army; "which," they said, "was a Plot contrived by some Men who had lately tasted of Sovereignty; and, being lifted up above the ordinary Sphere of Servants, endeavoured to become Masters, and were degenerated into Tyrants." They therefore declared, "that they would neither be employed for the Service of *Ireland*, nor suffer themselves to be disbanded, till their desires were granted, and the Rights and Liberties of the Subjects should be vindicated, and maintained." This Apology, or Vindication, being signed by many inferior Officers, the Parliament declared them to be Enemies to the State; and caused some of them, who talked loudest, to be imprisoned. Upon which a new Address was made to their General; wherein they complained "how disdainfully they were used by the Parliament, "for whom they had ventured their Lives, and lost "their Blood: that the Privileges which were due "to them as Soldiers, and as Subjects, were taken "from them; and when they complained of the "Injuries they received they were abused, beaten, "and dragged into Goals.

Hereupon, the General was prevailed with to write a Letter to a Member of Parliament, who showed it to the House; in which he took notice of several Petitions, which were prepared in the City of *London*, and some other Counties of the Kingdom against the Army; and "that it was looked upon as "very strange, that the Officers of the Army might "not be permitted to petition, when so many Pe- "titions were received against them; and that "he much doubted that the Army might draw to a "Rendezvous, and think of some other way for "their own vindication.

This manner of proceeding by the Soldiers, but especially the General seeming to be of their mind, troubled the Parliament; yet they resolved not to suffer their Counsels to be censured, or their Actions controlled, by those who were retained by them, and who lived upon their pay. And therefore, after many high Expressions against the presumption of several Officers and Soldiers, they declared, "that who- "soever should refuse, being commanded, to engage "himself in the Service of *Ireland*, should be disbanded." The Army was resolved not to be subdued in their first so declared Resolution, and fell into a direct and high Mutiny, and called for the Arrears of pay due to them; which they knew where and how to Levy for themselves; nor could they be in any degree appeased, till the Declaration that the Parliament had made against them, was rased out of the Journal-Book of both Houses, and a Month's pay sent to them; nor were they satisfied with all this, but talked very loud, "that they knew how to make themselves as considerable as the Parliament, and where to have their Service better valued, and rewarded;" which so frighted those at *Westminster*, that they appointed a Committee of Lords and Commons, whereof some were very acceptable to the Army, to go to them, and to treat with a Committee chosen of the Officers of the Army, upon the best expedients that might be applied to the composing these distempers. Now the Army thought itself upon a Level with the Parliament, when they had a Committee of the one authorized to treat with a Committee of the other; which likewise raised the Spirits of *Fairfax*, who had never thought of opposing or disobeying the Parliament; and disposed him to more concurrence with the impetuous humor of the Army, when he saw it was so much complied with and submitted to by all Men.

Cromwell, hitherto, carried himself with that rare dissimulation (in which sure he was a very great Master) that he seemed exceedingly incensed against this Insolence of the Soldiers; was still in the House of Commons when any such Addresses were made; and inveighed bitterly against the presumption, and had been the Cause of the Commitment, of some of the Officers. He proposed, "that the General might "be sent down to the Army;" who, he said, "would "conjure down this mutinous Spirit quickly;" and he was so easily believed, that he himself was sent once or twice to compose the Army; where after he had stayed two or three days, he would again return to the House, and complain heavily "of the "great Licence that was got into the Army; that, "for his own part, by the Artifice of his Enemies, "and of those who desired that the Nation should "be again imbrewed in Blood, he was rendered so "odious unto them, that they had a purpose to kill "him, if, upon some discovery made to him, he had "not escaped out of their hands." And in these, and the like discourses, when he spake of the Nation's being to be involved in new troubles, he would weep bitterly, and appear the most afflicted Man in the world with the sense of the Calamities which were like to ensue. But, as many of the wiser sort had long discovered his wicked intentions, so his hypocrisy could not longer be concealed. The most active Officers and Agitators were known to be his own Creatures, and such who neither did, nor would do, any thing but by his direction. So that it was privately resolved by the principal Persons of the House of Commons, that when he came the next day into the House, which he seldom omitted to do, they would send him to the Tower; presuming, that if they had once severed his Person from the

Army, they should easily reduce it to its former temper and obedience. For they had not the least jealousy of the General *Fairfax*, whom they knew to be a perfect Presbyterian in his Judgment; and that *Cromwell* had the Ascendant over him purely by his Dissimulation, and pretence of Conscience and Sincerity. There is no doubt *Fairfax* did not then, nor long after, believe, that the other had those wicked designs in his heart against the King, or the least imagination of disobeying the Parliament.

This purpose of seizing upon the Person of *Cromwell* could not be carried so secretly, but that he had notice of it; and the very next morning after he had so much lamented his desperate misfortune in having lost all reputation, and credit, and authority in the Army, and that his life would be in danger if he were with it, when the House expected every minute his presence, they were informed that he was met out of the Town by break of day, with one Servant only, on the way to the Army; where he had appointed a Rendezvous of some Regiments of the Horse, and from whence he writ a Letter to the House of Commons, "that having the night before received a Letter from some Officers of his own Regiment, that the jealousy the Troops had conceived of him, and of his want of kindness towards them, was much abated, so that they believed, if he would be quickly present with them, they would all in a short time by his advice be reclaimed, upon this he had made all the haste he could; and did find that the Soldiers had been abused by misinformation; and that he hoped to discover the

"Fountain from whence it Sprung; and in the mean time defired that the General, and the other Officers in the Houfe, and fuch as remained about the Town, might be prefently fent to their Quarters; and that he believed it would be very neceffary in order to the fuppreffion of the late diftempers, and for the prevention of the like for the time to come, that there might be a general Rendezvous of the Army; of which the General would beft confider, when he came down; which he wifhed might be haftened." It was now to no purpofe to difcover what they had formerly intended, or that they had any jealoufy of a Perfon who was out of their reach; and fo they expected a better conjuncture; and in few days after, the General and the other Officers left the Town, and went to their Quarters.

The fame Morning that *Cromwell* left *London*, Cornet *Joyce*, who was one of the Agitators in the Army, a Taylor, a fellow who had two or three years before ferved in a very Inferior employment in Mr. *Hollis'* Houfe, came with a Squadron of fifty Horfe to *Holmby*, where the King was, about the break of day; and, without any interruption by the Guard of Horfe and Foot which waited there, came with two or three more, and knocked at the King's Chamber-door, and faid, "he muft prefently fpeak with the King." His Majefty, furprifed with the manner of it, rofe out of his bed; and, half dreffed, caufed the door to be opened, which he knew otherwife would be quickly broken open; they who waited in the Chamber being Perfons of whom he

Cornet Joyce feized upon the King at Holmby June 3. 1647.

had little knowledge, and lefs confidence. As foon as the door was opened, *Joyce*, and two or three more, came into the Chamber, with their Hats off, and Piftols in their hands. *Joyce* told the King, "that he muft go with him." His Majefty afked, "whither?" he anfwered, "to the Army." The King afked him, "where the Army was?" he faid, "they would carry him to the Place where it was." His Majefty afked, "by what Authority they came?" *Joyce* anfwered, "by this;" and fhowed him his Piftol; and defired his Majefty, "that he would caufe himfelf to be dreffed, becaufe it was neceffary they fhould make hafte." None of the other Soldiers fpoke a word; and *Joyce*, faving the bluntnefs, and pofitivenefs of the few words he fpoke, behaved himfelf not rudely. The King faid, "he could not ftir before he fpoke with the Committee to whom he had been delivered, and who were trufted by the Parliament;" and fo appointed one of thofe who waited upon him, to call them. The Committee had been as much furprifed with the noife as the King had been, and quickly came to his Chamber, and afked *Joyce*, "whether he had any Orders from the Parliament?" he faid, No. "From the General? No." What Authority he came by? to which he made no other Anfwer, than he had made to the King, and held up his Piftol. They faid, "they would write to the Parliament to know their pleafure;" *Joyce* faid, "they might do fo, but the King muft prefently go with him." Colonel *Brown* had fent for fome of the Troops who were appointed for the King's Guard, but they came not; he fpoke

OF THE REBELLION.

then with the Officer who Commanded thofe who were at that time upon the Guard, and found that they would make no refiftance: fo that after the King had made all the delays he conveniently could, without giving them caufe to believe that he was refolved not to have gone, which had been to no purpofe, and after he had broken his Faft, he went into his Coach, attended by the few Servants who were put about him, and went whither Cornet *Joyce* would Conduct him; there being no part of the Army known to be within twenty Miles of *Holmby* at that time; and that which adminiftered moft caufe of apprehenfion, was, that thofe Officers who were of the Guard, declared " that the Squadron which was Commanded " by *Joyce*, confifted not of Soldiers of any one Re- " giment, but were Men of feveral Troops, and " feveral Regiments, drawn together under him, " who was not the proper Officer;" fo that the King did in truth believe, that their purpofe was to carry him to fome place where they might more conveniently murder him. The Committee quickly gave notice to the Parliament of what had paffed, with all the circumftances; and it was received with all imaginable confternation; nor could any Body imagine what the purpofe and refolution was.

The Committee give notice of it.

Nor were they at the more eafe, or in any degree pleafed with the Account they received from the General himfelf; who, by his Letter, informed them, " that the Soldiers at *Holmby* had brought the King " from thence; and that his Majefty lay the next Night " at Colonel *Montague's* Houfe, and would be the " next day at *Newmarket:* that the Ground thereof

The General's Account of it to the Parliament.

"was from an Apprehension of some strength gathered to force the King from thence; whereupon he had sent Colonel *Whaley*'s Regiment to meet the King." He protested "that his remove was without his consent, or of the Officers about him, or of the Body of the Army, and without their desire, or privity; that he would take care for the security of his Majesty's Person from danger;" and assured the Parliament, "that the whole Army endeavoured Peace, and were far from opposing Presbytery, or affecting Independency, or from any purpose to maintain a Licentious freedom in Religion, or the Interest of any particular Party, but were resolved to leave the absolute determination of all to the Parliament."

It was upon the third of *June* that the King was taken from *Holmby* by Cornet *Joyce*, well nigh a full year after he had delivered himself to the *Scots* at *Newark*; in all which time, the Army had been at leisure to contrive all ways to free itself from the Servitude of the Parliament, whilst the Presbyterians believed, that in spite of a few Factious Independent Officers, it was entirely at their Devotion, and could never prove disobedient to their Commands; and those few wise Men, who discerned the foul designs of those Officers, and by what degrees they stole the Hearts and Affections of the Soldiers, had not credit enough to be believed by their own Party. The joint confidence of the unanimous Affection of the City of *London* to all their purposes, made them despise all opposition; but now, when they saw the King taken out of their hands in this manner, and with

these

these circumstances, they found all their Measures broke by which they had formed all their Counsels. And as this Letter from the General administered too much cause of Jealousy of what was to succeed, so a positive information about the same time by many Officers, confirmed by a Letter which the Lord Mayor of *London* had received, that the whole Army was upon it's march, and would be in *London* the next day by noon, so distracted them that they appeared besides themselves: however, they Voted, "that the " Houses should sit all the next day, being *Sunday*; " and that Mr. *Marshall* should be there to pray for " them: That the Committee of Safety should sit up " all that night to consider what was to be done: " That the Lines of Communication should be " strongly Guarded, and all the Trained-bands of " *London* should be drawn together upon pain of " death." All Shops were shut up, and such a general Confusion over all the Town, and in the faces of all Men, as if the Army had already entered the Town. The Parliament writ a Letter to the General, desiring him, " that no part of the Army might come within " five-and-twenty Miles of *London*; and that the " King's Person might be delivered to the former " Commissioners, who had attended upon his Ma- " jesty at *Holmby*; and that Colonel *Rossiter*, and his " Regiment, might be appointed for the Guard of " his Person." The General returned for Answer, " that the Army was come to St. *Albans* before the " desire of the Parliament came to his hands; but " that, in Obedience to their Commands, he would " advance no farther; and desired that a Month's

BOOK X.

The King brought to Newmarket where he was allowed his Chaplains by the Army.

"pay might presently be sent for the Army." In which they deferred not to gratify them; though as to the redelivery of the King to the former Commissioners, no other Answer was returned, than "that they might rest assured, that all care should be taken for his Majesty's security."

From that time both *Cromwell* and *Ireton* appeared in the Council of Officers, which they had never before done; and their Expostulations with the Parliament, begun to be more brisk, and contumacious than they had been. The King found himself at *Newmarket* attended by greater Troops and superior Officers; so that he was presently freed from any Subjection to Mr. *Joyce*; which was no small satisfaction to him; and they who were about him appeared Men of better Breeding than the former, and paid his Majesty all the respect imaginable, and seemed to desire to please him in all things. All restraint was taken off from Persons resorting to him, and he saw every day the Faces of many who were grateful to him; and he no sooner desired that some of his Chaplains might have leave to attend upon him for his Devotion, but it was yielded to, and they who were named by him (who were Dr. *Sheldon*, Dr. *Morley*, Dr. *Sanderson*, and Dr. *Hammond*) were presently sent, and gave their attendance, and performed their Function at the ordinary hours, in their accustomed Formalities; all Persons who had a mind to it, being suffered to be present, to his Majesty's infinite satisfaction; who begun to believe that the Army was not so much his Enemy as it was reported to be; and the Army had sent an Address to him full of protestation of Duty,

and besought him "that he would be content, for
"some time, to reside among them, until the Affairs
"of the Kingdom were put into such a Posture as he
"might find all things to his own content, and secu-
"rity; which they infinitely desired to see as soon as
"might be; and to that purpose made daily instances
"to the Parliament." In the mean time his Majesty *His Majesty removes according to the marches of the Army.* sat still, or removed to such places as were most convenient for the March of the Army; being in all places as well provided for and Accommodated, as he had used to be in any Progress; the best Gentlemen of the several Counties through which he passed, daily resorted to him, without distinction; he was attended by some of his old Trusty Servants in the places nearest his Person; and that which gave him most encouragement to believe that they meant well, was, that in the Army's Address to the Parliament, they desired "that care might be taken for settling
"the King's Rights, according to the several Pro-
"fessions they had made in their Declarations; and
"that the Royal Party might be treated with more
"Candor, and less Rigor;" and many good Officers who had served his Majesty faithfully, were Civilly received by the Officers of the Army, and lived quietly in their Quarters; which they could not do any where else; which raised a great Reputation to the Army, throughout the Kingdom, and as much Reproach upon the Parliament.

The Parliament at this time had recovered its Spirit, when they saw the Army did not much nearer towards them, and not only stopped at St. *Albans*, but was drawn back to a farther distance;

which perſuaded them, that their General was diſpleaſed with the former advance: and ſo they proceeded with all paſſion, and vigor, againſt thoſe principal Officers, who, they knew, contrived all theſe Proceedings. They publiſhed Declarations to the Kingdom, "that they deſired to bring the King
" in honor to his Parliament; which was their buſi-
" neſs from the beginning, and that he was detained
" Priſoner againſt his Will in the Army; and that
" they had great reaſon to apprehend the ſafety of his
" Perſon." The Army, on the other hand," declared
" that his Majeſty was neither Priſoner, nor detained
" againſt his Will; and appealed to his Majeſty him-
" ſelf, and to all his Friends, who had liberty to
" repair to him, whether he had not more liberty,
" and was not treated with more reſpect, ſince he
" came into the Army than he had been at *Holmby*,
" or during the time he remained in thoſe places,
" and with that retinue that the Parliament had
" appointed?" The City ſeemed very unanimouſly devoted to the Parliament, and incenſed againſt the Army; and ſeemed reſolute, not only with their Trained-bands and Auxiliary Regiments to aſſiſt, and defend the Parliament, but appointed ſome of the old Officers who had ſerved under the Earl of *Eſſex*, and had been diſbanded under the new Model, as *Waller*, *Maſſey*, and others, to liſt new Forces; towards which there was not like to be want of Men out of their old Forces, and ſuch of the King's as would be glad of the employment. There was nothing they did really fear ſo much, as that the Army would make a firm conjunction with the King, and

Tranſactions in the City upon theſe occaſions.

unite with his Party, of which there was so much show; and many unskilful Men, who wished it, bragged too much; and therefore the Parliament sent a Committee to his Majesty, with an Address of another Style than they had lately used, with many professions of Duty; and declaring, "that if he was "not, in all respects, treated as he ought to be, and "as he desired, it was not Their fault, who desired "he might be at full liberty, and do what he would;" hoping that the King would have been induced to desire to come to *London*, and to make complaint of the Army's having taken him from *Holmby*; by which they believed the King's Party would be disabused, and withdraw their hopes of any good from the Army; and then, they thought, they should be hard enough for them.

The King was in great doubt how to carry himself; he thought himself so barbarously used by the Presbyterians, and had so ill an opinion of all the principal Persons who governed them, that he had no mind to put himself into their hands. On the other side, he was far from being satisfied with the Army's good intentions towards him; and though many of his Friends were suffered to resort to him, they found that their being long about him, would not be acceptable; and though the Officers and Soldiers appeared, for the most part, civil to him, they were all at least as vigilant, as the former Guards had been; so that he could not, without great difficulty, have got from them if he had desired it. *Fairfax* had been with him, and kissed his hand, and made such Professions as he could well utter; which was with no advantage in the delivery; his Authority was of no use, because he resigned himself entirely to *Cromwell*; who had been, and *Ireton* likewise, with the King, without either of them offering to kiss his hand; otherwise, they behaved themselves with good manners towards him. His Majesty used all the Address he could towards them to draw some promise from them, but they were so reserved, and stood so much upon their Guard, and used so few words, that nothing could be concluded from what they said: they excused themselves "for not seeing his Majesty " often, upon the great jealousies the Parliament " had of them, towards whom they professed all " fidelity." The Persons who resorted to his Majesty, and brought Advices from others who durst not yet offer to come themselves, brought several opinions to him; some thinking the Army would deal sincerely with his Majesty, others expecting no better from them than they afterwards performed: so that the King well concluded that he would neither reject the Parliament-Addresses by any neglect, nor disoblige the Army by appearing to have jealousy of them, or a desire to be out of their hands; which he could hardly have effected, if he had known a better place to have resorted to. So he desired both Parties " to hasten their Consultations, that the Kingdom " might enjoy Peace and Happiness; in which he " should not be without a share; and he would pray " to God to bring this to pass as soon as was " possible."

The news of the King's being in the Army, of his freedom in the exercise of his Religion, which he

had been so long without, and that some of his Servants, with whom he was well pleased had liberty to attend upon him, made every Body abroad, as well as those at home, hope well; and the King himself writ to the Queen, as if he thought his condition much better than it had been among the *Scots*. Sir *John Berkeley* after his Surrender of *Exeter*, and the spending his six Months allowed by the Articles to solicit his affairs where he would, had Transported himself into *France*, and waited upon the Queen at *Paris*, being still a menial Servant to her Majesty, and having a Friend in that Court that Governed, and loved him better than any Body else did. As soon as the reports came thither of the King's being with the Army, he repeated many Discourses he had held with the Officers of the Army, whilst they treated with him of the delivery of *Exeter*; how he had told them, "upon how slippery ground they
" stood; that the Parliament, when they had served
" their turn, would dismiss them with reproach,
" and give them very small rewards for the great
" Service they had done for them; that they should
" do well, seasonably to think of a safe retreat,
" which could be no where but under the Protection
" of the King; who by their Courage was brought
" very low; and if they raised him again; he must
" owe it all to them; and his Posterity, as well as
" himself, and all his Party, must for ever acknow-
" ledge it; by which they would raise their Fortunes,
" as well as their Fame, to the greatest degree Men
" could aim at;" which, he said, made such an impression upon this and that Officer, whom he

named, "that they told him at parting, that they should never forget what he had said to them; and that they already observed that every day produced somewhat that would put them in mind of it." In a word, "he had foretold all that was since come to pass, and he was most confident, that, if he were now with them, he should be welcome, and have credit enough to bring them to reason, and to do the King great Service;" and offered, without any delay, to make the Journey. The Queen believed all he said; and they who did not, were very willing he should make the experiment; for he that loved him best, was very willing to be without him; and so receiving the Queen's Letter of Recommendation of him to the King, who knew him very little, and that little not without some prejudice, he left *Paris*, and made all possible haste into *England*. John *Ashburnham*, who was driven from the King by the *Scots* after he had conducted his Majesty to them, had Transported himself into *France*, and was at this time residing in *Roan*; having found, upon his Address to the Queen at *Paris* upon his first Arrival, that his abode in some other place would not be ungrateful to her Majesty, and so he removed to *Roan*; where he had the society of many who had served the King in the most eminent Qualifications. When he heard where the King was, and that there was not the same restraint that had been formerly, he resolved to make an adventure to wait on him; having no reason to doubt but that his presence would be very acceptable to the King; and though the other Envoy from *Paris*, and He, did

margin:
Sir John Berkeley sent from the Queen to the King.

Mr. Ashburnham comes from France to the King.

not make their Journey into *England* together, nor had the least Communication with each other, being in truth of several Parties and Purposes, yet they arrived there, and at the Army, near the same time.

Berkeley first applied himself to those subordinate Officers with whom he had some acquaintance at *Exeter*, and they informing their Superiors of his Arrival, and Application, they were well pleased that he was come. They were well acquainted with his Talent, and knew his foible, that, by flattering and commending, they might govern him; and that there was no danger of any deep design from His contrivance; and so they permitted him freely to attend the King, about whose Person he had no title, or relation, which required any constant waiting upon him.

Ashburnham had, by some Friends, a recommendation both to *Cromwell*, and *Ireton*, who knew the credit he had with the King, and that his Majesty would be very well pleased to have his attendance, and look upon it as a Testimony of their respect to him. They knew likewise that he was an implacable Enemy to the *Scots*, and no Friend to the other Presbyterians, and though he had some ordinary craft in insinuating, he was of no deep and piercing judgment to discover what was not unwarily exposed, and a free speaker of what he imagined: so they likewise left Him at liberty to repair to the King; and these two Gentlemen came near about the same time to his Majesty, when the Army was drawing together, with a purpose, which was not yet published, of marching to *London;* his Majesty being

Sir John Berkeley and Mr Ashburnham's Transactions with some Officers of the Army.

still quartered in those places which were more proper for that purpose.

They were both welcome to his Majesty, the one bringing a special recommendation from the Queen, and, to make himself the more valuable, assuring his Majesty "that he was sent for by the Officers of "the Army, as one they would trust, and that they "had received him with open Arms; and, without "any scruple, gave him leave to wait upon him:" The other, needed no recommendation, the King's own inclinations disposing him to be very gracious to him; and so his Majesty wished them "to cor- "respond with each other, and to converse with "his several Friends, who did not yet think fit to "resort to him; and to receive their advice; to "discover as much as they could of the Intentions "of both Parties, and impart what was fit to the "King, till, upon a farther discovery, his Majesty "might better judge what to do." These two were the principal Agents (they conferring with all his Majesty's Friends, and, as often as they desired, with the Officers of the Army) upon whose Information, and Advice, his Majesty principally depended, though they rarely conferred together with the same Persons, and never with any of the Officers, who pretended not to trust one another enough to speak with that freedom before each other, as they would to one of them; and their Acquaintance among the Officers not being principally with the same Men, their Informations and Advices were often very different, and more perplexed than informed his Majesty.

The very high contests between the Parliament and the Army, in which neither side could be persuaded to yield to the other, or abate any of their asperity, made many prudent Men believe that both sides would, in the end, be willing to make the King the Umpire; which neither of them ever intended to do. The Parliament thought that their Name and Authority, which had carried them through so great undertakings, and reduced the whole Kingdom to their obedience, could not be overpowered by their own Army, raised and paid by themselves, and to whose Dictates the People would never submit. They thought the King's presence amongst them, gave them all their present reputation; and were not without apprehension that the Ambition of some of the Officers, and their malice to the Parliament, when they saw that they could obtain their ends no other way, might dispose them to an entire conjunction with the King's Party and Interest; and then, all the Penalties of Treason, Rebellion, and Trespasses, must be discharged at their costs; and therefore they labored, by all the public and private means they could, to persuade the King to own his being detained Prisoner by the Army against his Will, or to withdraw himself by some way from them, and repair to *White-Hall*; and, in either of those Cases, they did not doubt, first, to divide the Army (for they still believed the General fast to them) and by degrees to bring to reason, and to be disbanded, as many as were not necessary for the Service of *Ireland*; and then, having the King to themselves, and all his Party being obnoxious to those penalties for their

BOOK
X.

The different designs of the Parliament and Army at this time relating to the King.

Delinquency, they should be well able, by gratifying some of the greatest Persons of the Nobility with immunity and indemnity, to settle the Government in such a manner, as to be well recompensed for all the Adventures they had made, and hazards they had run.

On the other hand, the Army had no dread of the Authority and Power of the Parliament; which they knew had been so far prostituted, that it had lost most of its reverence with the People. But it had great apprehension, that, by its conjunction with the City, it might indeed recover credit with the Kingdom, and withhold the pay of the Army, and thereby make some Division amongst them; and if the Person of the King should be likewise with them, and thereby his Party should likewise join with them, they should be to begin their work again, or to make their Peace with those who were as much provoked by them as the King himself had been. And therefore they were sensible that they enjoyed a present benefit by the King's being with them, and by their treating him with the outward respect that was due to his Majesty, and the civilities they made profession of towards all his Party, and the permission of his Chaplains, and other Servants, to resort to him; and cultivated all these Artifices with great Address, suppressing, or discountenancing the Tyranny of the Presbyterians in the Country-Committees, and all other places, where they exercised notable rigor against all who had been of the King's Party, or not enough of theirs (for Neuters found no excuse for being of no Party) When they found it fit to make any lusty Declaration against the Parlia-

ment, and exclaim against their Tyrannical proceedings against the Army, they always inserted somewhat that might look like Candor and Tenderness towards the King's Party, complained of "the
" Affront, and Indignity done to the Army by the
" Parliament's not obferving the Articles which had
" been made upon Surrender of Garrifons, but proceeding against thofe on whofe behalf thofe Articles were made, with more feverity than was
" agreeable to juftice, and to the Intention of the
" Articles; whereby the honor and faith of the
" Army fuffered, and was complained of; all which,
" they faid, they would have remedied." Whereupon many hoped that they fhould be excufed from making any compofitions, and entertained fuch other imaginations as pleafed themfelves, and the other Party well liked; knowing they could demolifh all thofe Structures as foon as they received no benefit by them themfelves.

The King had, during the time he ftayed at *Holmby*, writ to the Houfe of Peers, that his Children might have leave to come to him, and to refide for fome time with him. From the time that *Oxford* had been Surrendered, upon which the Duke of *York* had fallen into their hands, for they would by no means admit that he fhould have liberty to go to fuch place as the King fhould direct, which was very earneftly preffed, and infifted on by the Lords of the Council there, as long as they could; but appointed their Committee to receive him with all refpect, and to bring him to *London*; from that time, I fay, the Duke of *York* was committed to the care of the Earl

BOOK X.

of *Northumberland*, together with the Duke of *Gloucester*, and the Princess, who had been by the King left under the Tuition of the Countess of *Dorset*, but from the Death of that Countess the Parliament had presumed, that they might be sure to keep them in their power, to put them into the Custody of the Lady *Vere*, an old Lady much in their favor, but not at all Ambitious of that Charge, though there was a competent allowance assigned for their support. They were now removed from her, and placed all together with the Earl of *Northumberland*, who received, and treated them, in all respects, as was suitable to their Birth, and his own Duty; but could give them no more liberty to go abroad, than he was, in his Instructions from the Parliament, permitted to do; and they had absolutely refused to gratify the King in that particular; of which his Majesty no sooner took notice to *Fairfax*, than he writ a Letter to the Parliament, "that the King much
"desired to have the sight and company of his Children, and that if they might not be allowed to be longer with him, that at least they might dine with him;" and he sent them word that, on such a day, the King, who attended the motion of the Army and was Quartered only where they pleased,

The King allowed to see his Children at Maidenhead and Caversham.

"would dine at *Maidenhead*." There his Children met him, to his infinite content and joy; and he being to Quarter and stay some time at *Caversham*, a House of the Lord *Craven's*, near *Reading*, his Children were likewise suffered to go thither, and remained with him two days; which was the greatest satisfaction the King could receive; and the receiving whereof, he imputed to the Civility of the General, and the good difpofition of the Army; which made fo much the more impreffion upon him, in that he had never made any one Propofition in which he had been gratified, where the Prefbyterian Spirit had power to deny it.

In the Houfe of Commons, which was now the Scene of all the Action that difpleafed and incenfed the Army (for the Houfe of Peers was fhrunk into fo inconfiderable a Number, and their Perfons not confiderable after the Death of the Earl of *Effex;* except thofe who were affected to, or might be difpofed by the Army) they were wholly guided by *Hollis,* and *Stapleton, Lewis,* and *Glyn,* who had been very popular and notorious from the beginning, and by *Waller,* and *Maffey,* and *Brown,* who had Served in Commands in the Army, and performed at fome times very fignal Service, and were exceedingly beloved in the City, and two or three others who followed their Dictates, and were fubfervient to their Directions. Thefe were all Men of Parts, Intereft, and fignal Courage, and did not only heartily abhor the Intentions which they difcerned the Army to have, and that it was wholly to be difpofed according to the defigns of *Cromwell,* but had likewife declared Animofities againft the Perfons of the moft active and powerful Officers; as *Hollis* had one day, upon a very hot debate in the Houfe, and fome rude expreffions which fell from *Ireton,* perfuaded him to walk out of the Houfe with him, and then told him, " that he fhould prefently go over the Water and " fight with him." *Ireton* replying, " his Confcience "would not suffer him to fight a Duel:" *Hollis*, in choler, pulled him by the Nose; telling him, "if his Conscience would keep him from giving Men satisfaction, it should keep him from provoking them." This affront to the third Person of the Army, and to a Man of the most Virulent, Malicious, and Revengeful Nature of all the Pack, so incensed the whole Party, that they were resolved one way or other to be rid of him, who had that power in the House, and that reputation abroad, that when he could not absolutely control their designs, he did so obstruct them, that they could not advance to any coclusion.

The Army impeach eleven Members of the House of Commons.

They resorted therefore to an expedient, which, they had observed, by the Conduct of those very Men against whom they meant to apply it, had brought to pass all that they desired; and, in the Council of Officers, prepared and impeachment of High-Treason in general Terms against Mr. *Hollis*, and the Persons mentioned before, and others, to the number of eleven Members of the House of Commons. This impeachment twelve Officers of the Army, Colonels, Lieutenant-Colonels, Majors, and Captains, presented to the House; and within few days after, when they saw the same Members still inveigh against, and arraign their proceedings, the General and Officers writ a Letter to the House, "that they would appoint fit Persons on their and the Kingdom's behalf, to make good the charge against those Members whom they had accused; and that they desired, that those Members impeached might be forthwith suspended from

fitting

"fitting in the House; since it could not be thought
"fit that the same Persons who had so much injured
"and provoked the Army, should sit Judges of their
"own Actions." This was an Arrow that the House
of Commons did not expect would have been shot
out of that Quiver; and though they were unspeakably dismayed, and distracted with this presumption, they answered positively, "that they neither
"would, nor could, sequester those Members from
"the House, who had never said, or done any thing
"in the House worthy of Censure, till proof were
"made of such particulars as might render them
"guilty." But the Officers of the Army replied,
"that they could prove them guilty of such practices
"in the House, that it would be just in the House to
"suspend them: that by the Laws of the Land, and
"the Precedents of Parliament, the Lords had, upon
"the very presentation of a general Accusation with
"out being reduced in form, sequestered from their
"House and committed the Earl of *Strafford*, and
"the Arch-Bishop of *Canterbury*; and therefore
"they must press, and insist upon the suspending
"at least of those accused Members from being
"present in the House, where they stood impeached;
"and without this, they said, the Army would not
"be satisfied." However the House of Commons
seemed still resolute, the accused Members themselves, who best knew their temper, thought it safer
for them to retire, and by forbearing to appear in the
House, to allay the heat of the present Contest.

Upon this so palpable Declension of Spirit in the
House, the Army seemed much quieter, and

BOOK X.

The temper of the City and the Changes of their Militia at this time.

resolved to set other Agents on their work. that they might not appear too busy and active upon their own concernment. It is very true that the City, upon whose influence the Parliament much depended, appeared now entirely Presbyterian; the Court of Aldermen, and Common-Council, consisted chiefly of Men of that Spirit; the Militia of the City was committed to Commissioners carefully and factiously chosen of that Party; all those of another temper having been put out of those Trusts, at or about the time that the King was delivered up by the *Scots*, when the Officers of the Army were content that the Presbyterians should believe, that the whole power of the Kingdom was in them; and that they might settle what Government they pleased; If there remained any Persons in any of those employments in the City, it was by their dissimulation, and pretending to have other Affections; most of those who were notorious to be of any other faction in Religion, had been put out; and lived as neglected and discountenanced Men; who seemed rather to depend upon the Clemency, and Indulgence of the State, for their particular liberty in the exercise of that Religion they adhered to, than to have any hope or ambition to be again admitted into any share, or part in the Government: yet, after all this dissimulation *Cromwell* and *Ireton* well knew, that the multitude of inferior People were at their disposal, and would appear in any conjuncture they should think convenient; and that many Aldermen and substantial Citizens were quiet, and appeared not to contradict or oppose the Presbyterians, only by their directions; and would

be ready upon their call. And now, when they faw thofe leading Men, who had governed the Parliament profecuted by the Army, and that they forbore to come to the Houfe, there flocked together great Numbers of the loweft, and moft inferior People, to the Parliament, with Petitions of feveral Natures, both with reference to Religion, and to the Civil Government; with the noife and clamor whereof, the Parliament was fo offended and difturbed, that they made an Ordinance, " that it fhould be Criminal " to gather, and folicit the Subfcription of hands. " to Petitions." But this Order fo offended all Parties, that they were compelled, within two days, to revoke it, and to leave all Men to their natural Liberty. Whilft this Confufion was in the City and Parliament, the Commiffioners, which had been fent to the Army to treat with the Officers, had no better fuccefs; but returned with the pofitive and declared Refolution of the Army, " that a Declara-
" tion fhould be publifhed by the Parliament againft
" the coming in of Foreign Force:" for they apprehended, or rather were willing that the People fhould apprehend, a new Combination by the *Scots*. " that
" the Pay of the Army fhould be put into a conftant
" Courfe, and all Perfons who had received Money,
" fhould be called to an account: that the Militia of
" *London* fhould be put into the hands of Perfons
" well affected, and thofe who had been formerly
" trufted: that all Perfons imprifoned for pretended
" Mifdemeanours, by Order of Parliament, or their
" Committees, might be fet at Liberty; and, if
" upon trial they fhould be found Innocent, that

"they might have good Reparation." And they particularly mentioned *John Lilburn*, *Overton*, and other Anabaptists and Fanatics, who had been committed by the Parliament for many Seditious Meetings, under pretence of Exercise of their Religion, and many insolent Actions against the Government. Upon the report of these demands the Parliament grew more enraged; and Voted, " that the yielding " to the Army in these particulars, would be against " their Honor, and their Interest, and destructive " to their Privileges;" with many expressions against their presumption, and insolence: yet, when a new Rabble of Petitioners demanded, with loud Cries, most of the same things, they were willing to compound with them; and consented that the Militia of the City of *London* should be put into such hands as the Army should desire.

The Militia of the City had been in the beginning of *May*, shortly after the King's being brought to *Holmby*, settled with the consent, and upon the desire, of the Common-Council, by Ordinance of Parliament, in the hands of Commissioners, who were generally of the Presbyterian Party, they who were of other inclinations being removed; and, as is said before, seemed not displeased at their disgrace; and now, when upon the Declarations and Demands of the Army, seconded by the clamorous Petitions, they saw this Ordinance reversed, in *July*, without so much as consulting with the Common Council according to custom, the City was exceedingly startled; and said, " that if the Imperious Command of the " Army, could prevail with the Parliament to reverse

"such an Ordinance as that of the Militia, they
"had reason to apprehend they might as well repeal
"the other Ordinances for the security of Money, or
"for the purchase of Bishops and Church-Lands, or
"whatsoever else that was the proper security of the
"Subject." And therefore they caused a Petition to
be prepared in the name of the City, to be presented
by the two Sheriffs, and others deputed by the Common-Council to that purpose. But, before they were
ready, many thousands, Apprentices and young Citizens, brought Petitions to the Parliament; in which
they said, "that the Command of the Militia of the
"City was the Birth-right of the City, and belonged
"to them by several Charters which had been confirm-
"ed in Parliament; for defence whereof, they said,
"they had ventured their Lives as far and as frankly
"as the Army had done; and therefore, they desired
"that the Ordinance of Parliament of the fourth of
"*May*, which had passed with their consent, might
"stand inviolable." They first presented their Petition to the House of Peers, who immediately revoked
their late Ordinance of *July*, and confirmed their
former of *May*; and sent it down to the Commons
for their consent; who durst not deny their concurrence, the Apprentices behaving themselves so insolently, that they would scarce suffer the door of the
House of Commons to be shut; and some of them
went into the House.

And in this manner the Ordinance was reversed
that had been made at the desire of the Army, and
the other of *May* ratified and confirmed; which was
no sooner done than the Parliament adjourned till

A tumultuous Petition of Apprentices, and others, to both Houses concerning their Militia.

Friday, that they might have two or three days to consider how they should behave themselves, and prevent the like violences hereafter. The Army had quickly notice of these extraordinary proceedings, and the General writ a very sharp Letter to the Parliament from *Bedford*; in which he put them in mind, " how civilly the Army had complied with their " desire, by removing to a greater distance, upon " presumption that their own Authority would " have been able to have secured them from any " rudeness, and violence of the People; which it " was now evident it could not do, by the unparalleled " violation of all their Privileges, on the " *Monday* before, by a Multitude from the City " which had been encouraged by several Common-" Council-Men, and other Citizens in Authority; " which was an Act so prodigious and horrid as must " dissolve all Government, if not severely and exemplarily " chastised: that the Army looked upon " themselves as accountable to the Kingdom, if this " unheard of outrage, by which the Peace and settlement " of the Nation, and the relief of *Ireland*, had " been so notoriously interrupted, should not be " strictly examined, and justice speedily done upon " the Offenders." Upon *Friday*, to which both Houses had adjourned, the Members came together, in as full Numbers as they had used to meet, there being above one hundred and forty of the House of Commons; but, after they had sat some time in expectation of their Speaker, they were informed that he was gone out of the Town early that Morning; and they observed that Sir *Henry Vane*, and some few

Margin: BOOK X. Upon this the General writ a very sharp Letter to the Parliament.

OF THE REBELLION.

other Members who used to concur with him, were likewise absent. The House of Peers found likewise that the Earl of *Manchester*, their Speaker, had withdrawn himself, together with the Earl of *Northumberland*, and some other Lords; but the Major part still remained there, full of Indignation against those who were absent, and who they all concluded were gone to the Army. Hereupon both Houses chose new Speakers; who accepted the Office; and the Commons presently voted, "that the eleven "Members who stood impeached by the Army, "and had discontinued coming to the House, should "presently appear, and take their places." They made an Ordinance of Parliament, by which a Committee of safety was appointed to join with the City Militia, and had Authority to raise Men for the defence of the Parliament; which they appeared so vigorously resolved on, that no Men in the Houses, or in the City, seemed to intend any thing else. The News of this roused up the Army, and the General presently sent a good Party of Horse into *Windsor*, and marched himself to *Uxbridge*, and appointed a general Rendezvous for the Army upon *Hounslow*-Heath, within two days; when there appeared twenty thousand Foot and Horse, with a Train of Artillery, and all other provisions proportionable to such an Army.

As soon as the Rendezvous was appointed at *Hounslow* Heath, at the same time the King removed to *Hampton*-Court; which was prepared, and put into as good order for his reception, as could have been done in the best time. The Houses seemed for some

BOOK X.

time to retain their Spirit and Vigor, and the City talked of lifting Men, and defending themselves, and not suffering the Army to approach nearer to them; but, when they knew the day of the Rendezvous, those in both Houses who had been too weak to carry any thing, and so had looked on whilst such Votes were passed as they liked not and could not oppose, now when their Friend the Army was so near, recovered their Spirits, and talked very loud; and persuaded the rest, " to think in time of making their " peace with the Army, that could not be with-" stood." And the City grew every day more appalled, irresolute, and confounded, one Man proposing this, and another somewhat contrary to that, like Men amazed and distracted. When the Army met upon *Hounslow*-Heath at their Rendezvous, the Speakers of both Houses, who had privately before met with the Chief-Officers of the Army, appeared there with their Maces, and such other Members as accompanied them; complaining to the General, " that they had not freedom at *Westminster*, but " were in danger of their lives by the Tumults;" and appealed to the Army for their protection.

Both Speakers, and the other Members, appear in the Army on Hounslow-Heath.

This looked like a new Act of Providence to vindicate the Army from all reproaches, and to justify them in all they had done, as absolutely done for the preservation of the Parliament and Kingdom. If this had been a retreat of Sir *Harry Vane* and some other discontented Men, who were known to be Independents, and Fanatics in their opinions in Religion, and of the Army-faction, who being no longer able to oppose the wisdom of the Parliament, had fled to their Friends for protection from Justice, they would have got no reputation, nor the Army been thought the better of for their Company; but neither of the Speakers were ever looked upon as inclined to the Army; *Lenthall* was generally believed to have no malice towards the King, and not to be without good inclinations to the Church; and the Earl of *Manchester*, who was Speaker of the House of Peers, was known to have all the prejudice imaginable against *Cromwell*; and had formerly accused him of want of Duty to the Parliament; and the other hated him above all Men, and desired to have taken away his life. The Earl of *Manchester*, and the Earl of *Warwick*, were the two Pillars of the Presbyterian Party; and that they two, with the Earl of *Northumberland*, and some other of the Lords, and some of the Commons, who had appeared to disapprove all the proceedings of the Army, should now join with Sir *Harry Vane*, and appeal to the Army for protection, with that formality as if they had brought the whole Parliament with them, and had been entirely driven and forced away by the City, appeared to every stander by so stupendous a thing, that it is not to this day understood otherwise, than that they were resolved to have their particular shares in the Treaty, which they believed the Chief-Officers of the Army to have near concluded with the King. For that they never intended to put the whole power into the hands of the Army, nor had any kindness to, or confidence in the Officers thereof, was very apparent by their carriage and behaviour after, as well as before; and if they had continued together, considering how much the City was devoted to them, it is probable that the Army would not have used any force; which might have received a fatal repulse; but that some good Compromise might have been made by the Interposition of the King. But this Schism carried all the Reputation and Authority to the Army, and left none in the Parliament; for though it presently appeared, that the Number of those who left the Houses was small in comparison of those who remained behind, and who proceeded with the same Vigor in declaring against the Army, and the City seemed as resolute in putting themselves into a posture, and preparing for their defence, all their Works and Fortifications being still entire, so that they might have put the Army to great trouble if they had steadily pursued their Resolutions (which they did not seem in any degree to decline) yet this rent made all the accused Members, who were the Men of parts, and reputation to conduct their Counsels, to withdraw themselves upon the astonishment; some concealing themselves, till they had opportunity to make their Peace, and others withdrawing and transporting themselves beyond the Seas; whereof *Stapleton* died at *Calais* as soon as he Landed, and was denied Burial, upon imagination that he had died of the Plague: others remained a long time beyond the Seas; and, though they long after returned, never were received into any trust in those times, nor in truth concurred, or acted in the public Affairs, but retired to their own Estates, and lived very privately.

The Chief Officers of the Army received the two Speakers, and the Members who accompanied them,

as so many Angels sent from Heaven for their good;
paid them all the respect imaginable, and professed all
submission to them, as to the Parliament of *England*;
and declared "that they would re-establish them in
" their full power, or perish in the attempt," took
very particular care for their accommodations, before the General; and assigned a Guard to wait upon
them for their security; acquainted them with all
their consultations, and would not presume to resolve
any thing without their approbation: and they had
too much modesty to think they could do amiss,
who had prospered so much in all their undertakings.
No time was lost in pursuing their Resolution to
establish the Parliament again at *Westminster*; and
finding that the rest of the Members continued still
to sit there with the same Formality, and that the
City did not abate any of their Spirit, they seemed to
make a halt, and to remain quiet, in expectation of
a better understanding between them, upon the Messages they every day sent to the Lord-Mayor, and
Aldermen, and Common-Council (for of those at
Westminster they took no notice) and Quartered
their Army about *Brentford*, and *Hounslow*, *Twitten-
ham*, and the adjacent Villages, without restraining
any Provisions, which every day according to custom
were carried to *London*, or doing the least Action
that might disoblige, or displease the City; the Army
being in truth under so excellent discipline, that no
body could complain of any damage sustained by
them, or any provocation by word or deed. However, in this calm, they sent over Colonel *Rainsborough*
with a Brigade of Horse and Foot, and Cannon,

BOOK X.

at *Hampton*-Court, to poffefs *Southwark*, and thofe works which fecured that end of *London*-Bridge; which he did with fo little Noife, that in one Night's march, he found himfelf Mafter without any oppofition, not only of the Borough of *Southwark*, but of all the Works and Forts which were to defend it; the Soldiers within, fhaking hands with thofe without, and refufing to obey their Officers which were to Command them: So that the City, without knowing that any fuch thing was in agitation, found in the morning that all that Avenue to the Town was poffeffed by the Enemy; whom they were providing to refift on the other fide, being as confident of this that they had loft, as of any Gate of the City.

This ftruck them dead; and put an end to all their Confultation for defence; and put other thoughts into their heads, how they might pacify thofe whom they had fo much offended, and provoked; and how they might preferve their City from Plunder, and the fury of an enraged Army. They who had ever been of the Army-party, and of late had fhut themfelves up, and not dared to walk the Streets for fear of the People, came now confidently amongft them, and mingled in their Councils; declared, "that the
" King and the Army were now agreed in all parti-
" culars, and that both Houfes were now with the
" Army, and had prefented themfelves to the King;
" fo that to oppofe the Army would be to oppofe
" the King and Parliament, and to incenfe them as
" much as the Army." Upon fuch confident difcourfes and infinuations from thofe with whom they would not have converfed, or given the leaft credit

to, three days before, or rather upon the confusion and general distraction they were in, they sent six Aldermen and six Commoners to the General; who lamented, and complained, "that the City should "be suspected, that had never acted any thing against "the Parliament; and therefore, they desired him "to forbear doing any thing that might be the occa- "sion of a new War." But the General little considered this Message, and gave less countenance to the Messengers; but continued his slow marches towards the City: whereupon they sent an humble Message to him, "that since they understood that the "reason of his march so near *London* was to restore, "and settle the Members (the Lords and Commons) "of Parliament to the Liberty and Privilege of "sitting securely in their several Houses (to which "the City would contribute all their power, and "service) they prayed him, with all submission, that "he would be pleased to send such a Guard of Horse "and Foot as he thought to be sufficient for that "purpose; and that the Ports and all Passages "should be open to them; and they should do any "thing else that his Excellency would Command." To which, he made no other Answer but "that he "would have all the Forts of the West-side of the "City to be delivered immediately to him; those "of the other side being already, as is said, in the "hands of *Rainsborough* and his other Officers." The Common-Council, that sat Day and Night, upon the receipt of this Message, without any pause returned "that they would humbly submit to his "Command; and that now, under Almighty-God,

The City sends six Aldermen to the General, and submits

"they did rely only upon his Excellency's honor-
"able word for their protection, and security."
And so they caused their Militia to be forthwith
drawn off from the Line, as well as out of the Forts,
with all their Cannon and Ordnance; and the General appointed a better Guard to both. At *Hyde*
Park the Mayor and Aldermen met him, and humbly
congratulated his arrival; and besought him "to
"excuse what they had, out of their good meaning
"and desire of Peace, done amiss;" and as a Testimony of their Affection and Duty, the Mayor, on
the behalf of the City, presented a great gold Cup to
the General; which he sullenly refused to receive,
and, with very little Ceremony, dismissed them.

The General conducts the two Speakers and other Members to their several Houses of Parliament.

He himself waited upon the two Speakers, and
conducted them, and their Members, to the several
Houses, where the other Members were then sitting;
even in the Instant when the Revolters, as they
called them, entered into the Houses, the old Speakers
assumed their places again, and entered upon their
business, as if there had been no separation. The first
thing they did, was calling in the General into both
Houses, and making him a large acknowledgment
in the name of each House, of the great favors he had
done to them; they thanked him "for the Protec-
"tion he had given to their Persons, and his Vindi-
"cation of the Privileges of Parliament." Then
they voted "all that had been done by themselves in
"going to the Army, and in residing there, and all
"that had been done by the Army, to be well and
"lawfully done;" as, some time after, they also
voted, "that all that had been done in the Houses

" since their departure, was against Law, and Privilege of Parliament, invalid and void:" Then they adjourned to the next day, without questioning or punishing any Member who had acted there.

The Army of Horse, Foot, and Cannon, marched the next day through the City (which, upon the desire of the Parliament, undertook forthwith to supply a hundred thousand pounds for the payment of the Army) without the least disorder, or doing the least damage to any Person, or giving any disrespective word to any Man; by which they attained the reputation of being in excellent Discipline, and that both Officers and Soldiers were Men of extraordinary temper and sobriety. So they marched over *London*-Bridge into *Southwark*, and to those Quarters to which they were assigned; some Regiments were Quartered in *Westminster*, the *Strand*, and *Holborn*, under pretence of being a Guard to the Parliament, but intended as a Guard upon the City. The General's head-Quarters were at *Chelsea*, and the rest of the Army Quartered between *Hampton*-Court and *London*, that the King might be well looked to; and the Council of Officers, and Agitators, sat constantly, and formally, at *Fulham*, and *Putney*, to provide that no other settlement should be made for the Government of the Kingdom than what they should well approve.

Whilst these things were thus agitated between the Army and the Parliament and the City, the King enjoyed himself at *Hampton*-Court, much more to his content than he had of late; the respects of the Chief-Officers of the Army seeming much greater than they had been; *Cromwell* himself came oftener to him, and had longer conferences with him; talked with more openness to Mr. *Ashburnham* than he had done, and appeared more cheerful. Persons of all conditions repaired to his Majesty of those who had served him; with whom he conferred without reservation; and the Citizens flocked thither as they had used to do at the end of a Progress, when the King had been some Months absent from *London*: but that which pleased his Majesty most, was, that his Children were permitted to come to him, in whom he took great delight. They were all at the Earl of *Northumberland*'s House, at *Sion*, from the time the King came to *Hampton*-Court, and had liberty to attend his Majesty when he pleased; so that sometimes he sent for them to come to *Hampton*-Court, and sometimes he went to them to *Sion*; which gave him great satisfaction.

The King's discourse and conversation with his Children that were in the parliament's Power.

In this conversation, as if his Majesty had foreseen all that befel him afterwards, and which at that time sure he did not suspect, he took great care to instruct his Children how to behave themselves if the worst should befal him that the worst of his Enemies did contrive, or wish; and "that they should preserve unshaken their Affection and Duty to the Prince their Brother." The Duke of *York* was then about fourteen years of Age; and so, capable of any information or instruction the King thought fit to give him. His Majesty told him, "that he looked upon himself as in the hands and disposal of the Army, and that the Parliament had no more power to do him good or harm, than as the Army should

"should direct or permit; and that he knew not, in
"all this time he had been with them, what he
"might promise himself from those Officers of the
"Army at whose devotion it was: that he hoped
"well, yet with much doubt and fear; and there-
"fore he gave him this general direction, and com-
"mand, that if there appeared any such alteration
"in the affection of the Army, that they restrained
"him from the liberty he then enjoyed of seeing his
"Children, or suffered not his Friends to resort to
"him with that freedom that they enjoyed at present,
"he might conclude they would shortly use him
"worse, and that he should not be long out of a
"Prison; and therefore that from the time he dis-
"covered such an alteration, he should bethink
"himself how he might make an escape out of their
"power, and Transport himself beyond the Seas."
The place he recommended to him, was *Holland*;
where he presumed his Sister would receive him very
kindly, and that the Prince of *Orange* her Husband
would be well pleased with it, though, possibly,
the States might restrain him from making those
Expressions of his Affection his own inclination
prompted him to. He wished him to think always
of this, as a thing possible to fall out, and so spake
frequently to him of it, and of the circumstances and
cautions which were necessary to attend it.

The Princess *Elizabeth* was not above a year or
two younger than the Duke, a Lady of excellent
Parts, great Observation, and an early Understanding; which the King discerned, by the Account
she gave him both of Things and Persons, upon

the experience she had had of both. His Majesty enjoined her, " upon the worst that could befal him, " never to be disposed of in Marriage without the " consent and approbation of the Queen her Mother, " and the Prince her Brother; and always to per- " form all Duty and Obedience to both those; and " to Obey the Queen in all things, except in matter " of Religion; in which he commanded her, upon " his Blessing, never to hearken or consent to her; " but to continue firm in the Religion she had been " Instructed and Educated in, what discountenance " and ruin soever might befal the poor Church, at " that time under so severe prosecution."

The Duke of *Glocester* was very young, being at that time not above seven years old, and so might well be thought incapable of retaining that advice, and injunction, which in truth ever after made so deep impression in him. After he had given him all the advice he thought convenient in the matter of Religion, and commanded him, positively, " never " to be persuaded or threatened out of the Reli- " gion of the Church, in which he hoped he would " be well Instructed, and for the Purity and Integ- " rity whereof he bid him remember that he had " his Father's Testimony, and Authority;" his Majesty told him, " that his Infancy, and the tenderness " of his years, might persuade some Men to hope " and believe, that he might be made an Instrument, " and Property, to advance their wicked designs; " and if they should take away his Life, they might, " possibly, the better to attain their own ends make " him King; that under him, whilst his Age would

" not permit him to Judge, and Act for himself,
" they might remove many obstructions which lay
" in their way; and form and unite their Councils;
" and then they would destroy Him too. But he
" commanded him, upon his Blessing, never to
" forget what he said to him upon this occasion, nor
" to accept, or suffer himself to be made King, whilst
" either of his elder Brothers lived, in what part of
" the World soever they should be: that he should
" remember that the Prince his Brother was to suc-
" ceed him by the Laws of God and Man; and, if
" he should miscarry, that the Duke of *York* was to
" succeed in the same Right; and therefore that he
" should be sure never to be made use of to interrupt,
" or disturb either of their Rights; which would in
" the end turn to his own destruction." And this
discourse the King reiterated to him, as often as he
had liberty to see him, with all the earnestness, and
passion he could express; which was so fixed in his
Memory that he never forgot it. And many years
after, when he was sent out of *England*, he made
the full relation of all the particulars to Me, with
that commotion of Spirit, that it appeared to be
deeply rooted in him; and made use of one part of
it very seasonably afterwards, where there was more
than an ordinary attempt made to have perverted
him in his Religion, and to persuade him to become Roman-Catholic for the advancement of his
Fortune.

In this manner, and with these kind of reflections,
the King made use of the Liberty he enjoyed; and
considered as well, what remedies to apply to the

BOOK X.

worst that could fall out, as to Caress the Officers of the Army in order to the improvement of his Condition; of which he was not yet in despair; the Chief-Officers, and all the Heads of that Party, looking upon it as their wisest Policy to cherish the King's hopes by the Liberty they gave him, and by a very flowing Courtesy towards all who had been of his Party; whose expectation, and good word, and testimony, they found did them much good both in the City and the Country.

At this time the Lord *Capel*, whom We left in *Jersey*, hearing of the difference between the Parliament and the Army, left his two Friends there; and made a Journey to *Paris* to the Prince, that he might receive his Highness' approbation of his going for *England*; which he very willingly gave; well knowing that he would improve all opportunities, with great diligence, for the King his Father's Service: and then that Lord Transported himself into *Zealand*, his Friends having advised him to be in those parts before they endeavoured to procure a Pass for him; which they easily did, as soon as he came thither; and so he had liberty to remain at his own House in the Country, where he was exceedingly beloved, and hated no where. And in this general and illimited indulgence, he took the opportunity to wait upon the King at *Hampton*-Court; and gave him a particular Account of all that passed at *Jersey*, before the Prince's remove from thence, and of the reasons which induced those of the Council to remain still there, and of many other particulars, of which his Majesty had never before been thoroughly informed,

The Lord Capel waits on the King at Hampton-Court from Jersey.

and which put it out of any Body's power to do the Chancellor of the Exchequer any ill Offices: and from thence the King writ, with his own hand, a very gracious and kind Letter to the Chancellor at *Jerſey*; full of hope, "that he ſhould conclude ſuch "a Treaty with the Army and Parliament that he "ſhould ſhortly draw Him, and ſome other of his "Friends, to him." He thanked him "for under-"taking the work he was upon; and told him, he "ſhould expect ſpeedily to receive ſome contribu-"tion from him towards it;" and, within a very ſhort time afterwards, he ſent to him his own Memorials (or thoſe which by his Command had been kept, and were peruſed, and corrected by himſelf) of all that had paſſed from the time he had left his Majeſty at *Oxford*, when he waited upon the Prince into the Weſt, to the very day that the King left *Oxford* to go to the *Scots*; out of which Memorials, as hath been ſaid before, the moſt important paſſages in the Years 1644, and 1645, are faithfully collected. To the Lord *Capel*, his Majeſty imparted all his Hopes and all his Fears; and what great Overtures the *Scots* had again made to him; and "that he did really "believe that it could not be long before there "would be a War between the two Nations; in "which the *Scots* promiſed themſelves an univerſal "concurrence from all the Preſbyterians in *England*; "and that, in ſuch a conjuncture, he wiſhed that "his own Party would put themſelves in Arms, "without which he could not expect great benefit "by the ſucceſs of the other:" and therefore deſired *Capel* "to watch ſuch a conjuncture, and draw his

BOOK X.

The Subſtance of the King's Letter to the Chancellor of the Exchequer.

Z 3

BOOK X.

"Friends together;" which he promised to do effectually; and did, very punctually, afterwards, to the loss of his own Life. Then the King enjoined him "to write to the Chancellor of the Exchequer, that "whenever the Queen, or Prince, should require "him to come to them he should not fail to yield "Obedience to their Command," and himself writ to the Queen, "that whenever the Season should "be ripe for the Prince to engage himself in any "action, she should not fail to send for the Chan- "cellor of the Exchequer to wait upon him in it." And many things were then adjusted, upon the foresight of future contingencies, which were afterwards thought fit to be executed.

The Marquis of Ormond likewise waits on the King at Hampton-Court.

The Marquis of *Ormond* had, by special Command and Order from the King whilst he was with the *Scots* at *New-Castle*, delivered up the City of *Dublin* to the Parliament, after the *Irish* had so infamously broken the Peace they had made with the King, and brought their whole Army before *Dublin* to Besiege it; by which he was reduced to those straits that he had no other election than to deliver it to the *Irish*, or to the Parliament; of which his Majesty being informed, determined, he should give it to the Parliament; which he did, with full Conditions for all those who had served his Majesty; and so Transported himself into *England*, and, from *London*, presented himself to the King at *Hampton*-Court; who received him with extraordinary Grace, as a Person who had served him with great Zeal and Fidelity, and with the most universal Testimony of all good Men that any Man could receive. He used less Application to the

Parliament and Army than other Men, relying upon the Articles the Parliament had signed to him; by which he had liberty to stay so many Months in *England*, and at the end thereof to Transport himself into the parts beyond the Seas, if in the mean time he made no composition with the Parliament: which he never intended to do; and though he knew well that there were many jealous Eyes upon him, he repaired frequently to present his Duty to the King; who was exceedingly pleased to confer with him, and to find that he was resolved to undertake any Enterprise that might Advance his Service; which the King himself, and most other Men who wished well to it, did at that time believe to be in no desperate Condition. And no Men were fuller of professions of Duty, and a Resolution to run all hazards, than the *Scottish* Commissioners; who, from the time they had delivered up the King, resided at *London* with their usual Confidence, and loudly complained of the presumption of the Army in seizing upon the Person of the King; insinuated themselves to all those who were thought to be most constant, and inseparable from the Interest of the Crown, with passionate undertaking that their whole Nation would be united, to a Man, in any Enterprise for his Service. And now, from the time his Majesty came to *Hampton*-Court, they came to him with as much presumption as if they had carried him to *Edinborough*; which was the more notorious, and was thought to signify the more, because their Persons were known to be most odious to all the great Officers in the Army, and to those who now governed in the

And Scottish Commissioners.

BOOK X.

The Army begins to be less regardful of the King.

Parliament. Here the foundation of that engagement was laid, which was endeavoured to be performed the next year ensuing, and which the *Scots* themselves then communicated to the Marquis of *Ormond*, the Lord *Capel*, and other trusty Persons; as if there was nothing else intended in it than a full vindication of all his Majesty's Rights and Interest.

When the Army had thus subdued all opposition, and the Parliament and They seemed all of a piece, and the refractory humors of the City seemed to be suppressed, and totally tamed, the Army seemed less regardful of the King than they had been; the Chief Officers came rarely to *Hampton*-Court, nor had they the same countenances towards *Ashburnham*, and *Berkeley*, as they used to have; they were not at leisure to speak with them, and when they did, asked captious Questions, and gave Answers themselves of no signification. The Agitators, and Council of Officers, sent some Propositions to the King, as ruinous to the Church and destructive to the Regal Power, as had been yet made by the Parliament; and, in some respects, much worse, and more dishonorable; and said, "if his Majesty would consent thereunto, they would apply themselves to the Parliament, and do the best they could to persuade them to be of the same opinion." But his Majesty rejected them with more than usual indignation, not without some reproaches upon the Officers, for having deluded him, and having prevailed in all their own designs, by making the World believe that they intended his Majesty's Restoration and Settlement, upon better Conditions than the Parliament was willing to admit.

By

By this manner of refentment, the Army took itfelf to be difobliged, and ufed another Language in their difcourfe of the King than they had, for fome Months, done; and fuch Officers who had formerly ferved the King, and had been civilly treated and fheltered in the Quarters of the Army, were now driven from thence. They who had been kind to them, withdrew themfelves from their Acquaintance; and the Sequeftrations of all the Eftates of the Cavaliers, which had been intermitted, were revived with as much rigor as ever had been before practifed, and the declared Delinquents racked to as high compofitions; which if they refufed to make, their whole Eftates were taken from them, and their Perfons expofed to affronts, and infecurity; but this was imputed to the prevalence of the Prefbyterian humor in the Parliament againft the judgment of the Army: and it is very true, that though the Parliament was fo far fubdued, that it no more found fault with what the Army did, nor complained that it meddled in determining what Settlement fhould be made in the Government, yet, in all their own Acts and Proceedings, they profecuted a Prefbyterian Settlement as earneftly as they could. The Covenant was preffed in all places, and the Anabaptifts and other Sects, which begun to abound, were punifhed, reftrained, and difcountenanced; which the Army liked not, as a violation of the Liberty of tender Confciences; which, they pretended, was as much the Original of the Quarrel, as any other Grievance whatfoever.

In this year, 1647, they had begun a Vifitation of the Univerfity of *Oxford*; which they finifhed not

The Univerfity of Oxford vifited by the Parliament.

till the next year; in which the Earl of *Pembroke* had been contented to be employed as Chancellor of the University, who had taken an Oath to defend the Rights and Privileges of the University; notwithstanding which, out of the extreme weakness of his Understanding, and the miserable compliance of his Nature, he suffered himself to be made a Property in joining with *Brent*, *Pryn*, and some Committee-Men, and Presbyterian Ministers, as Commissioners for the Parliament to reform the Discipline, and erroneous Doctrine of that Famous University, by the Rule of the Covenant; which was the Standard of all Men's Learning, and ability to govern; all Persons of what Quality soever being required to subscribe that Test; which the whole Body of the University was so far from submitting to, that they met in their Convocation, and, to their eternal Renown (being at the same time under a strict and strong Garrison, put over them by the Parliament; the King in Prison; and all their hopes desperate) passed a public Act, and Declaration against the Covenant, with such invincible Arguments of the Illegality, Wickedness, and Perjury contained in it, that no Man of the contrary Opinion, nor the Assembly of the Divines (which then sat at *Westminster*, forming a new Catechism, and Scheme of Religion) ever ventured to make any Answer to it; nor is it indeed to be answered, but must remain to the World's end, as a Monument of the Learning, Courage, and Loyalty, of that excellent place, against the highest Malice and Tyranny that was ever exercised in, or over any Nation, and which those Famous Commis-

The Oxford Reasons against the Covenant passed in Convocation at this time.

sioners only answered by Expelling all those who refused to submit to their Jurisdiction, or to take the Covenant; which was, upon the matter, the whole University; scarce one Governor and Master of College or Hall, and an incredible small Number of the Fellows, or Scholars, submitting to either; whereupon that desolation being made, they placed in their rooms, the most notorious Factious Presbyterians, in the Government of the several Colleges or Halls; and such other of the same Leven in the Fellowships, and Scholars places, of those whom they had Expelled, without any regard to the Statutes of the several Founders, and the Incapacities of the Persons that were put in. The Omnipotence of an Ordinance of Parliament, confirmed all that was this way done; and there was no farther contending against it.

It might reasonably be concluded that this wild and barbarous depopulation, would even extirpate all that Learning, Religion, and Loyalty, which had so eminently flourished there; and that the succeeding ill Husbandry, and unskilful Cultivation, would have made it fruitful only in Ignorance, Prophanation, Atheism, and Rebellion; but, by God's wonderful blessing, the goodness and richness of that Soil could not be made barren by all that stupidity and negligence. It choked the Weeds, and would not suffer the poisonous Seeds, which were sown with industry enough, to spring up; but after several Tyrannical Governments, mutually succeeding each other, and with the same malice and perverseness endeavouring to extinguish all good Literature and Allegiance, it yielded a Harvest of extraordinary good

A a 2

BOOK X.

and found knowledge in all parts of Learning; and many who were wickedly introduced, applied themselves to the Study of good Learning, and the practice of Virtue; and had inclination to that duty and obedience they had never been taught; so that when it pleased God to bring King *Charles* the second back to his Throne, he found that University (not to undervalue the other, which had nobly likewise rejected the ill infusions which had been industriously poured into it) abounding in excellent Learning, and devoted to Duty and Obedience, little inferior to what it was before its desolation; which was a lively instance of God's mercy, and purpose, for ever so to provide for his Church, that the Gates of Hell shall never prevail against it; which were never opened wider, nor with more Malice, than in that time.

These violent Proceedings in all places, blasted all the King's hopes, and put an end to all the rest and quiet he had for some time enjoyed; nor could he devise any remedy. He was weary of depending upon the Army, but neither knew how to get from them, nor whither else to resort for help. The Officers of those Guards which were assigned to attend his Person, and who had behaved themselves with good Manners, and Duty towards him, and very civilly towards those of his Party who had used to wait upon his Majesty, begun now to murmur at so great resort to him, and to use many, who came, rudely; and not to suffer them to go into the Room where the King was; or, which was worse, put them out when they were there; and when his Majesty seemed to take notice and be troubled at it, they appeared

appeared not to be concerned, nor anfwered him with that Duty they had ufed to do. They affronted the *Scottifh* Commiffioners very notably, and would not fuffer them to fpeak with the King; which caufed an expoftulation from the Parliament; which removed the obftruction for the future, but procured no fatisfaction for the injury they had received, nor made the fame Officers more civil towards their Perfons. *Afhburnham*, and *Berkeley*, received many Advertifements from fome Officers with whom they had moft converfed, and who would have been glad that the King might have been reftored by the Army for the preferments which they expected might fall to their fhare, "that *Cromwell*, and *Ireton* refolved never "to truft the King, or to do any thing towards his "Reftoration;" and they two fteered the whole Body; and therefore it was advifed, "that fome way "might be found to remove his Majefty out of their "hands." Major *Huntington*, one of the beft Officers they had, and Major to *Cromwell*'s own Regiment of Horfe, upon whom he relied in any Enterprife of importance more than upon any Man, had been imployed by him to the King, to fay thofe things from him which had given the King the moft confidence, and was much more than he had ever faid to *Afhburnham*; and the Major did really believe that he had meant all he faid, and the King had a good opinion of the Integrity of the Major, upon the Teftimony he had received from fome he knew had no mind to deceive his Majefty; and the Man merited the Teftimony they gave him. He, when he obferved *Cromwell* to grow colder in his Expreffions for the

King than he had formerly been, expostulated with him in very sharp terms, for "abusing him, and "making him the Instrument to cozen the King;" and, though the other endeavoured to persuade him that all should be well, he informed his Majesty of all he had observed; and told him, "that *Cromwell* "was a Villain, and would destroy him if he were not "prevented;" and, in a short time after, he gave up his Commission, and would serve no longer in the Army. *Cromwell* himself expostulated with Mr. *Ashburnham*, and complained "that the King could not "be trusted; and that he had no affection or confi- "dence in the Army, but was jealous of them, and "of all the Officers: that he had Intrigues in the "Parliament, and Treaties with the Presbyterians "of the City, to raise new troubles; that he had a "Treaty concluded with the *Scottish* Commissioners "to engage the Nation again in blood; and there- "fore he would not be answerable if any thing fell "out amiss, and contrary to expectation;" and that was the reason, besides the old Animosity, that had drawn on the Affront, which the Commissioners had complained of. What that Treaty was, and what it produced, will be mentioned in a more proper place.

END OF THE EIGHTH VOLUME.

www.ingramcontent.com/pod-product-compliance
Lightning Source LLC
Chambersburg PA
CBHW030305240426
43673CB00040B/1072